Learning English

Challenge 21

Band 1

Herausgegeben von

Ulrich Brößkamp
Maria Dashöfer
Hermann Fischer
Beate Hegemann
Alexander Hick
Harald Peter
Barbara Ware-Thürwächter
Ephrem Wellenbrock

Ernst Klett Verlag
Stuttgart Düsseldorf Leipzig

Learning English

Challenge 21 Band 1

Herausgegeben von

OStR Ulrich Brößkamp, Bochum; OStR'n Maria Dashöfer, Mannheim; StR Hermann Fischer, Münster; StD'n Beate Hegemann, Gladbeck; StR Alexander Hick, Weinheim; StD Harald Peter, Kirchzarten; StR'n Barbara Ware-Thürwächter, MA, Karlsruhe; OStR Ephrem Wellenbrock, Dortmund.

Beratende Mitarbeit

StD Günther Klein, Bad Schönborn; StD Ewald Farkas-Baumann, Fachleiter für Englisch am Staatlichen Seminar für Schulpädagogik (Berufliche Schulen), Karlsruhe.

Tonträger zu Challenge 21 Band 1

2 CDs mit ausgewählten Texten und Liedern, Klettnummer 510515 (auch als **Kassette** erhältlich, Klettnummer 510514)

CD mit den Hörverstehenstexten, Klettnummer 510518 (auch als **Kassette** erhältlich, Klettnummer 510516)

Symbols used

dialogue or predominantly oral task

supplementary activity

Special attention necessary!

Text is recorded on CDs/cassettes accompanying student's book (Klett number: 510515/510514)

Text is recorded on CD/cassette of additional listening comprehension material (Klett number: 510518/510516)

1. Auflage

A 1 6 5 4 3 | 2005 2004 2003 2002 2001

Alle Drucke dieser Auflage können im Unterricht nebeneinander benutzt werden, sie sind untereinander unverändert. Die letzte Zahl bezeichnet das Jahr dieses Druckes.

Internetadresse: http://www.klett-verlag.de

Redaktion: Gillian Bathmaker, BA (hons), Virginia Maier, M.A.

Gestaltung: Andrea Thieme, Asperg.
Umschlaggestaltung & Grafik: Hanjo Schmidt, Stuttgart.
Satz: DTP-Verlag.
Repro: Lihs GmbH, Medienhaus, Ludwigsburg.
Druck: Aprinta Druck GmbH, Wemding.
Printed in Germany.
ISBN 3-12-510510-2

Contents

1 Who cares what I think?

First impressions

First impressions: the way you feel about someone or something the first time you see them or it.

Describing people →

- What is your first impression of the young people in these photographs? Think of adjectives to describe each of them. *Example:* ***friendly, relaxed, angry***
- Compare your ideas with your partner's. Talk about any differences and similarities. Then try to find the opposites of the adjectives you have both found.
  Example: ***friendly - unfriendly***
- How important are first impressions for you? What is most important for you when you are getting to know people: physical appearance – age – clothes – interests – …?
- Look at the young people in the photographs. Say which of them you would most and which you would least like to meet. Give reasons.

Rebels

Write out the poem below in the correct order by choosing the correct line on the right to go after each line on the left.
Example: When everybody has short hair,
The rebel lets his hair grow long.

← **Creating a poem**

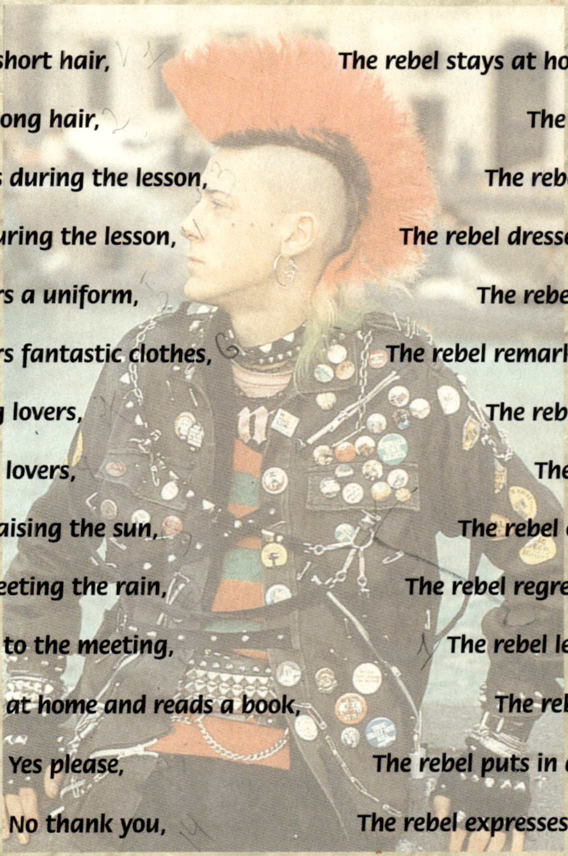

The Rebel

When everybody has short hair,	***The rebel stays at home and reads a book.***
When everybody has long hair,	**The rebel says, Yes please.**
When everybody talks during the lesson,	**The rebel says, No thank you.**
When nobody talks during the lesson,	***The rebel dresses in fantastic clothes.***
When everybody wears a uniform,	***The rebel goes to the meeting.***
When everybody wears fantastic clothes,	***The rebel remarks on the need of rain.***
In the company of dog lovers,	***The rebel doesn't say a word.***
In the company of cat lovers,	***The rebel dresses soberly.***
When everybody is praising the sun,	***The rebel creates a disturbance.***
When everybody is greeting the rain,	***The rebel regrets the absence of sun.***
When everybody goes to the meeting,	***The rebel lets his hair grow long.***
When everybody stays at home and reads a book,	***The rebel cuts his hair short.***
When everybody says, Yes please,	***The rebel puts in a good word for dogs.***
When everybody says, No thank you,	***The rebel expresses a preference for cats.***

It is very good that we have the rebels,
You may not find it very good to be one.

By D. J. Enright from Rhyme Times Rhyme, *London: Chatto & Windus, 1974, p. 9.*

to remark on to comment on

soberly *here: opp. of* extravagantly

disturbance [-'--] trouble

preference ['prefrns] Vorliebe

← **Comprehension**

1. In your own words write a key sentence to sum up what kind of person the rebel is.
2. Look at the last two lines. What do you think the author means by them? Do you agree or disagree?

← **Grammar**

The present tense
See *grammar files* on pp. 142 & 143.

Work with a partner.
a) Ask your partner five questions about the rebel. Use the simple present tense.
Example: When does the rebel let his hair grow long?
b) Change roles and answer your partner's questions.

Over to you

- Make a list of other things which 'rebels' do or don't do. Then use your list to write your own poem. Present your poem in the form of a rap to your class, choosing suitable music to go with it.

Personal appearance

Talk about it →

- How important is a person's appearance? • What kind of groups or organisations usually have rules about clothes, hairstyles or wearing jewellery? Why? • Should there be any rules about appearance at your school? • In what ways do your parents restrict you or advise you about your appearance?
- Would you be prepared to dress differently to get a job? Give reasons.

1 **AP** *short for* Associated Press
2 **on grounds that** because of
3 **spike** (see photo) – **hairdo** hairstyle
4 **appeal** request for a legal case to be judged again
7 **studded** (see photo) – **collar** *here:* a band worn round the neck
9 **up to standards** satisfactory
10 **industrial tribunal** a group of officials who settle disputes between employees and employers – **port** a town with a harbour
11 **to dismiss** to fire
12 **to sport** *here:* to wear
14 **safety hazard** danger – **to project** [-'-] to stick out
16 **supervisor** manager of a department
17 **adhesive / glue** *Klebstoff* – **to mould** to shape or form
18 **to deny** to say s.th. is untrue

Fired from Rolls Royce for Dangerous Hair

Bristol, England (AP)
An 18-year-old punk rocker, fired by Rolls Royce on grounds that the four-inch spikes of his hairdo endangered the eyes of his co-workers, lost an appeal against the decision on Tuesday.

Peter Mortiboy, whose unusual dress includes 18 earrings, a studded dog collar, steel armlets and a stud through his nose, was repeatedly warned by Rolls that his appearance was not up to company standards, an industrial tribunal in this west coast port was told.

The luxury car maker dismissed him from the Rolls Royce Technical College and his £120-a-week job as an apprentice technician when he began sporting spikes last June, training manager Howard Parry testified.

"His hairstyle represented a safety hazard," Parry said. "The spikes projected from the surface of his head for some distance and an accidental movement could have injured a supervisor leaning over him."

Mortiboy, who said he used industrial adhesive and glue to mould his black hair into stiff, vertical spikes, denied that the spikes are dangerous.

"They would be if they were three feet long," he said. "I mix with people all the time in crowded nightclubs and I have never injured anyone," he said. "I didn't cut them off because I'm not happy unless I look the way I want to look ... The only trouble I have is sleeping. I have to lie on my stomach."

From True and Tacky Weird Stories From the World's Newswires *by Monica Hoose and Carolyn Naifeh (ed.), New York: Topper Books/Pharos Books, 1990, p. 24.*

Comprehension →

1. Why did Peter Mortiboy lose his job?
2. Why didn't he change his appearance?
3. What do you think of the way Peter was treated and the way he reacted?

Translation →

Translate ll. 2 to 13:
"An 18-year-old punk rocker ... Howard Perry testified."

Translating
See *skills file* on pp. 122 & 123.

Grammar →

1. Complete the sentences below by copying the structure and tenses used in this sentence from the text: *"I mix with people all the time [...] and I have never injured anyone."* (ll. 19–20)
   I go to school every day but/and ▬ • I always learn my English vocabulary but/and ▬
   I have a shower every morning but/and ▬ • We travel to Italy every year but/and ▬
2. Write four sentences of your own using the present and present perfect tenses.
3. Now rewrite all the sentences using the third person.
   Example: Peter mixes with people all the time but he has never injured anyone.

Present perfect
See *grammar file* on pp. 142 & 144.

Role play

Peter is interviewed by a newspaper reporter about his case.
Work with a partner. One of you should take Peter's role, the other should play the role of the reporter. Make notes of what you want to say before you start, but don't write the interview out in full. Practise the interview together and be prepared to present it to your class.

Reporter
It's 10 am when Peter arrives at your office. Greet him, then offer him a seat and something to drink.
Tell him a photographer will be coming to take his photo soon and find out if that is OK.
Find out the following things:
- when Peter started working for Rolls Royce;
- how much he earned there;
- whether he has always been a punk rocker;
- how he makes his hair stick up;
- his reasons why he likes his appearance like this;
- whether he was warned that he might be dismissed;
- the reasons given for his dismissal;
- why he didn't change his haircut;
- what he thinks of the decision;
- what his job prospects are now/what he now plans to do.

Thank Peter for coming to meet you. Wish him all the best for the future. Tell him when the report will be in the paper.

Peter
Return the reporters greeting.
Accept or decline a drink.
Agree to having a photo taken.

Use facts from the text on page 8 to answer the reporter's questions as far as possible.
Where no answer is given in the text decide on your own answers. (The answers you gave to the comprehension questions may help you.)

Remember to say 'please' and 'thank you' as often as possible!

Who cares what I think?

Over to you

- Teenagers often feel that they are not taken seriously by adults. How do you feel you are treated by your parents/teachers/other adults that you know?

Answer the following questions and use your answers to draw up an illustrated personal fact sheet which can be displayed in your classroom.

1. How would you describe yourself?
2. Who are your heroes?
3. What's your idea of a 'best friend'?
4. What do you hope to achieve in your life?
5. In what way would you like to 'make a difference' in society?
6. What's your idea of a 'good citizen'?
7. If you could live in any country in the world (including your own), which one would you pick and why?
8. It is often said that politicians cannot be trusted. Is this true or false in your opinion? Why?
9. What role do you think Germany will play in Europe and the world in 50 years?
10. What could you do that might help your country to be a better place?

★ **Listening comprehension**
Listen to an American teenager answering similar questions to those you have just answered.

Time and money

Collecting information

1. Answer the following questions.
   a) How much pocket money do you get each month?
   b) What do you spend most of your money on?
   c) How much do you spend every month on music and on clothes?
   d) How much time do you spend every day a) on the telephone and b) watching television?

2. Ask two other members of your class these questions and make a note of their answers.

Making comparisons

Write sentences comparing the results of your answers and your two friends' answers to the questions above. Try to use each of the following phrases at least once:

… less (than) • … more (than) • as … as
(the) most • (the) least

Example: *Susanne spends less time every day watching television than I do.*

> **Comparisons**
> See *grammar file* on p. 149.

> **Charts**
> Statistical information is often presented in charts. Three common types of charts are:
>
> Bar charts 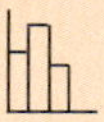
>
> Graphs 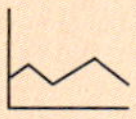
>
> Pie charts 
>
> See also *skills file* on p. 131.

1. Pocket money

Amount of pocket money received each week by 10- to 13-year-olds. Percentage responses.

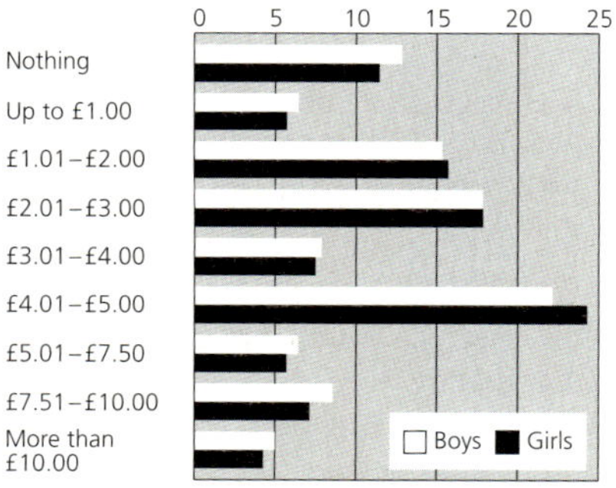

2. After school

Percentage of 14- to 15-year-olds who spent more than three hours watching TV. Percentage who spent none doing homework.

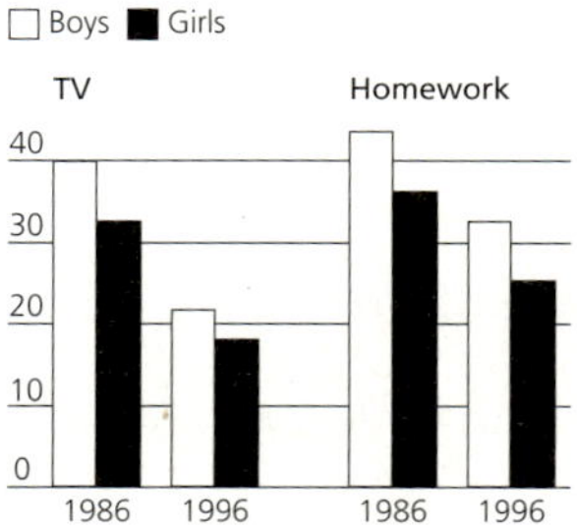

Source: University of Exeter

From The Guardian, *August 28, 1997.*

Talking about statistics

Look at the bar charts. Complete the sentences below using information from the charts and the words and phrases given in the boxes on the left.

> almost a quarter of • around 12 % of • one third of • roughly the same amount

> between • more … less … than • in the same period • dropped by almost • from over … to just over

1. Pocket money

a) ___ boys and girls get £2 pocket money or less per week.
b) ___ boys and girls get more than £7.50 pocket money per week.
c) ___ all boys and girls get between £4 and £5 pocket money per week.
d) Boys and girls get ___ of pocket money.

2. After school

a) In 1986 teenagers watched ___ TV and did ___ homework ___ in 1996.
b) ___ 1986 and 1996 the percentage of teenage boys who watched TV for three hours ___ 20 %.
c) ___ the percentage of boys who did no homework dropped by 10 % ___ 40 % ___ 30 %.

Over to you

- Work in pairs. Make further sentences about the statistics presented in the charts. Be prepared to present your information to your class.

Music makes the world go round for teenagers

Music is the central focus of teenagers' lives and their spending, a survey reveals today, *writes Clare Longrigg.*

The news comes after tickets for an Oasis tour sold out in hours at the weekend as fans jammed hotlines. Seconds after 300 special phone lines opened at 9am, they were blocked by callers, who bought 156,000 tickets at £17.50.

Fans had slept outside the six venues across Britain to be first in line when the box office opened. By dawn on Saturday, 2,000 fans were queueing outside Olympia in London.

The scale of the turnout endorses a TSB survey which shows that music is the single most important thing in the lives of nearly a quarter of teenagers. Teenagers could also be the most important thing in the lives of record companies: some boys spend more than £50 a month on music.

Almost half the teenagers questioned also said their clothes were influenced by pop stars. However, the survey of 500 16- to 20-year-olds is bad news for song-writers with a message. The report says that teenagers buy a record because they like the tune, rather than for its social or political content. In fact, 75 per cent say they will listen to music even if they don't like what it stands for.

The confusion of messages is even greater when it comes to drugs. Forty-three per cent of teenagers surveyed said that Liam Gallagher's caution for possessing drugs made them lose some respect for him, but it did not stop them voting Oasis albums the top two records of the 1990s.

By John Carvel, The Guardian, *August 28, 1997.*

4 **to jam** to block
6 **venue** place where an event is held
7 **to queue** to form a line
9 **scale** *here:* size – **turnout** crowd – **to endorse** to support– **TSB** Trustee Savings Bank *(Name einer Sparkasse)*
16 **tune** [tju:n] melody
17 **to stand for** to represent a certain point of view
18 **when it comes to** *(informal)* on the subject of
19 **caution** ['kɔ:ʃn] a formal warning

Comprehension

1. How did the Oasis tour confirm the findings of the TSB survey?
2. According to the survey how do young people spend money and how do they dress?
3. What did the survey find out about the importance of the texts of pop songs for young people?
4. What do teenagers think of pop stars who are involved in drugs, according to the survey?

Over to you

1. What is your favourite pop song in English? How much of the text do you know and how much do you understand?
2. a) Bring a CD or cassette of your favourite song to school and play it to your class. Explain what the song is about in your own words.
   b) Say why you like the song.
   c) Find out what your classmates think of the song you have chosen. Make sure they give a reason for their opinion.
3. What would you be prepared to do (or what have you already done) in order to get tickets for a concert by your favourite band?

A step further

1. a) In what ways does the language you hear in pop songs affect your own use of language? Think about songs in your mother tongue as well as in English.
   b) "I don't care about the text as long as the tune is good."
   How true is this statement for you and for other people in your class? Give reasons.
2. Which other ways can you think of in which pop stars influence their fans?
3. What or who in addition to pop music has the greatest influence on people of your age in your opinion? Give examples and reasons.

Every generation has its day

- Think about the way adults (your parents, teachers, etc.) behave towards you. Name three things which you think are very good and three which you disagree with. Say in what way you might behave differently when you are older. Give reasons for your choices.
- Work with a partner or in a group and make a diagram like the one on the left showing what has changed and what has remained the same over the last fifty years. Who do you think had an easier/better time as a teenager: your parents' generation, your grandparents' generation or your generation? Give reasons.

★ Listening
Listen to the pop song N'oubliez jamais *by Joe Cocker.*

Check the web
Get more information about Aids at:
http://www.avert.org

By the end of the 20th Century over 33 million people will have become infected by the Aids virus worldwide. Around 25 million of these are under 25 years old.

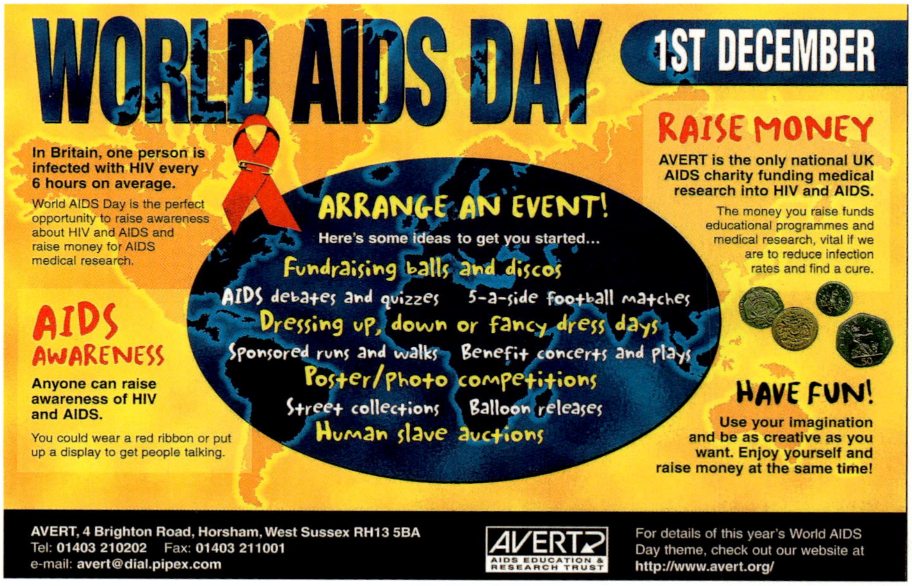

© AVERT 1999

on average *im Durchschnitt*
to raise awareness to cause people to be more informed
fundraising making money for a good cause
dressing up/down wearing formal/informal clothes – **fancy dress** a costume usu. worn at a party; it can be unusual, funny, etc.
sponsored run and walk activity where participants earn money for a good cause by running or walking
release *here:* letting (balloons) go
slave auction event where people are sold as 'slaves' for a day and the money is given to a good cause
ribbon *Schleife*

Young give up condoms as Aids fear fades

Britain's young people are turning their back on warnings about safe sex and putting themselves at greater risk of catching the Aids virus.

New research has revealed that increasing numbers of teenagers and young adults are having sex more often without using a condom, compared with five years ago. According to a study of the sexual behaviour of young people aged 16 to 24, compared to five years ago three times as many of them are having regular sex, almost a third fewer are using condoms and a quarter more have had at least four partners by the time they are 24.

The findings are supported by an increase in the levels of sexually transmitted diseases in young people – an indicator of the levels of unprotected sex. The incidence of gonorrhoea in teenagers has risen by almost 30 % since 1995.

Dr Nick Ford, a medical geographer from the University of Exeter who carried out the study and is still analysing the findings, said: "One reason for the change in

to fade [feɪd] to disappear slowly

1 **to turn one's back on** to ignore

11 **gonorrhoea** [ˌgɒnəˈriːə]
12 **medical geographer** [dʒɪˈɒgrəfə] s.o. who analyzes medical trends in a region

attitude is that young people are taking longer periods of their lives before settling down. This means they are having a series of sexual partners. Their lifestyles have implications not only for the transmission of HIV and sexually transmitted diseases but also marriage, family formation and childbearing."

He said the change in behaviour could largely be attributed to a sea change in the views of young women. "The 'romantic' attitude of women towards relationships has been eroded. They are now much more at ease with casual relationships," he said.

"Since the safe sex campaigns of the late 1980s and early 1990s the message hasn't been hammered as hard. Perhaps that is why this generation is behaving in what seems to be a less restrained manner," said Julian Roberts, health analyst from Somerset health authority who commissioned the report.

Dr Roger Ingham, director of the Centre for Sexual Health Research and a reader in psychology at Southampton University, said: "We know there is a lot of unprotected sex going on at a younger age in Britain at the moment."

Typical is Charlotte Davis, a 24-year-old estate agent from Bath, in Somerset. She admitted last week she was no longer as worried about the risk of contracting HIV through unprotected sex. "Like most young people during the late 1980s, I was terrified of becoming infected," she said.

"According to the hype, we would all know someone who was HIV positive by 1990, so naturally I insisted on using a condom with a partner. It simply hasn't happened so I'm not really concerned any more."

Davis, who lost her virginity at 17, said her priorities have changed over the years along with her nine different sexual partners. "The first time I made love was at college and I was terribly nervous about Aids – we both insisted on protection. Now if they're there, I'd use them but if not, I wouldn't bother. It just isn't a hard and fast rule for me or my friends anymore," she said.

Single motherhood and unwanted pregnancies hold more fears for people like Davis, a Cambridge University graduate. "These days we're all more likely to know a single mum than someone with Aids. The pill is the best safeguard against that," she said.

A 23-year-old insurance salesman from Weston-super-Mare, who declined to be identified, admitted he expects to have sex with a different partner "whenever the chance presents itself". That is usually every weekend and included Christmas Eve. "When I was younger I always used a condom because of the fear of Aids," he said. "Now, I don't bother, I am sure they will have a cure soon. Some people might think I'm being irresponsible but I reckon that's just the way things are in my generation."

A recent survey on attitudes to sex conducted by the Health Education Authority showed that 12 % (more than 1 in 10) of young people under 24 erroneously believe that there is a cure for Aids.

From the article by Cherry Norton and Simon Trump, The Times*, London, January 4, 1998.*

14 **to settle down** to stay with a long-term partner

16 **implication** significance

18 **to be attributed** [əˈtrɪbjʊtɪd] **to** to probably be explained by – **sea change** very big change

20 **to erode** to slowly destroy – **at ease** relaxed – **casual** *here:* not serious

23 **to hammer** *here:* to repeat

24 **restrained** reasonable

25 **authority** *Behörde* – **to commission** to give s.o. a task

29 **estate agent** s.o. who sells houses and flats for clients

30 **to contract** [-ˈ-] to become infected

33 **hype** [haɪp] hysteria

34 **to insist on** *bestehen auf*

36 **virginity** *Jungfräulichkeit*

39 **to bother** to take the trouble to do s.th. – **hard and fast** fixed; cannot be changed

43 **safeguard** protection

45 **to decline** to say 'no'

50 **to reckon** to suppose

51 **to conduct** [-ˈ-] to carry out

52 **erroneously** [-ˈ----] falsely

Collecting information

1. A useful way of getting information out of a text is to make a table. Design a table with the following headings and subheadings:
   a) *Heading:* *New research*
      Subheadings: *Findings* • *Reasons*
   b) *Headings:* *Charlotte* • *Insurance salesman*
      Subheadings: *Age* • *Job* • *Attitude by 1990* • *Attitude today* • *Reasons for behaviour today*
2. Compare your table with your partner's and decide which table you think is better.
3. Fill in the table you have chosen with information from the text.

Your opinion →

Give your opinion on the way Charlotte and the insurance salesman behave. These phrases may help you:

In my opinion • As far as I'm concerned • To my mind • I think that …

Do **not** use ***I mean***!

Working with words →

1. Which prepositions go with these phrases? All the phrases are used at least once in the text. Find an example of each.
   a) according ▬ – *according to (l.5: According to a study of sexual behaviour …)*
   b) to be more likely ▬
   c) to be terrified ▬
   d) to be worried ▬
   e) the change ▬
   f) to decline ▬
   g) an increase ▬
   h) to insist ▬
   i) at risk ▬
   j) a survey ▬

2. Work with a partner. Brainstorm to think of other 'dangers' which young people face, e.g. drugs, smoking. Use the phrases from task 1 to make sentences about them. Refer to the ideas you collected in your 'Lifestyles: then and now diagram' (see p. 12).
   Example: (According to) *According to critics surfing the net for hours can make people become isolated and depressed.*

Grammar →

1. Read ll. 3–37 again and find examples of the present perfect.
2. Now complete the sentences below using the correct form of the verbs on the right.
   ! Don't always use the present perfect!

Tenses
See *grammar files* on pp. 142 – 145.

a) Selena ▬ eight letters of application over the last two months but so far she ▬ to come for an interview.	send off • not be asked
b) One question employers often ▬ at interviews is: how long ▬ you ▬ English?	ask • learn
c) When my father ▬ a teenager he ▬ cycling every weekend but he ▬ any sports for years now because he says he ▬ time.	be • go • not do • not have
d) I … my friends from my old school since we ▬ in the summer.	not see • leave

3. Show that you understand how to use the present perfect by forming three sentences of your own using the present perfect in a typical way.

Over to you →

Having a discussion
See *skills files* on pp. 131 & 132.

- Which holds more fears for you: an unwanted pregnancy or Aids (see ll. 41–42)? Discuss in groups.
- How can you protect yourself against the sexually transmitted disease gonorrhoea (l. 11) and the Aids virus? What are the symptoms and consequences of these sexually transmitted diseases? What kind of medical treatment is available for sufferers? Find information in reference books and, if possible, on the internet. Write at least five sentences outlining your results.

Under pressure

Before you read

- Form groups of three or four and brainstorm ideas of when you feel under pressure. Think about situations at school, at home and with your friends.
- Who do you usually turn to for help when you are under pressure?
- Most human beings are capable of absorbing a lot of mental and emotional punishment. Sadly, some aren't. What might young people under pressure feel driven to do?
- The following text is a scene from a play called The Pressure Cooker which was written by teenagers about teenagers. What is a pressure cooker? What do you think the play might be about?

The Pressure Cooker (1)

pressure cooker metal pot in which food is cooked quickly under high pressure
Graham ['greɪəm]

Characters: ANDREA, GRAHAM, DAWN, ANDREA'S MOTHER, IAN

The story so far: In scene 1 Andrea and Graham meet outside school. They have just got their mock exam results. Andrea worked hard for her exams but she has done much worse than she expected to. She is disappointed because she knows if she gets bad results she won't be able to go to drama college. She also knows her mother will be really angry with her for doing so badly. Graham got bad results, but he doesn't care and makes fun of Andrea for worrying so much. Dawn, who always does well in her exams even without doing any revision, joins the couple and invites them to her house to watch a video. They both decide to go to Dawn's house even though Andrea's mother has asked her to come home and cook tea because she has to go to a meeting. Now read Scene 2.

mock exam a practice school exam

Scene 2

(MOTHER is getting ready to go out. ANDREA enters: she is surprised at seeing MOTHER still in.)

ANDREA: Oh!
MOTHER: So you've come home. What time do you call this?
ANDREA: Sorry, Mum, I was at Dawn's watching a video.
MOTHER: Watching a video! Never mind about getting tea ready; never mind your mother's got a meeting to go to. Andrea's at Dawn's watching a video. Very nice indeed. Well, thank you Andrea.
ANDREA: I said I was sorry.
MOTHER: Honestly, Andrea, it's not fair. I work all day so that you can have a decent home. I get no help from you. You do nothing in the home. Not a thing.
ANDREA: That's not true.
MOTHER: When was the last time you hoovered or dusted? God knows it's hard enough without your father. I thought you might help out a bit.
ANDREA: I do. You know I do.
MOTHER: Well, maybe you could do a bit more. For instance, you could cook the meal when you know I've got a meeting to go to.
ANDREA: Alright, Mum, don't go on.
MOTHER: 'Don't go on!' That's a fine thing to say: 'Don't go on'. Thank you, Andrea. Anyway, because you weren't here, I had to cook the meal. There's some meat in the oven and potatoes and carrots in the pressure cooker.
ANDREA: You know I don't like spuds out of the pressure cooker. They go all soggy.

15 **to hoover** *(BE)* to vacuum
25 **spud** *(informal)* potato
26 **soggy** wet and soft

28 **in a rush** in a hurry

29 **lid** a cover for a pot – **to hiss** to make a sound like a long "sss"

37 **to let s.o. down** to disappoint s.o.

43 **revision** studying, usu. before an exam

44 **loads of s.th.** *(informal)* lots of s.th.

60 **cheeky** showing no respect

73 **to see** *here:* to meet her boyfriend

79 **retake** another attempt to pass an exam

Mother: Perhaps you should have thought of that when you were watching the video. I had to use the pressure cooker because I'm in a rush. So you'll have to like it. And don't try to take the lid off before it stops hissing. You're lucky to get anything at all.

Andrea: Sorry.

Mother: I should think so ... Pass my lipstick, will you, it's on the side.

Andrea: Here.

Mother: Thank you – oh yes, another thing; you were getting your results today. How did you get on?

Andrea: *(quietly)* OK.

Mother: Oh, Andrea, you've not let me down, have you?

Andrea: Did my best.

Mother: What do you mean, you did your best? How bad were they?

Andrea: Bad.

Mother: How bad is 'bad'?

Andrea: Very bad.

Mother: Andrea! I give up with you. How much revision did you do?

Andrea: Loads. You know I stayed in and worked.

Mother: You obviously didn't work hard enough. How did the others do? How did Dawn do? I bet she did well, didn't she? I bet she did a lot of revision.

Andrea: Didn't do any.

Mother: But I'm sure she got good marks, didn't she? Andrea, you've got to work harder. If you don't, you'll never get to university.

Andrea: I don't want to go to university. I want to go to drama college.

Mother: Don't be stupid, Andrea. We've talked about this. Just because you're in the school play you think you're going to be a great actress.

Andrea: I want to go to drama college!

Mother: I'm not discussing this any more. We've decided that you're going to university.

Andrea: *You*'ve decided.

Mother: I want you to do well for yourself. Like Ian.

Andrea: It's always Ian, isn't it? Ian this. Ian that. Isn't Ian wonderful?

Mother: Don't be so cheeky.

Andrea: You want me to be Ian.

Mother: No I don't. Don't be so silly.

Andrea: I'm not Ian, I'm me. I want to do what I want to do, not what everyone else wants me to do. It's my life.

Mother: That's right. And I want the best for you. I want you to go to university and get a decent job and do well. I want what's best for you.

Andrea: What's best for me is what I want to do.

Mother: Getting bad results?

Andrea: I didn't mean to get bad results.

Mother: You didn't mean to get good ones either. If you had, you'd have spent more time revising instead of seeing *him*.

Andrea: Who?

Mother: You know who I mean. You see far too much of that boy.

Andrea: He's got a name, mum. He's called Graham.

Mother: Yes, that's him. Graham. I don't know what you see in him. Honestly, I don't. How did *he* get on in the exams?

Andrea: What's it matter how he got on?

Mother: I see, as badly as you, I imagine. I've told you, Andrea, I'm not letting you stay on to do retakes.

Andrea: Mum, I worked as hard as I could, honestly.

MOTHER: You still went out though.
ANDREA: I can't stay in all the time.
MOTHER: It wouldn't hurt! Perhaps if you had, you might have got better results. Ian never went out, and he got good results.
ANDREA: Ian again. Ian. Little favourite Ian. Goody-goody Ian. *(mimics mother)* Oh, Ian's so clever. Andrea's so thick. My son Ian, he's at university. I love Ian so much. He's a lovely boy. Is that why Dad left? Because you loved Ian so much?
(MOTHER slaps ANDREA'S face. ANDREA starts to cry)
MOTHER: Don't you ever talk to me like that. It was because of you that he left – not Ian. You. Left me to bring up both of you. And I will. And you'll get good qualifications and good jobs. I'll make sure you do. If you can't help yourself, then I'll have to do it for you. Understand? First of all, you're staying in. No more going out until the exams are over.
ANDREA: You can't make me.
MOTHER: Can't I? Just you see. For a start, you're not going to that party tomorrow.
ANDREA: You said I could!
MOTHER: Well, after tonight, I've changed my mind.
ANDREA: But I've told Graham I'm going.
MOTHER: That's another thing – no more seeing him. You've got work to do.
ANDREA: That's not fair.
MOTHER: I don't care what's fair, Andrea. You're staying in, and that's that.
ANDREA: I hate you.
MOTHER: You'll thank me in the long run.
ANDREA: *(running out and slamming the door)* No I won't. I hate you.

From The Pressure Cooker *by Steve Skidmore and Steve Barlow in* New Plays 1: Contemporary One-Act Plays, *Peter Terson, ed., London: Oxford University Press, 1989, pp. 106–110.*

86 **thick** *(informal)* stupid
89 **to slap** to hit s.o. with the flat of your hand
91 **to bring up** *here: aufziehen*
106 **to slam** to shut loudly

Comprehension

1. Make a list of all the things which Andrea and her mother disagree or argue about.
2. How does Andrea feel about her brother Ian? Why do you think she feels that way?
3. In what context is the pressure cooker referred to in this scene? In what way is this symbolic of Andrea's relationship with her mother?

Grammar

Question tags
See *grammar file* on p. 150.

In spoken English it is common to use question tags, as in l. 37: *"Oh, Andrea, you've not let me down, have you?"*

1. Find further examples of question tags in the text.
2. Add question tags to these sentences from the text:
   a) You could cook the meal when you know I've got a meeting to go to, ___ ? (ll. 18/19)
   b) You obviously didn't work hard enough, ___ ? (l. 45)
   c) Left me to bring up both of you, ___ ? (l. 91)
3. Make sentences with question tags to go with these situations.
   a) You think your partner isn't listening to you.
   b) You went to a very good film with your partner last night.
   c) You can't find your pen and you think your partner might have put it in his/her pencil case.
4. Ask your partner to respond to your statements. Some responses are given on the right.

Possible responses: Yes, of course, I am. • Yes, I thought so, too. • Yes, you're right. • No, I don't think so. • No, I'm afraid not.

Over to you

- Look at the information given to you about Scene 1 on p.15. Write the conversation between Andrea and Graham and between them and Dawn. Then act out the scene.
- How do you think the play continues? What do you think happens in the end?
- How do your parents react towards your school results?

The Pressure Cooker (2)

The Pressure Cooker *has five scenes altogether. This is the last scene.*

Scene 5

(Outside Andrea's house Dawn rings the doorbell. Ian answers.)

DAWN: Oh, hello. Is Andrea in?
IAN: No.
DAWN: Oh. Um – you're Ian, aren't you? Andrea's brother?
IAN: That's right. Are you a friend of Andrea's?
DAWN: Yes – at least – we had a bit of a row … she hasn't been at school for a day or two. I wondered …
IAN: Are you Dawn?
DAWN: Yes.
IAN: You'd better come in. Through here – in the kitchen. I'm just cooking supper. I don't want to leave it.

(The pressure cooker is whistling.)

DAWN: What's that noise?
IAN: Pressure cooker. I'm doing the spuds. The safety valve's letting off a bit of steam. I'll turn the heat down: it'll stop in a minute.
DAWN: Makes a racket, doesn't it?
IAN: You've got to have a safety valve on a pressure cooker. Could blow up if you didn't.
DAWN: Will Andrea be home soon?
IAN: No.
DAWN: Well, I could come back tomorrow.
IAN: How'd she been? These last few days?
DAWN: Well …
IAN: Bit upset would you say?
DAWN: A bit, yeah.
IAN: Any idea about what?
DAWN: Well, exams. And she was worried her mum might not let her go to drama college.
IAN: And?
DAWN: We had a bit of a row, like. About a boy. I wanted to make it all up.
IAN: That all?
DAWN: Well, there was this letter. In a magazine.
IAN: I found the magazine.
DAWN: We was laughing about it. At school. Didn't know it was her. She was upset. A bit.
IAN: A bit. Just a bit. Only a bit.
DAWN: Look, can I see Andrea?
IAN: Andrea's in hospital.
DAWN: What?
IAN: That's why I'm here. Mum called me at university.
DAWN: But – what? – I mean – was it an accident?
IAN: Not an accident. She swallowed mum's sleeping pills. Nearly a whole bottle. Mum was out.
DAWN: Oh my God … I never thought … not Andrea. Why?
IAN: Don't you know?
DAWN: I can't believe it.
IAN: You can go and see her – she's all wired up like Frankenstein's monster – tubes going in, tubes coming out, in her arms, down her throat.
DAWN: I'll go and see her – or is your mum …?

7 **row** [raʊ] a noisy or violent discussion

15 **safety valve** a device that lets off steam or pressure when it becomes too great

17 **racket** a loud and unpleasant noise

25 **upset** angry, unhappy

31 **to make s.th. up** *here: wieder gut machen*

35 **we was** *(informal; grammatically incorrect!)* we were

43 **to swallow** *here:* to take

49 **tube** [tju:b]

Dear Auntie Emily,
I'm writing to you because I don't know what else to do. I haven't got a dad, only a mum, and I can't talk to her, she's always out at meetings. Anyway she doesn't listen. She wants me to go to university. We keep having rows about it. I want to go to drama college, but I've mucked up all my exams. On top of that, she's told me to stop seeing my boyfriend. I really love him, but he's started going out with my best mate …

IAN: Mum's at a meeting.
DAWN: At a *meeting*? Not at the hospital?
IAN: There's no point. Andrea's in a coma. Know what that means?
DAWN: Course I know what it means. Don't the doctors know when she'll wake up?
IAN: The doctors don't know *if* she'll wake up. They said they'd ring if anything happened.
DAWN: Oh, God, it's my fault. Poor Andrea.
IAN: Bit late to be sorry, isn't it?
DAWN: What d'you mean?
IAN: Pity you weren't sorrier a bit earlier – you and this Graham.
DAWN: How d'you know about ... how did you know who I was?
IAN: She mentioned your names. In the note.
DAWN: Note?
IAN: They always leave a note. *(Pause)* There, see, it's stopped.
DAWN: What?
IAN: The noise from the steam. That means the pressure's back to normal. Unless the safety valve's got blocked. I've heard of that happening. Then you could be in dead trouble. You can't always tell, can you?
(In another part of the house, the telephone starts to ring.)

69 **dead** *here:* serious

From The Pressure Cooker *by Steve Skidmore and Steve Barlow in* New Plays 1: Contemporary One-Act Plays, *Peter Terson, ed., London: Oxford University Press, 1989, pp. 119–121.*

Comprehension

1. At the end of the play the phone is ringing. Who do you think it is? What do you think the news will be?
2. Look at the things Ian says about the way a pressure cooker works. In which specific situations can someone's life be compared to a pressure cooker?
3. When someone attempts suicide, things have often been building up for weeks, months or even years. Go through the last scene again and make a note of all the things that happened leading up to Andrea's suicide attempt.

Letter writing

Letter writing
See *skills files* on pp. 136 & 137.

Look at Andrea's letter on p. 18 and write either your own letter to an 'Agony Aunt' or a reply to Andrea's letter.

Over to you

Project: Creating a poster

Work with a partner. Copy the mind map below onto a large (A3) piece of paper. Think about what you have covered in this chapter and add more areas and ideas of your own. Find illustrations in magazines, newspapers, etc. or design your own illustrations to go with the bubbles you create. Present your poster to your class, explaining the different areas you have included.

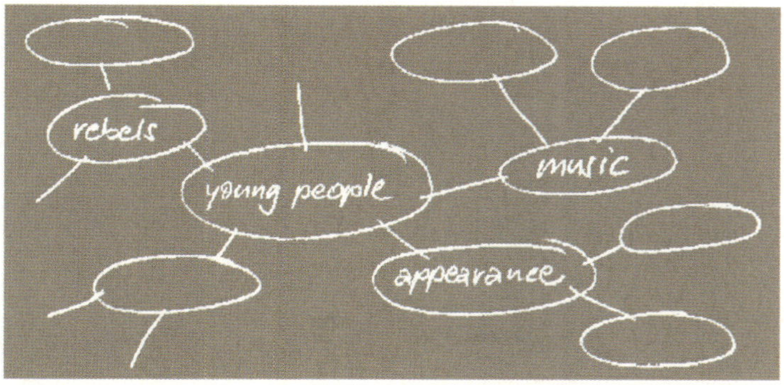

Mind maps
See *skills file* on p. 121.

Projects
See *skills file* on p. 139.

Check the web
Get more information about many youth related issues at:
http://www.youthnet.org
and
http://www.thesite.org

2 A British jigsaw

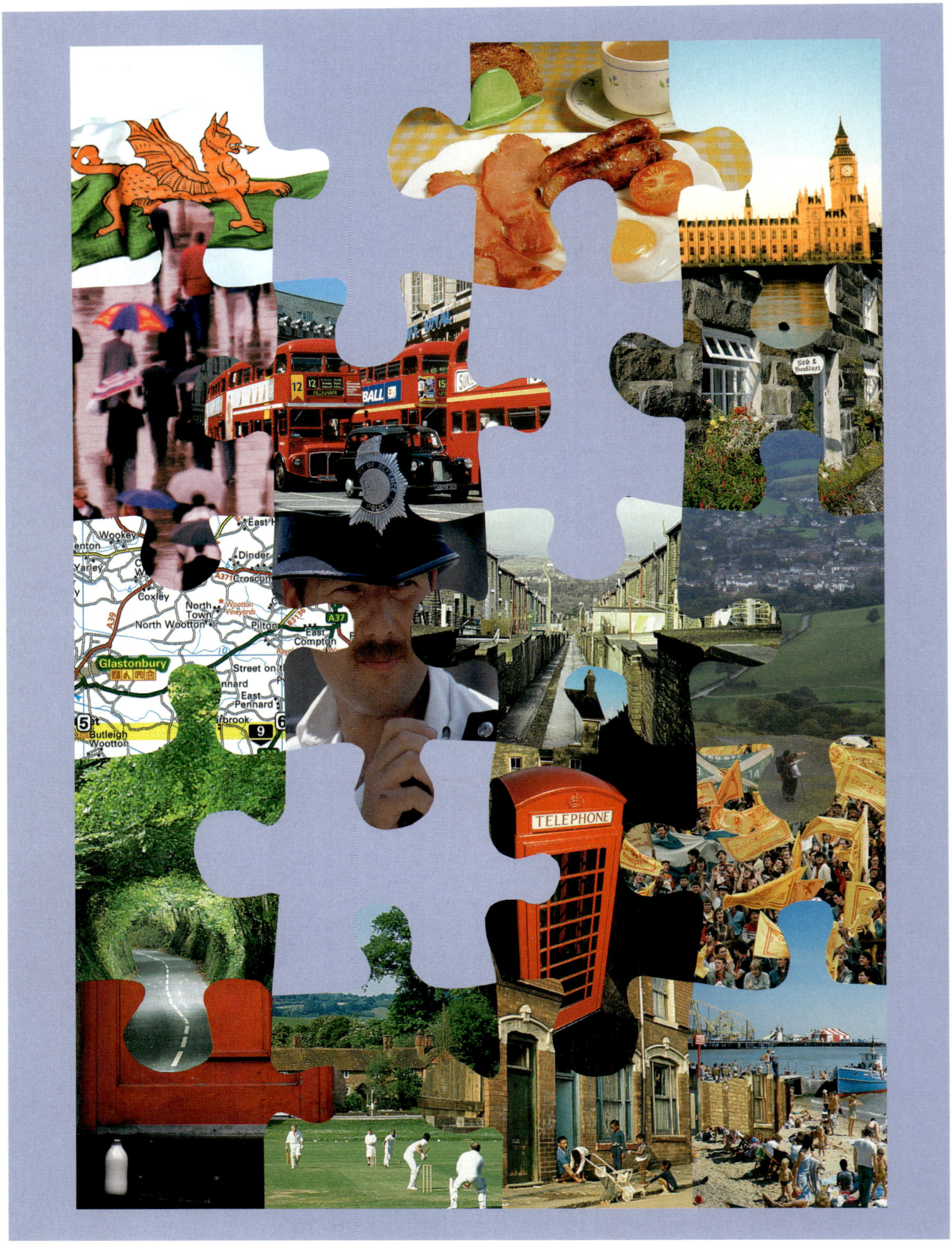

A British jigsaw

Looking at the jigsaw puzzle

1. Work with a partner. Think of a title for each of the pictures in the jigsaw puzzle on p. 20.
2. Which two pictures in the jigsaw give the most typical view of Britain in your opinion? Which picture means the least to you? Give reasons and compare your answers with others in your class.

Talking about clichés

1. When you think of Britain and the British, what do you think of? Think of products, places, people, etc.
2. a) Write down at least three 'clichés' about Britain and the British. Compare your ideas with others in your class.
   b) Is your own view of Britain and the British based on clichés or on first-hand knowledge? Explain your answer.
3. If you were asked to make a 'German Jigsaw' what pictures would you choose? Brainstorm ideas with a partner. Try to come up with a list of ten things that you agree on as being typically German. Find out what other people in your class think and try to agree on ten ideas for your class.

Clichés & stereotypes
See *glossary* on pp. 152 & 153.

Fact finding

1. Where can you look to find information about Britain? Brainstorm ideas in class.
2. a) Find out the following information about England, Scotland, Wales and N. Ireland and make a table showing it:
      capital city • main industries • languages spoken • natural resources
   b) Compare your results with others in your class making corrections and additions where necessary.
   c) Add two further categories to your table, for example, famous people, sports, etc. and fill in the relevant information in your table.

Abbreviations & acronyms

Abbreviations and acronyms are often used in Britain and also internationally, for example, in business language and on the Internet. You can find a comprehensive list of frequently used abbreviations and acronyms in most good dictionaries.

Work out which words the acronyms and abbreviations below stand for. Start a file of acronyms and abbreviations and add to it whenever you come across new items.

a.k.a.	You use another name, which might be better known.
a.s.a.p.	very quickly
c/o	used to contact a person through someone else
CV	(Latin) written details about yourself for an employer
e.g.	(Latin) *exempli gratia*. Can you give the meaning in English?
i.c.	(used on the Internet) Say this aloud and understand it!
i.e.	(Latin) *id est*. Can you give the meaning in English?
IOU	You give this to someone when you have borrowed money from them. If you say it aloud you should understand it!
No.	*Example:* Tel. no.: ++ 49 121 472 3837
p.a.	every year
p.t.o.	written at the bottom of a page to tell you to look at the next one
s.a.e.	You send one of these in order to get a reply in the post.
VIP	someone of great importance
w/o	opposite of 'with'

An **abbreviation** is a shortened way of writing a word. An **acronym** is a way of writing a phrase using only the first letters of each word.

Over to you

- Work in groups and invent an acronym for use in your English lessons! See if the other groups can work out what you mean.

About Britain

Britain is made up of England, Scotland, Wales and Northern Ireland. Each country has its own capital although the government of all four countries is in London. Britain is a member state of the European Union. Its full name is the United Kingdom of Great Britain and Northern Ireland.

Urban and rural population
Half of all Britain's people live in just seven super cities such as Manchester, Birmingham and London, which were formed from smaller towns that grew together. Many of the cities grew up as a result of industries which began to develop in the 19th century. At the beginning of the 19th century 8 out of 10 people lived in the countryside – then Britain had a rural population. Nowadays about 8 out of 10 people in Britain live in a city or town – so Britain has a mainly urban population.

Geographical facts
- Highest mountain: Ben Nevis, in the Highlands of Scotland, at 1,343 m
- Longest river: the Severn, 354 km long, which rises in central Wales and flows through Shrewsbury, Worcester and Gloucester in England to the Bristol Channel
- Largest lake: Lough Neagh, Northern Ireland, at 396 sq km
- Highest waterfall: Eas a Chual Aluinn, from Glas Bheinn, in the Highlands of Scotland, with a drop of 200 m
- Deepest cave: Ogof Ffynnon Ddu, Wales, at 308 m deep
- Closest point to mainland continental Europe: Dover, Kent. The Channel Tunnel, which links England and France, is a little over 50 km long, of which nearly 38 km are actually under the Channel.

Britain is made up of different landscapes from beautiful mountain ranges and flat open spaces, where few people live, to towns and cities which are densely populated. Not only are the areas of Britain different, they are always changing, for example when factories close down and workers become unemployed or when a new industry moves into an area and creates new jobs.

Population
Britain covers a small area compared with many other countries, but it has a large number of people living in it. The approximate population is 58,395,000 (England 48,708,000, Wales 2,913,000, Scotland 5,132,000, N. Ireland 1,642,000).
The population is spread unevenly across Britain and the way it is spread depends on things like climate, resources, landscape and past history. Population density in England is higher than the rest of Britain, with 375 people per sq km. The whole population is now growing, but only very slowly.

Shrewsbury ['ʃrəʊzbrɪ] – **Worcester** ['wʊstə] – **Gloucester** ['glɒstə] – **Neagh** [neɪ] – **Eas a Chual Aluinn** [es ə 'xu:ɑ:l 'ælɪn] – **Glas Bheinn** [glɑ:s ven] – **Ogof Ffynnon** [ɒgɒ 'fɪnɒn] – **Ddu** [ði:]

Climate
Britain's climate is generally mild and temperate. There are frequent weather changes but few extremes of temperature. In general the daily weather is influenced by depressions moving eastward from the Atlantic. Winds are mostly south-westerly. There is more rainfall in the mountainous areas in the west and north than in central and eastern parts.

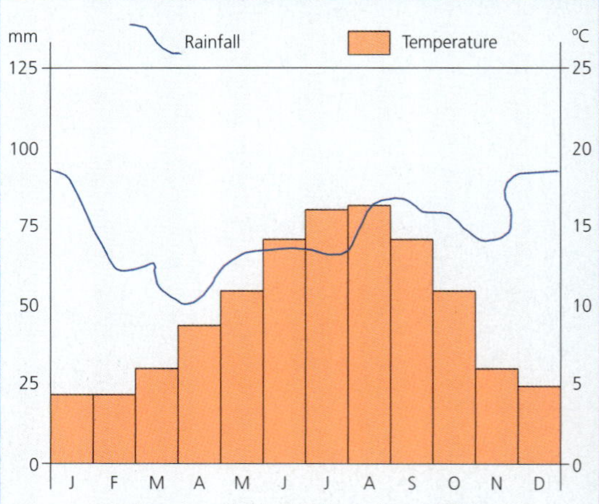

Figures supplied by the Meteorological Office

With an area of about 242,000 sq km, Britain is just under 1,000 km from the south coast to the extreme north of Scotland and just under 500 km across at the widest point. The coastline of Britain is 14,549 km long including islands. The most northerly point on the mainland is Dunnet Head, north-east Scotland and the most southerly point is Lizard Point, Cornwall.

Dunnet ['dʌnɪt]

Comprehension

1. Three of the boxes on p. 22 have no heading. Think of suitable headings to go with them.
2. What are the most important factors which affect population distribution in Britain according to the information in the boxes? Find as many details as posssible.

Working with words

1. Find the words in the boxes on p. 22 which mean:
   a country which belongs to a larger group of countries • the countries of Europe other than Britain • information about mountains, rivers, etc.
2. Explain the following words from the boxes in your own words. Use a dictionary if necessary:
   a rural population • an urban population • densely populated • population density
3. Copy and continue the mind maps below with words from the boxes. Then add any more suitable words that you know.

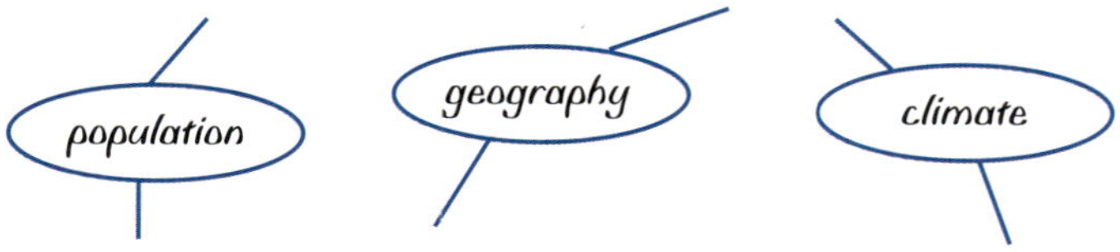

Over to you

- Make a set of ten questions based on the information in the boxes.
  - Use as many different question types as possible.
  - Make a note of the answers to your questions on a separate piece of paper.
  - Decide how many points to give for each answer according to the difficulty of the question.
  - Test your partner and ask your partner to test you.

Listening comprehension
Listen to Charlotte Trew talking about Wales and the Welsh.

Looking at links to Britain

The Channel Tunnel was opened in 1994, forming the first and only land link between Britain and mainland Europe.

1. a) Why do you think it was important for Britain to be linked to Europe via a tunnel?
   b) Why do you think many people in Britain were sceptical about the tunnel while it was being built?
2. a) Name the forms of transport illustrated below.
   b) What other ways are there of getting to Britain?
   c) What are the advantages and disadvantages of the different types of transport? Think about convenience, cost, effect on the environment, employment, business and economy.
3. If you were travelling to Britain, which form of transport would you choose? Why?

The British way of life

Get a copy of the latest official handbook from:
The Stationery Office,
The Publications Centre,
PO Box 276,
London SW8 5DT

Check the web
Get more information from Her Majesty's Stationery Office (HMSO) at:
http://www.hmso.gov.uk

Every year an official handbook about Britain is published by the Office for National Statistics. The following article summarizes information from Britain 1999.

The new Brits: single, stoned and selfish

We now live longer, marry later, and are more likely to try drugs and to put pleasure before responsibility, reports Richard Thomas

They are both single. He lives alone, feeding off takeaways between 12-hour shifts at the office. She is divorced and juggles care for her daughter with a demanding career. Both have taken drugs, both have jobs in financial services and neither belongs to a trade union. Welcome to the new British way of life.

A comprehensive analysis of the state of our society shows that family life is declining in importance, the growth of communications makes geographical distances less significant, people are eschewing gender and age stereotypes – and cats have overtaken dogs as the modern Briton's pet of choice.

Britain 1999, published by the Office for National Statistics, shows that the size of the average household is now 2.4, down from 3.1 at the beginning of the 1960s. The proportion of households made up of single people has risen from 14 per cent to 27 per cent – with the fastest growth in single male adult households. Divorce plays a large part: the UK leads the European league table for marital breakdowns.

Women make up 45 per cent of the workforce, and now return to work more quickly after having children. But they are still bumping against a glass ceiling: women make up 5 per cent of company directors, 7 per cent of university professors and 10 per cent of judges. Trade unions, once the voice of male manufacturing workers, now attract 30 per cent of the workforce.

Both men and women are marrying later and living longer, with life expectancy rising by two years for every post-war decade, the Office for National Statistics found.

Martin Hayward, director of consumer consultancy at the Henley Centre and a social and economic forecaster, says age and gender are becoming less important in the way people live their lives. One sign of this is a move to study later in life – 50 per cent of university students are now over 25.

Hayward says that social, economic and demographic changes have also downgraded the family. 'In the 1960s, people were married in their early twenties and had three kids, so a huge chunk of their life was family time.

'Today we are getting married in our late twenties, having one and a bit kids – reducing the child-focused period – and then living ten years longer at the end. We are probably more selfish, with less of our life taken up by other people.'

Communications technology has revolutionised the home: 35 per cent of households own an answerphone or subscribe to a voicemail service; 29 per cent own a computer, 15 per cent are on the Internet and 22 per cent own at least one mobile phone.

We have become more financially cautious [...]. But dreams of serious riches still prompt 75 per cent of households to regularly buy tickets for the National Lottery draw. Spending on leisure pursuits has grown by more than 20 per cent this decade. Eating out, visits to the cinema and fitness pursuits are on the rise, although one in five men list snooker or pool as their physical activity in the last month. The same proportion of women list yoga.

At home, television remains the favourite activity: 80 per cent of teenagers have one in their room and 82 per cent of households own a video. Two thirds of us have a CD player, up from 15 per cent at the end of the 1980s. But despite the rise of electronic entertainment, libraries remain strong, with 60 per cent of adults carrying a library card and 500 million books borrowed a year.

Other traditions are tumbling. One in 10 Britons now attends a religious service on a weekly basis, while half never or scarcely ever do. Even the bulldog is under threat: the nation's 7 million pet dogs are now outnumbered by 8 million cats.

From the article by Richard Thomas, The Observer, *January 10, 1999.*

Col. 1:
1 **to feed off** *(informal)* to eat
3 **to juggle** *here:* to do several things at one time
4 **demanding** taking up a lot of time and effort
7 **trade union** *Gewerkschaft*
13 **significant** important – **to eschew** [ɪs'tʃu:] *(formal)* to avoid – **gender** sex, i.e. male or female
26 **marital** relating to marriage
30 **glass ceiling** *(here fig.)* invisible yet unbreakable barrier stopping s.o.'s being promoted *(befördert)*
41 **Henley Centre** *(GB)* company which observes consumer behaviour for commercial reasons
42 **forecaster** s.o. who says what will happen using information

Col. 2:
11 **selfish** concerned only with o.s.
15 **to subscribe to s.th.** to pay beforehand for the regular use of a service or product
20 **cautious** ['kɔ:ʃəs] careful
27 **pursuit** [pə'sju:t] activity

← **Comprehension**

1. In your own words say what has changed in Britain according to the text in terms of:
   a) family life
   b) leisure pursuits.
2. *"Hayward says that social, economic and demographic changes have also downgraded the family."* (Col. 2, ll. 1–3)
   a) Find one example of social change and one of economic change in the text.
   b) Think of an example of your own to show that you understand what is meant by demographic change.
3. Which – if any – of the changes described in the text do you think are specific to Britain and which do you think might equally apply to Germany?

← **Asking questions**

1. Look at col. 1, ll. 27–35 *"Women make up 45 per cent ... of the workforce."* Write down the questions the interviewers had to ask women in order to obtain all this information.
2. Comment on the information in the last three paragraphs by comparing it with the situation in your class:
   a) Decide on a set of suitable Yes/No questions to ask.
   b) Ask your questions in class and carry out a handcheck.
   c) Summarize the results of your handcheck in a style similar to that of the text.

← **Vocabulary**

1. a) Find compound nouns in the text which mean:
      • a meal bought in a restaurant but eaten at home.
      • a special service which records messages for you and which you can call and listen to at a suitable time.
   b) Find two more compound nouns in the text and explain them in your own words.
2. Find phrases in the text meaning:
   • to increase in number • to decrease in number

← **Grammar**

1. Find an example in the text of each of the following tenses:
   simple present • present continuous • present perfect • simple present passive • simple past
2. a) Find two examples in the text of the use of the gerund.
   b) Use a gerund to join the sentences below without changing the meaning.
      • People travel long distances nowadays. It is no problem for them anymore.
      • One in five men play snooker regularly. This is the only physical exercise they do!

The gerund
See *grammar file* on p. 150.

← **Understanding the cartoon**

'Let us try to remember the Lord's Prayer'

1. Who is the clergyman in this cartoon talking to: regular church goers or people who rarely attend a church service? How do you know?
2. Find a reference/references to the British attitude towards religion in the text. Does the cartoon reflect what the text says?

Talking about cartoons
See *skills file* on p. 130.

← **Your view**

- The text gives facts about the current way of life in Britain, but does not give an opinion on why these changes are taking place. Why do you think British society is changing in the ways pointed out in the text?

Notes from a small island

Bill Bryson is an American journalist and writer who lived in England for almost twenty years. In his book Notes from a Small Island *he describes Britain and the British as he came to know them. Three short extracts from his book follow here.*

While you read →

- Which elements in the extract below are illustrated in the British jigsaw on p. 20?

Part 1: Marmite and village fêtes

Suddenly, in the space of a moment, I realized what it was that I loved about Britain – which is to say, all of it. Every last bit of it, good and bad – Marmite, village fêtes, country lanes, people saying 'mustn't grumble' and 'I'm terribly sorry but', people apologizing to me when I conk them with a careless elbow, milk in bottles, beans on toast, haymaking in June, stinging nettles, seaside piers, Ordnance Survey maps, crumpets, hot-water bottles as a necessity, drizzly Sundays – every bit of it.

What a wondrous place this was – crazy as fuck, of course, but adorable to the tiniest degree. What other country, after all, could possibly have come up with place names like Tooting Bec and Farleigh Wallop, or a game like cricket that goes on for three days and never seems to start? Who else would think it not the least odd to make their judges wear little mops on their heads, compel the Lord Chancellor to sit on something called the Woolsack, or take pride in a naval hero whose dying wish was to be kissed by a fellow named Hardy? ('Please, Hardy, full on the lips, with just a bit of tongue.') What other nation in the world could have given us William Shakespeare, pork pies, Christopher Wren, Windsor Great Park, the Open University, *Gardeners' Question Time,* and the chocolate digestive biscuit? None, of course.

How easily we lose sight of all this. What an enigma Britain will seem to historians when they look back on the second half of the twentieth century. Here is a country that fought and won a noble war, dismantled a mighty empire in a generally benign and enlightened way, created a far-seeing welfare-state – in short, did nearly everything right – and then spent the rest of the century looking on itself as a chronic failure. The fact is that this is still the best place in the world for most things – to post a letter, go for a walk, watch television, buy a book, venture out for a drink, go to a museum, use the bank, get lost, seek help, or stand on a hillside and take in a view.

From Notes from a Small Island *by Bill Bryson, London: Black Swan, 1996, pp. 351–352.*

Marmite *(brand name) (Hefeextrakt)* salty topping, spread thinly on bread – **fête** [feɪt] kind of bazaar held to make money for charity
4 **to conk** *(informal)* to hit
5 **stinging nettle** plant which 'burns' the skin when touched *Brennnessel* – **pier** [pɪə] structure with a deck built over water, usu. used as a promenade – **Ordnance Survey** *(GB)* official map-making body
6 **crumpet** a small, light cake, eaten toasted and buttered – **drizzly** ['drɪzlɪ] raining lightly
8 **tiniest degree** even the little things
9 **Farleigh** ['fɑːlɪ]
11 **to compel s.o.** to force s.o.
12 **Woolsack** ['wʊlsæk] – **naval hero** reference to Horatio Nelson who died in the Battle of Trafalgar (1805)
15 **pie** [paɪ] *Torte* – **Christopher Wren** (1632–1723) architect
16 **biscuit** [[bɪskɪt] *Keks*
17 **enigma** [-'--] s.th. mysterious and puzzling
19 **to dismantle** to take apart
20 **benign** [bɪ'naɪn] kind – **enlightened** well-informed
21 **chronic** [ɒ]

Language & comprehension →

1. a) Find the adjectives in the text which Bill Bryson uses to describe Britain and the British.
   b) In your own words say what impression of Britain and the British Bill Bryson creates by using these adjectives.
2. Do you think it is an advantage or a disadvantage that Bill Bryson is a foreigner in terms of the way he describes the British?

Looking at style →

What rhetorical and literary devices does Bill Bryson use to make his writing more interesting? Give examples to illustrate your choice. Add to your list when you are reading the other two extracts on pp. 27 and 28.

Rhetorical and literary devices
See *glossary* on p. 153.

Over to you

- Choose one of the following items mentioned in the text. Find out as much as possible about it and prepare an illustrated talk on it for your class:
  Ordnance Survey maps (l. 5) • cricket (l. 9) • the Lord Chancellor/the Woolsack (ll. 11–12) • William Shakespeare (ll. 14–15) • Christopher Wren (l. 15) • the Open University (l. 15)

Giving a talk
See *skills file* on p.129.

Style
See *glossary* on p. 151.

- While reading the next extract from *Notes from a Small Island* pay attention to Bill Bryson's style and note similarities and differences compared with the first extract.

← ***While you read***

Part 2: A lonely island

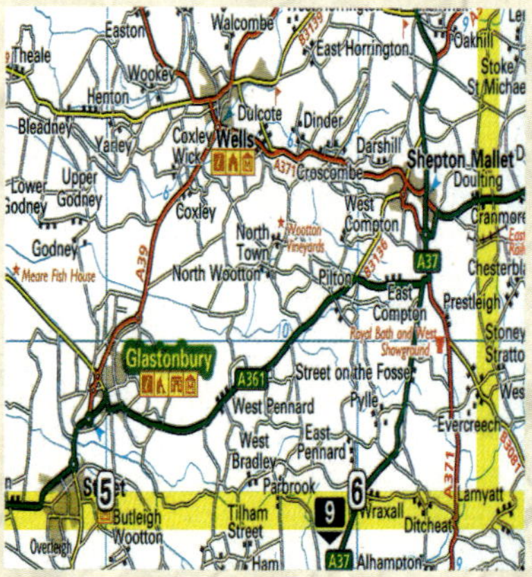

There are certain idiosyncratic notions that you quietly come to accept when you live for a long time in Britain. One is that British summers used to be longer and sunnier. Another is that the England football team shouldn't have any trouble with Norway. A third is the idea that Britain is a big place. This last is easily the most intractable.

If you mention in the pub that you intend to drive from, say, Surrey to Cornwall, a distance that most Americans would happily go to get a taco, your companions will puff their cheeks, look knowingly at each other, and blow out air as if to say, 'Well, now *that's* a bit of a tall order,' and then they'll launch into a lively and protracted discussion of whether it's better to take the A30 to Stockbridge and then the A303 to Ilchester or the A361 to Glastonbury via Shepton Mallet. [...]

The fact is that the British have a totally private sense of distance. This is most visibly seen in the shared pretence that Britain is a lonely island in the middle of an empty green sea. Oh, yes, I know you are all aware, in an abstract sort of way, that there is a substantial landmass called Europe near by and that from time to time it is necessary to go over there to give old Jerry a drubbing or have a holiday on the Med, but it's not nearby in any meaningful sense in the way that, say, Disney World is. If your concept of world geography was shaped entirely by what you read in the papers and saw on television, you would have no choice but to conclude that America must be about where Ireland is, that France and Germany lie roughly alongside the Azores, that Australia occupies a hot zone somewhere in the region of the Middle East, and that pretty much all the other sovereign states are either mythical (viz., Burundi, El Salvador, Mongolia and Bhutan) or can only be reached by spaceship. [...]

I can remember, after I had been living about a year in Bournemouth and bought my first car, fiddling with the car radio and being astounded at how many of the stations it picked up were in French, then looking at a map and being even more astounded to realize that I was closer to Cherbourg than I was to London. I mentioned this at work the next day and most of my colleagues refused to believe it. Even when I showed them on a map, they frowned doubtfully and said things like, 'Well, yes, it may be closer in a strict *physical* sense,' as if I were splitting hairs and that really a whole new concept of distance was required once you waded into the English Channel – and of course to that extent they were right.

From Notes from a Small Island *by Bill Bryson, London: Black Swan, 1996, pp. 29, 32–33.*

1 **idiosyncratic** [ˌɪdɪəʊsɪŋˈkrætɪk] being typical of the thinking of a specific group

8 **intractable** difficult to influence

14 **a tall order** *(informal)* s.th. that is difficult to do

15 **protracted** long

16 **Ilchester** [ˈɪltʃɪstə]

17 **Glastonbury** [ˈglæstnbrɪ]

19 **pretence** action that is untrue but is made to appear true

22 **give Jerry a good drubbing** *(informal, old)* reference from World War II to defeating the German army

24 **entirely** completely

27 **Azores** [əˈzɔːz] three groups of islands in the North Atlantic

28 **sovereign** [ˈsɒvrɪn] having a monarch

29 **viz.** namely – **Bhutan** [buːˈtɑːn]

31 **Bournemouth** [ˈbɔːnməθ]

32 **astounded** very surprised

36 **to frown** to have a disapproving look on one's face

37 **to split hairs** to mention a small difference unnecessarily

Comprehension →

1. The author says that *"[…] the British have a totally private sense of distance"* (l. 18). What do you think he means by this in terms of:
   Britain itself • Britain and Europe • Britain and the world?
2. a) Can you think of an explanation for the attitude described?
   b) Is it acceptable to think in this way in your opinion?

Language →

1. Find words and phrases in the text which mean:
   to plan to do s.th. • That's expecting too much of s.o./s.th. • a long serious talk about s.th. • to be totally influenced by s.th. • to be very surprised
2. Rewrite these sentences from the text replacing the words underlined with your own words:
   - *The fact is that the British <u>have a totally private sense of distance.</u>* (l. 18)
   - *I mentioned this at work the next day and <u>most of my colleagues refused to believe it.</u>* (ll. 34–35)
   - *[…] they frowned doubtfully and said things like, 'Well, yes, it may be closer in a strict physical sense,' <u>as if I were splitting hairs.</u>* (ll. 36–37)

Translation →

Translate the last paragraph of the text (ll. 31–39: *"I can remember … they were right."*). Try to copy Bill Bryson's style in your translation.

Translating
See *skills file* on pp. 122 & 123.

Part 3: Two nations

One of the great surprises to me upon moving North was discovering the extent to which it felt like another country. Partly it was from the look and feel of the North – the high, open moors and big skies, the wandering drystone walls, the grimy mill towns, the snug stone villages of the Dales and Lakes – and partly, of course, it was to do with the accents, the different words, the refreshing if sometimes startling frankness of speech. Partly it was also to do with the way Southerners and Northerners were so extraordinarily, sometimes defiantly, ignorant of the geography of the other end of the country. It used to astonish me, working on newspapers in London, how often you could call out a question like 'Which of the Yorkshires is Halifax in?' and be met with a tableful of blank frowns. And when I moved North and told people that I'd previously lived in Surrey near Windsor, I often got the same look – a kind of nervous uncertainty, as if they were afraid I was going to say, 'Now you show me on the map just where that is.'

Mostly what differentiated the North from the South, however, was the exceptional sense of economic loss, of greatness passed, when you drove through places like Preston or Blackburn or stood on a hillside like this. If you draw an angled line between Bristol and the Wash, you divide the country into two halves with roughly twenty-seven million people on each side. Between 1980 and 1985, in the southern half they lost 103,600 jobs. In the northern half in the same period they lost 1,032,000 jobs, almost exactly ten times as many. And still the factories are shutting. Turn on the local television news any evening and at least half of it will be devoted to factory closures (and the other half will be about a cat stuck up a tree somewhere; there is truly nothing direr than local television news). So I ask again: what do all those people in all those houses do – and what, more to the point, will their children do?

3 **moor** high area of open, unused land – **grimy** dirty, polluted
4 **snug** [ʌ] protected
5 **startling** surprising
6 **frankness** honesty
7 **defiantly** [dɪˈfaɪəntlɪ] refusing to do s.th.
10 **frown** disapproving look
14 **to differentiate** to show the difference between two things
16 **angled** which is neither horizontal nor vertical
23 **devoted** *here:* to be dedicated to
25 **dire** [aɪ] very bad

From Notes from a Small Island *by Bill Bryson, London: Black Swan, 1996, pp. 212–213.*

Comprehension

1. List the north-south differences mentioned in this extract.
2. Suggest answers to Bill Bryson's question *"What do all those people in all those houses do – and what, more to the point, will their children do?"* (ll. 27–29)

Creative writing

- Write a story or news report based on the photo on p. 28. Write about 250 words.

Looking at style

Compare the style of this extract with the style used in the other two extracts from *Notes from a Small Island* (pp. 26 and 27).

1. Which literary devices does Bill Bryson use in all three extracts?
2. Why do you think he changes his style and the type of language used at different points?
3. Which extract did you prefer in terms of style? And in terms of content? Why?

Literary devices
See *glossary* on pp. 152 & 153.

Over to you

- Bill Bryson claims that in England Northerners and Southerners know almost nothing about each other. How much do you know about other regions of Germany? Are there similar regional differences in your country?

The two Ashingtons

	Ashington Northumberland	Ashington West Sussex
Average house	£40,000	£85,000
Households without a car	40%	9.9%
Low rent housing	35%	10.5%
Pubs and clubs	25	2
Last election results	Labour majority: 36%	Conservative majority: 40%

Comprehension

1. Compare the information about the two Ashingtons given above. (Use the figures to support your statements but don't simply quote the statistics.)
   Example: *In Ashington, Northumberland houses are much cheaper than in West Sussex, in fact they cost only half as much.*
2. What conclusions can you draw from these figures about life in Ashington, Northumberland compared to life in Ashington, W. Sussex?

Role play

Roles: *Role A:* Unemployed 17-year-old from Ashington, Northumberland
Role B: 18-year-old trainee bank clerk from Ashington, West Sussex.

Situation: You are both at an open-air concert in Birmingham in the summer and you are standing next to each other in a queue waiting to get drinks. You start talking to each other.

Dialogue: Start with 'small talk'. For example, you could talk about the music at the concert and/or the weather, etc.
Then find out your partner's name and where he/she is from and express surprise when you find out you are both from a town called Ashington. ("What a coincidence!")
Find out as much as possible about the 'other' Ashington.
Arrange to meet in one of the Ashingtons at a later date.

Small talk
See *skills file* on p. 128.

City streets

A Government urban pollution study published in 1999 came to the conclusion that air quality in some northern industrial towns in Britain is improving whilst southern towns are heavily polluted. The article on this page looks at the results for Britain as a whole. The article on p. 31 focuses on Wolverhampton, an industrial town in the Midlands.

Revealed: Britain's filthiest air

LONDON'S most fashionable districts are becoming more polluted than decaying northern industrial towns, the first health check of Britain's city streets reveals.

Roads in Mayfair, Knightsbridge, Kensington and around Hyde Park will soon be the dirtiest in the country. Streets in Newcastle, Wakefield, Jarrow, Sunderland and Wolverhampton will be among the cleanest. [...]

Liverpool is becoming the second dirtiest city, the study shows, followed by Manchester, Birmingham, Leeds, Leicester and Nottingham. While some southern towns are heavily polluted, air quality in larger northern industrial centres is improving dramatically.

The streets of Bristol are becoming more polluted than roads in Glasgow, Newcastle, Cardiff and Hull. Children living near busy roads in Portsmouth will be more likely to contract asthma than youngsters in Bolton, Doncaster, Stockport or Derby. [...]

Professor John Whitelegg, a former adviser to Prescott (Minister of the Environment, 1999) added: 'Unless we change tack, we are heading for a public health disaster like the smogs of the Fifties. Particle levels are rising, nitrogen dioxide levels are far too high and, as we approach the summer, ground-level ozone is rising. [...]'

Traffic is responsible for three-quarters of nitrogen dioxide emissions in towns and cities. The gas attacks the respiratory system causing asthma, lung disease and viral infections. A cut of 30 per cent in emissions from cars, buses and lorries would reduce the number of roads breaking the pollution targets from 761 to 116, environmentalists say.

Friends of the Earth want Ministers to set a national target to cut traffic levels by 10 per cent of 1990 levels by 2010, and to implement radical proposals to charge motorists for driving into city centres. They say company car parking should be taxed and councils given new powers to improve bus services. [...]

Number of city streets forecast to exceed nitrogen dioxide targets

London	**499**
Liverpool	**37**
Manchester	**32**
Birmingham	**31**
Leeds	**22**
Leicester	**19**
Nottingham	**11**
Bristol	**10**
Portsmouth	**6**
Glasgow	**4**
Newcastle	**2**
Edinburgh	**1**
Sunderland	**1**
Wolverhampton	**1**

7 **Leicester** ['lestə] a city in central England, in Leicestershire
12 **to contract** [-'-] *here:* to become ill with
13 **Derby** ['dɑːbɪ] a city in central England, in Derbyshire
16 **to change tack** to use a different method
17 **particle** *here:* tiny amounts of dust in the air
18 **nitrogen dioxide** ['naɪtrədʒən daɪ'ɒksaɪd] *Stickstoffdioxyd*
23 **respiratory** ['respərɪtrɪ] related to the parts of the body which allow one to breathe
30 **to charge** to make s.o. pay

From the article by John Arlidge, The Observer, *March 21, 1999.*

Comprehension →

1. A quick way to draw a rough map of Britain is simply to draw a triangle (see diagram on the right). Look at the map at the front of the book and on your own sketch map mark the towns mentioned in the text and in the table. Number each town according to its ranking in the road pollution table.
2. In one sentence each explain the problem, the consequences and the solution discussed in the text.
3. Why were the results of the survey considered surprising?

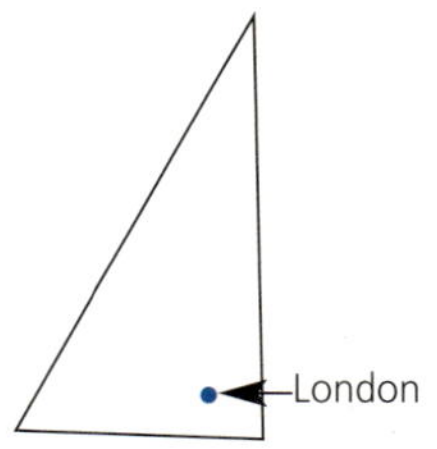

Britain can be depicted in sketch form as a simple triangle.

Vocabulary →

Collect all the words from the text belonging to the semantic field 'pollution' and arrange them in a topic web.

Semantic field
See *skills file* (Collecting words) on p. 133.

← Would you consider Wolverhampton to be a green city judging by the photo? Why? Why not?

Greening of the Midlands grime

by John Arlidge

For a town once so grimy that Queen Victoria refused even to look as she passed through it, topping the green list has come as a surprise. When *The Observer* broke the news on Friday, locals at first refused to accept it.

"This place? The cleanest?" said John Young, 62, who runs a flower stall outside grey, Sixties-built Mander Shopping Centre. "No, you got on the wrong train, mate. You want Winchester or Warminster. This is Wolverhampton. It's a shithole."

But after a look at the pollution study, some locals began to see the green side of Wolverhampton. "It has got a lot better lately," said Gerald Kells, a 40-year-old playwright and environmentalist who grew up in London and moved to the Midlands to escape smog. "I can remember when Wolverhampton had a rotten reputation. That image is out of date now ... You can tell the air is cleaner."

Walking her 16-month-old daughter, Rebecca, in West Park, Sonia Colabella, 29, said she was relieved that after years of smog she could bring up her children safely.

"My husband gets asthma, and I am worried that Rebecca and my second child will suffer too," she said. "The cleaner the air is here, the happier I am. I was thinking of moving, but perhaps now I'll stay."

Col. 1:
3 **grimy** [graɪmɪ] dirty
4 **Queen Victoria** (1837–1901) the queen of Great Britain and Ireland
9 **to break the news** to tell people s.th.

Col. 2:
11 **playwright** s.o. who writes plays

Col. 3:
1 **to be out of date** old-fashioned

From the article by John Arlidge, The Observer, *March 21, 1999.*

← **Comprehension**

What do you find out in the text about:
- Queen Victoria • Wolverhampton • John Young • Mander Shopping Centre • Gerald Kells • Sonia Colabella?

← **Grammar: adverbs**

a) Find three adverbs of time and one adverb of manner in the text.
b) Explain what the adverbs mean giving either a synonymous expression or the opposite.

← **Sentence structure**

"The cleaner the air is here, the happier I am." (Col. 3, ll. 14–15)
1. How would you translate this very common English sentence structure into German?
2. Copy the structure and make sentences using the following words and phrases:
   - more traffic/more polluted air • live close to busy roads/likely to suffer from asthma
   - clean air in Wolverhampton/good reputation of town

Over to you

- Consider in what ways the area you live in has become more or less environmentally friendly in recent years. Summarize your ideas in a short news report like the one above. Ask members of staff and other pupils for their opinion and quote them in your report.

Focus on Birmingham

Birmingham is the second largest city in Britain (after London). It is situated in the Midlands in central England, further from the sea than any other British city! It is a city of historical importance especially in terms of industrial development. Today Birmingham is an important political, commercial and industrial centre. The following tables give details of the structure of the population in Birmingham compared to Britain as a whole.

Preparation →

- Look at the tables and make sure you understand all the vocabulary used in them before doing the tasks on p. 33. Use a dictionary, if necessary.

Table 1: Population in the 1990s

Age structure	Total number in Birmingham	% of population in Birmingham	% of population in GB
0 – 4 years	78,500	7.7	6.5
5 – 15 years	158,000	15.5	14.0
16 – 44 years	432,100	42.5	41.0
45 – pensioner	176,100	17.3	20.2
Pensioners	172,700	17.0	18.2

Table 2: Socio-economic figures in the 1990s

Characteristics	Total number in Birmingham	% of population in Birmingham	% of population in GB
White	754,274	78.5	94.5
Black Caribbean, African & Other	56,376	5.8	1.6
Indian, Pakistani, Bangladeshi	129,899	13.5	2.7
Chinese & Other	20,492	2.1	1.2
Households with no car	168,559	45.0	33.4
One parent households	21,793	5.8	4.2

Check the web
Get more information at:
http://www.go-wm.gov.uk/region/birmingham.html

Table 3: Employment

Employment (1995/96)	Total number in Birmingham	% in Birmingham	% in GB
Employees	446,500	91.2	86.4
– in manufacturing	105,800	23.7	18.3
– in services	320,100	71.7	75.8
– other employees	20,600	4.6	5.9
– part-time	106,200	23.8	28.2
Self-employed	34,900	7.1	12.8
Work related govt. training schemes	8,100	1.7	0.8

During 1995/96 a total number of 24,814,000 people were employed in Britain, 489,500 of them in Birmingham.

Table 4: Unemployment

Unemployment (April 1997)	Birmingham	Great Britain
% unemployed:		
– aged under 25 years	27.9	26.1
– unemployed 6 months +	60.5	53
– unemployed 12 months +	44.1	35.8

In April 1997 1,624,103 people were unemployed in Britain, 44,100 of them in Birmingham.

Source: Government Office for the West Midlands, *http://www.go-wm.gov.uk/region/birmingham.html*

← **Expressing figures**

1. Look at the statistics on p. 32 and comment on when a comma (,) and when a decimal point (.) is used in English.
2. a) Which of the possibilities below is the correct way to say the number: 21,793?
   - Twenty-one thousand and seven hundred and ninety-three
   - Twenty-one thousand seven hundred and ninety-three
   - Twenty-one thousand seven hundred ninety-three
   - Twenty-one thousands seven hundreds and ninety-three

   b) Which of the possibilities below is the correct way to say the number: 86.4 %?
   - eighty-six comma four per cent
   - eighty-six point four per cent
   - sixty-eight point four per cent
   - eight six point four per cent
3. Work with a partner. Choose a different table each and dictate the figures in your table to your partner and vice versa. (Write down the numbers dictated to you without looking at the table!) Afterwards check that you have written the figures down correctly.
4. Think of situations at the workplace and at home when it can be important to be able to quote complex numbers like these.

← **Drawing conclusions**

1. The approximate population of the UK is 58,395,000 (see p. 22). Work out what percentage of the UK population lives in Birmingham using the statistics in Table 1.
2. a) Which of the statistics for Birmingham in Tables 2, 3 and 4 differ the most significantly from those for Britain as a whole?

   b) What (if anything) can you conclude about life in Birmingham from this?
3. The population density of Birmingham is 38.1 persons per hectare. The population density for Britain as a whole is 2.5 persons per hectare. What effects do you think this high population density has on the cost of living and living conditions in Birmingham?
4. a) Which of the statistics do you find the most useful and which do you find the least useful in terms of getting an impression of Birmingham? Give reasons.

   b) What other statistical information (if any) would you have found more useful or more interesting?
5. a) Find Birmingham on the map of Britain at the front of this book and describe its location.

   b) Why do you think Birmingham's location contributes to it being a major political and economic centre in national and international terms?

Talking about statistics
See *skills file* on p. 131.

Over to you

- Prepare a talk on the socio-economic profile of Birmingham based on the statistics given.
  - Present at least one of the tables in the form of a bar chart and one in the form of a pie chart.
  - Comment on any of the statistics which you find particularly interesting, surprising, positive or worrying.
  - Say how you think the facts shown in the statistics might affect life and culture in the city.

Giving a talk
See *skills file* on p. 129.

Check the web
Get more information about Birmingham at:
www.birmingham.gov.uk

Further information
There is more information about Birmingham on pp. 34 and 35.

Quick & Quirky: Facts about Birmingham

These Quick & Quirky (Q&Q) facts were found on the website ***www.birmingham.gov.uk*** *under the menu 'Tourism and Leisure'. Additional information on many of the facts is also provided on the website as well as further links to other related websites.*

- Make an alphabetical listing of any words in the Quick & Quirky facts that you don't understand and look them up in an English/English dictionary.

Q&Q Birmingham is said to have more canals than Venice. The first canal was opened in 1769 and linked Birmingham to Wednesbury.

Q&Q Birmingham's international partner cities include Chicago (USA), Frankfurt (Germany), Johannesburg (South Africa), Leipzig (Germany), Lyon (France) and Milan (Italy).

Q&Q Birmingham is home to Cadbury's Chocolate. George Cadbury and his brother Richard moved their successful chocolate manufacturing business from Bull Street, Birmingham to Bourneville in 1879.

Q&Q X-Ray photography was invented by Major John Hall Edwards; he took the first x-ray in Birmingham in 1896.

Q&Q There are 3 universities and over 450 schools in the city.

Q&Q William Murdock, who worked for Boulton and Watt at Soho, Handsworth, invented gas lighting. His cottage at Soho Foundary was the first domestic building to be lit by gas (1798).

Q&Q How many miles is it from Birmingham to …?

Paris	302
Moscow	1,578
Tokyo	5,929
Bonn	396
Rome	983
London	110
Washington	3,594
Ottawa	3,244

Q&Q Birmingham's basketball team are the "Bullets" and there are three professional soccer teams: the "Blues", the "Villains" and the "Baggies".

Q&Q James Watt, who lived in Birmingham 1775–1819, developed the steam engine. Through it, the firm Boulton and Watt sold the Industrial Revolution to the world. Watt also invented the letter copying machine, forerunner of the photocopier. And his name stays in our vocabulary through the light bulb measurement – 60 Watts, 40 Watts.

Q&Q State education was pioneered in Birmingham in the 1850s.

Q&Q The population of Birmingham is approximately 1 million people; 6 million people live within 50 miles of the city.

Q&Q Nigel Mansell, Indy and Formula One Champion was born, lived and worked in Birmingham.

Q&Q The pneumatic tyre was invented in Birmingham by John Dunlop in 1888.

Q&Q Clean Sweep! … Council street cleaners regularly sweep 1,300 miles of road and empty 4,000 litter bins – helping to make Birmingham officially the UK's cleanest large city.

Q&Q Two of the four biggest banks in Britain were founded in Birmingham – Lloyds (1765) and Midland (1836).

Q&Q Alec Issigonis was one of the most colourful car designers of modern times. He designed the world famous, Birmingham-made 'Mini', which started production in 1959 at Longbridge, Birmingham and is still in production today.

Source: Birmingham Assist, *http://www.birmingham.gov.uk*

Comprehension

1. What kind of information is given in the Q&Q facts?
   a) Identify different categories and group the facts according to them.
   b) Give each category an appropriate heading, e.g. Industry and Economy, Famous People, ….
2. What kind of information – if any – about Birmingham is missing from your point of view as a young person? Why is this missing information important to you?
3. In your own words say what your impression of Birmingham is, taking into consideration the Q&Q facts and the information you acquired on pp. 32 and 33.

Grammar

1. Identify the use of the passive and the active voice in the following sentences and rewrite the sentences substituting the active for the passive voice and vice versa.
   a) George and Richard Cadbury moved their factory from Bull Street to Bourneville in 1879.
   b) The mini was designed by Alec Issigonis and production of it was started at Longbridge, Birmingham in 1959.
   c) X-ray photography was invented by Major John Hall Edwards; he took the first x-ray in Birmingham in 1896.
   d) James Watt developed the steam engine and invented the letter copying machine at Soho Factory in Birmingham.
   e) William Murdock invented gas lighting at the end of the 18th century.
   f) The pneumatic tyre was invented in Birmingham by John Dunlop in 1888.
   g) Council street cleaners regularly sweep 1,300 miles of road in Birmingham.
2. Explain why the passive voice is frequently used to present information like this.

The passive
See *grammar file* on p. 147.

Working on the Internet

1. Go to the Birmingham Assist website (*www.birmingham.gov.uk*) and find out as much as you can about:
   - the website
   - the Quick and Quirky fact (or facts) that interests you most.
2. Collect your findings so that you can present them to your class. Remember to keep a record of the websites you visit and the paths you take to find information.

Giving a talk or presentation
See *skills file* on p. 129.

Over to you

Project: Presenting a town / region

Work in groups.
Aim: To produce a brochure of information about your town or region for visitors from Britain.
Target groups: Choose one of the target groups below (or identify your own target group):
a) a group of students from a college in England visiting your town as part of an educational exchange
b) a delegation from a British company considering opening an office in your area.
Facts: Be certain to include the following:
- geographical aspects
- socio-economic information
- tourist attractions
- history and heritage
- cultural attractions
- points of particular interest for your target group.

Projects & group work
See *skills file* on p. 139.

The British political system

The Constitution

The British constitution is not set down in a single document, instead it is made up of a whole range of laws and conventions, which have been established over the centuries. The constitution can be changed by Act of Parliament to adapt to changing political conditions.

The Monarchy

Check the web
Get more information about the monarchy at:
http://www.royal.gov.uk

The Monarchy is the oldest institution of government. The Monarch is the official Head of State, the head of the executive and of the judiciary, the commander-in-chief of the armed forces and the 'supreme governor' of the Church of England. The Monarch formally appoints many important government office holders, including the Prime Minister (PM). However, the Monarch's real powers are now very limited and the Monarch's duties are largely ceremonial.

Parliament

Check the web
Get more information about Parliament at:
http://www.parliament.uk

Parliament is made up of the House of Commons, the House of Lords and – officially – the Sovereign (Monarch). The House of Lords and The House of Commons are situated in London at the Palace of Westminster, so Parliament is often referred to as Westminster. A Parliament has a maximum duration of five years but in practice General Elections are usually held before the end of this period. The Prime Minister decides exactly when a General Election is to be held within the five year term.

The House of Commons

The House of Commons is where new laws are passed and the main business of government is done. The House of Commons is elected by universal suffrage and consists of 659 Members of Parliament (MPs), one from each of the constituencies (see p. 38, *The Electoral System*). The MPs elect the Speaker who presides over the House but does not take part in discussions or votes.

The House of Lords

He'll have his father's nose, but not his seat in the Lords.

The House of Lords acts in a mainly controlling and advisory capacity but it can delay Bills for up to a year. Until November 1999 it was made up of the most important ministers of the Church of England (two archbishops and 24 bishops), the hereditary peers (over 750 in 1997) and the life peers (over 400 in 1997). When Labour won the 1997 General Election it made a commitment to reform the House of Lords with the intention of making the Lords more democratic and more representative of all sections of British society. In November 1999, in the first stage of reform, the right of hereditary peers to sit and vote in the House of Lords, which they had held since the 14th Century, was abolished. 92 hereditary peers were elected to retain their seats in the House of Lords alongside the life peers and members of the Church until the second stage of reform was completed. At the time no concrete plans were made regarding the further stages of reform.

p. 36
constitution document which states the laws and people's rights in a country – *2* **convention** official agreement – *3* **Act** law *(Gesetz)* – *5* **judiciary** [dʒuːˈdɪʃərɪ] *Rechtswesen* – **armed forces** army, navy, airforce, etc. – *9* **ceremonial** related to a ceremony – *13* **General Elections** main government elections – *17* **universal suffrage** the right of both men and women to vote in elections – *18* **constituency** area represented by an MP – *21* **to delay** to cause to happen later – **Bill** law which has not yet been passed – *23* **hereditary** passed on in a family from one generation to the next – **peer** person with a title (Lord/Lady) – *25* **commitment** promise – *29* **to retain** to keep

p. 37
15 **devolution** transfer of power from central government to regional governments – *16* **predominantly** mainly – *22* **virtually** nearly – *24* **respectively** in that order

Government and Opposition

The party which wins the most seats (though not necessarily the most votes) at a General Election forms the Government. The Leader of the party is appointed Prime Minister by the Sovereign. The Prime Minister's official residence is Number 10 Downing Street. The Prime Minister forms a Cabinet by appointing ministers who are usually in charge of a government department. Most ministers are known as 'Secretary of State' or 'Minister' unless they have a special title, such as the Chancellor of the Exchequer, who is responsible for financial and monetary issues. Other important Ministers are the Home Secretary, responsible for internal affairs and the Foreign Secretary, responsible for foreign affairs.

The largest minority party in the House of Commons becomes the official Opposition with its own leader and 'shadow cabinet'.

Traditionally Britain has been governed centrally from Westminster (London) with Scotland and Wales being represented there by Secretaries of State. Since June 1998 Northern Ireland has had its own assembly (the New Northern Ireland Assembly) and since 1999 Wales and Scotland have had their own assemblies with some – limited – powers. (See p. 39, *Devolution*.)

Check the web
Get more information about 10 Downing Street at:
http://www.number-10.gov.uk

Check the web
Get more information about the government at:
http://www.open.gov.uk

The Political Parties

For the past 150 years a predominantly two party system has existed in Britain. Since 1945 power has been held by the Conservative Party (Tories), a right of centre party, eight times and by the Labour Party, a left of centre party, seven times. No other party has held power in this time. The Liberal Democrats make up the third biggest party in Britain. The party was formed in 1988 when the Liberals and the Social Democrats joined together. There is a Green Party in Britain but it is not represented in parliament, partly because the electoral system gives small parties virtually no chance of winning any seats. (See p. 38, *The Electoral System*.) There are two nationalist parties: Plaid Cymru (Welsh Nationals) and the Scottish National Party which play an important role in Wales and Scotland respectively. In Northern Ireland the most important parties are the Ulster Unionist Party, the Social Democratic and Labour Party, the Democratic Unionist Party and Sinn Fein, the political wing of the IRA.

Check the web
Scottish National Party:
http://www.snp.org.uk
Plaid Cymru:
http://www.plaidcymru.org/

Labour

Check the web:
http://www.labour.org.uk

Green Party

Check the web:
http://www.greenparty.org.uk/

CONSERVATIVE

Check the web:
http://www.conservative-party.org.uk

Check the web:
http://www.libdems.org.uk

LIBERAL DEMOCRATS

The Electoral System

Current system

For electoral purposes Britain is divided into 659 constituencies. Each constituency is represented by one MP in the House of Commons. With a few exceptions British citizens over the age of 18 can vote but voting is not compulsory.

The current system used at General Elections in the UK is the simple majority or 'first-past-the-post' (FPTP) system. Each elector has one vote. Electors vote for the candidate of their choice in their constituency. The candidate who gets the most votes in a constituency wins the seat. Under FPTP all the votes cast for non-winning candidates are wasted. The percentage of seats gained by a party and the percentage of votes cast for it (in total) is often disproportionate. In 1997, for example, Labour gained 65.2 % of the seats in Parliament having won only 43.2 % of the total vote. (See below, *UK General Election results*) The main advantages of FPTP are that it is simple to understand, it tends to produce strong single party governments rather than coalitions, and it provides a close link between MPs and their constituencies.

Proposals for reform

There are currently calls for reform of the electoral system to include some form of proportional representation. Proposals include the following:

Alternative Vote Plus (AV+): This is a two vote system. The first vote is for a constituency MP. The second vote is a 'top-up' vote for a national party list. It is designed to make the representation of the parties representative of the percentage of votes they receive overall.

Party list: This system was used at the European Parliament Elections in Britain in 1999. It is a system of proportional representation in its most basic form. Voters vote for a party, not a candidate. All votes are added together and the percentage of seats won is proportional to the percentage of votes a party gets.

Additional Member: This system was used in the elections for the Scottish Parliament and Welsh Assembly in May 1999. It is a two vote system as used in Germany. Voters have one vote for a constituency MP (FPTP) and a second vote for a (regional) party list (proportional representation).

4 **compulsory** s.th. which must be done

10 **disproportionate** unequal

15 **proposal** suggestion

17 **proportional representation** system of voting in which the percentage of seats a party wins is equal to the percentage of votes it gets

Check the web

Get more information about electoral reform and electoral systems at:
http://www.electoral-reform.org.uk

UK General Election results, May 1997

Party	*Seats won*	*% of votes*
Labour	418	43.2
Conservatives	165	30.7
Liberal Democrats	46	16.8
Referendum	0	2.6
Scottish National Party	6	2.0
Northern Ireland parties*	18	2.1
Plaid Cymru	4	0.5
Others	2	0.0
(Others	0	2.1)
Total	***659***	***100***

**** Northern Ireland parties:***
Ulster Unionist: 10 seats
Social Democrats and Labour Party: 3 seats
Democratic Unionist: 2 seats
Sinn Fein: 2 seats
United Kingdom Unionist: 1 seat

Seats won by party by region

	Labour	**Conservative**	**Liberal Democrat**	**SNP**	**Plaid Cymru**	**Other**	***Total***
England	328	165	34	–	–	2	529
Wales	34	–	2		4		40
Scotland	56	–	10	6	–	–	72
N.Ireland*	–	–	–	–	–	18	18
Britain	418	165	46	6	4	20	659

Devolution

Northern Ireland

On 10th April 1998, in what is known as the Good Friday Agreement, a Northern Ireland Assembly was proposed. A referendum was held on 22nd May 1998 in which the people of Northern Ireland voted in favour of a New Northern Ireland Assembly. Elections were held on 25th June 1998. 108 members were elected by proportional representation (six from each of the 18 existing constituencies). The Assembly has been set the task of creating a North-South Council accountable to the Northern Ireland Assembly and the Irish Parliament. Whilst Westminster retains power in many areas, the Assembly will have closer links with the Irish Government. Legislation over matters of mutual interest, such as transport, will be discussed, agreed and made jointly.

Check the web
Get more information about the New Northern Ireland Assembly at:
http://www.ni-assembly.gov.uk

Scotland

On the 11 September 1997 a referendum was held in Scotland in which the people of Scotland voted overwhelmingly in favour of a Scottish Parliament (Yes: 74 %; No: 26 %). On May 6th 1999 elections to the Scottish Parliament were held for the first time in 300 years. 129 members (MSPs) were elected: 73 from the constituencies on the first past the post system and 56 additional members on a proportional basis from party lists. Each elector had two votes: one for a constituency MSP and one for the party (or individual) of their choice. Elections will be held every four years.

The new Scottish Parliament has been given limited powers to legislate (to make 'Acts of the Scottish Parliament') whilst the Westminster Parliament continues to be the sovereign parliament of the United Kingdom and has the power to legislate about any matter. However, the Westminster Parliament will not normally make laws concerning devolved matters in Scotland without the agreement of the Scottish Parliament.

Check the web
Get more information about the Scottish Parliament at:
http://www.scottish.parliament.uk/
http://www.thescottishparliament.com

Scottish Parliamentary Election Results, May 1999

	Overall results	*First Vote*	*Second vote*
Labour	56	53	3
SNP	35	7	28
Conservative	18	0	12
Liberal Democrat	17	12	5
Other	3	1	2

Wales

On September 18th 1997 a devolution referendum was held in Wales in which the Welsh people voted by a margin of fewer than 7,000 votes in favour of having a Welsh Assembly. On 6th May 1999 elections for the new Assembly were held. The Assembly has 60 elected members, 40 of which are elected on the first past the post system and 20 by a form of proportional representation. Voters all have two votes and elections will be held every four years.

The Welsh Assembly does not have the same level of power or responsibility as the Scottish Parliament. It has been given only what is known as 'secondary legislative powers' in certain defined areas, with Westminster retaining control of 'primary legislative power' in all areas. This means that Westminster makes laws at a national level and the Welsh Assembly can make secondary legislation deciding exactly how these laws are interpreted in Wales.

Check the web
Get more information about the Welsh Assembly at:
http://www.wales.gov.uk

Welsh Assembly Election Results, May 1999

	Overall results	*First Vote*	*Second vote*
Labour	28	27	1
Plaid Cymru	17	19	8
Conservative	9	1	8
Liberal Democrat	6	3	3

2 **Good Friday** the Friday before Easter Sunday
7 **accountable to** answerable to
9 **legislation** making of laws
mutual interest of interest to both groups
13 **overwhelmingly** very strongly

3 Making the grade

Mission Statement

Our aim is to provide, in a supportive environment, high quality career and personal development to enhance individual aspirations and to reflect local, national and international needs through Higher and Further Education Training.

← *Left:* The front cover of a brochure produced by the Central College of Commerce, Glasgow

↑ *Above:* The Central College's 'Mission Statement'.

Education: What's the point?

Analyzing language & illustrations →

1. Make a table with three columns. List the words from the front cover of the brochure in the first column. In the second column write down what you think is meant by them, and in the third column write down what they mean to you in terms of your education.
2. Why do you think the cover designer chose these signs and a compass for the brochure?
3. Read the college's mission statement and find phrases which show that:
   the college aims to create a helpful learning atmosphere • the college wants to help students both at home and in their future jobs • the college knows that it is important to pay attention to developments outside the college walls.
4. Work in groups. Design a collage and/or write a 'mission statement' which reflect your reasons for continuing your education at a vocational college.

Collecting words

While reading the texts in this chapter make a **glossary** on 'education' by writing down all the words that belong to that category. Look up any words you don't know in a dictionary! See also *skills file* on p. 133.

Class opinion →

Look at the statements below and give each statement a rating of 1 (very true) to 5 (not true at all). Compare your results with a partner and then with others in your class. Each time try to agree on a top five so that in the end you find the five statements which best express the opinion of your class.

- Being trained is boring, being educated is not.
- 16+ students increasingly show no real commitment to their school work.
- 16+ students are frequently bored in class.
- 16+ students show a tendency not to care when they oversleep or miss classes.
- Education helps students develop a meaningful philosophy of life.
- 16+ students see further and higher education only as a means of increasing their income and becoming financially well-off.
- 16+ students today are 'consumers' of education. They want to be entertained.
- 16+ students do not view education as an opportunity to expand their minds.
- 16+ students go to school to prepare themselves for their future.
- Most 16+ students stay on at school simply to avoid having to get a job.

Having a discussion

See *skills files* on pp. 131 & 132.

16+

Eastbourne College of Arts and Technology (ECAT) included these case studies in their college brochure. Read the case studies and then do the tasks below.

Developing Potential

Claire Hafernik

Claire, from **Park College** and **Cavendish School** studied the one year **BTEC Foundation Art and Design** course.

She said,
"I found the course very challenging but it taught me to think in a professional way. The tutors encouraged me to expand on the set projects which definitely helped in my application to University. The printing facilities at the college are particularly good even compared to some Universities I've visited."

Claire will be studying for a degree in Textile Design and Surface Decoration at Buckinghamshire College.

Developing Potential

Richard Day

Richard came from **Hailsham Community College** to study **GNVQAdvanced Information Technology.**

He said,
"College life is always humorous. You work in a relaxed and informal way with mature and younger students alike. Tutors are helpful and supportive, making time to deal with your problems and questions thoroughly. You get guidance throughout the course and the opportunity to examine all aspects of the Computing Industry."

Richard is looking forward to studying a BSc Degree in Computer Science at Brighton University.

Developing Potential

Carla Keeley

Carla came from **Hampden Park School** to study **A Levels** in **Chemistry, Biology** and **Mathematics**.

She said,
"I have enjoyed College life, there is a great deal of independence compared to secondary school. This has meant a lot of organisation and self-motivation. My A Levels have been a challenge and harder than I expected."

Carla intends to study for a degree in Biological Science at the University of Birmingham and hopes, in the future, for a career in scientific research.

case study detailed study of a person or group

Claire
BTEC technical qualification
to encourage *anregen*
application *Bewerbung*
facility equipment, buildings, etc. serving a certain purpose
degree title given by a university or college when a student successfully completes a course

Richard
GNVQ General National Vocational Qualifications
mature [mə'tjʊə] grown up
supportive helpful, esp. to s.o. in a difficult position
thoroughly ['θʌrəlɪ] completely
guidance help and advice
BSc Degree Bachelor of Science degree

Tenses
See *grammar files* on pp. 142 – 145.

Role play

Work in pairs. In turns take on the role of the interviewer and one of the students above and devise role plays to go with two of the case studies. Pay attention to the tenses you use in your questions and answers. Be prepared to present your role play to the rest of the class.

Interviewer *(The student has just entered your office.)*
Greet him/her and offer him/her a seat.
Find out the student's name.
Explain that you want to ask a few questions that can be included in the next college brochure and that you are going to record the interview.
Ask if the student can give you a photo that can be used in the brochure. Give the student the information asked for. Find out:
... which school the student went to before coming to ECAT.
... what the student thinks of the college courses, the lecturers and the college as a whole.
... what the student's plans for the future are.
Remember to thank the student at the end of the interview and say goodbye.

Student *(You have just entered the interviewer's office.)*
Return the interviewer's greeting.
Remember to say please and thank you as often as possible!
When asked, find out what size of photo is needed and whether it should be black and white or colour. Offer to bring a photo the next day.
Use facts from the case study to answer the interviewer's questions as far as possible.
Where no answer is given in the text, decide on your own answer. Remember to say goodbye before you leave.

Over to you

Make a short statement about your reasons for staying on at your school. Include a photo of yourself and (on a computer) design a profile page about your class for a partner college.

School life in Britain

Collecting information

1. What do you know about school life in Britain? Make a mind map of the things you already know. You can add more information to your mind map as you work through this chapter. The following categories might help you:
   types of schools • school day • exams • school subjects • extra-curricular activities
   This is what the first stage of your mind map might look like:

Mind maps
See *skills file* on p. 121.

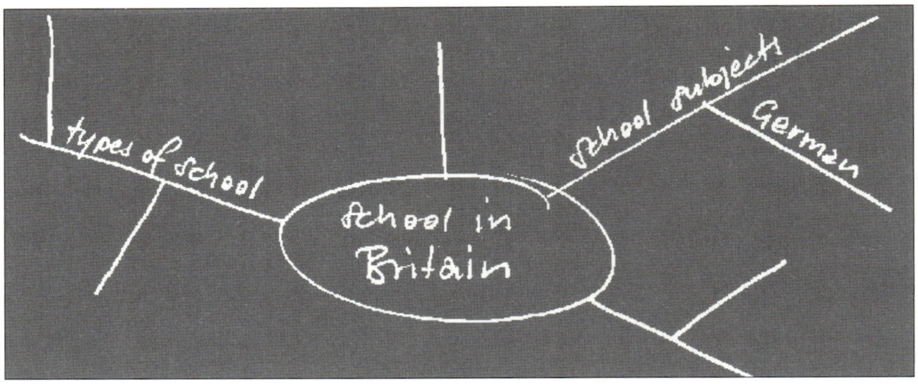

2. Make a similar mind map about school life in your country.

Fact finding & making questions

1. Read the information in the boxes on the next two pages. Add any new information to your mind map.
2. a) Write a question to go with each box. Try to make up as many different types of questions as possible. You should write at least one question from each of the categories on the right. Make a note of the answers to your questions on a separate sheet of paper.

   What ...? • When ...? • How many ...? • Where ... ? • Explain in your own words • Which ...? • Find the word/phrase which means ... • Give your opinion on ...

   b) Ask your partner to answer your questions and vice versa.

The school year in British schools starts early in September and continues into the following July. Classes are held from Mondays to Fridays from about 9 in the morning until 3 or 4 o'clock in the afternoon. Pupils can join in extra-curricular activities, such as sport and drama clubs, during the lunch break or after school.

A National Curriculum is taught in state schools. This sets out what subjects pupils should study, what they should be taught and what standards they should achieve.

Around the end of compulsory education at the age of 15–16, pupils take GCSEs (General Certificates of Secondary Education). GCSEs are available in a wide range of subjects, and pupils are tested by assessment of work during the course and by examinations.

compulsory obligatory

Religious education (RE) must be taught by law in all state schools and all schools must hold daily collective worship. Parents have the right to withdraw their children from this and from RE classes if they choose.

worship religious ceremony
to withdraw *here:* to take away

Over 85% of state secondary school pupils go to comprehensive schools. These take children of all abilities and provide a wide range of secondary education for most children aged from 11 to 16 or 18 years.

About 4% of pupils go to grammar schools. Grammar schools offer a mainly academic education for the 11- to 18-year-old age group. Other types of secondary schools provide a more general education up to the age of 16 (the minimum leaving age).

City Technology Colleges (CTCs) aim to give boys and girls a broad secondary education with a strong technological and business slant. They are independent secondary schools set up by the Government with the help of business sponsors who finance a large proportion of the initial capital costs and develop on-going links with schools. These schools charge no fees.

slant *here:* emphasis on particular subjects

Over 90 % of children in Britain go to publicly-financed schools known as state schools. Some eight million children attend schools in England alone. They start primary school at the age of five in the infants' school. At seven they move to the junior school and the usual age for transfer from junior to secondary school is 11.

TVEI (Technical and Vocational Educational Initiative) aims to help schools better prepare young people for work. The objective is to make the school curriculum more relevant to the working environment. Projects emphasize a practical, problem-solving approach to learning and encourage the use of the latest technologies.

Further Education (FE) provides a wide range of academic and vocational courses for students over the compulsory school age. Currently, some 70 % of 16-year-olds continue their full-time education. All 16- to 18-year-olds have a right to free education.

All pupils in their last year of compulsory education have the opportunity to go on work experience. During a placement they carry out particular jobs in much the same way as regular employees.

placement a period of practical experience e.g. in business

About seven per cent of children attend fee-charging independent or private schools in England. These range from small kindergartens to large day and boarding schools, and from new experimental schools to schools famous throughout the world. Some independent schools are known for historical reasons as 'public' schools, although they receive no state funding.

fee-charging requiring payment of a certain amount of money – **boarding school** school where students live during the term – **funding** *here:* money

All schools, colleges and universities provide careers education and guidance for students to raise their awareness of training and careers opportunities, and help them prepare for the future.

All children in Britain must by law receive education between the ages of five and 16 and more than 70 % of 16-year-olds stay on in full-time education. Other young people leave school at 16 to take up training for work or a job with training. Young people do not have to undertake training. The Government does not directly provide training for people in work.

There are three main kinds of post-16 qualification:
GCE A (Advanced) levels are academically demanding examinations, usually taken by pupils at 18 years and over. They are the main academic qualification for entry into higher education (universities).
GCE AS (Advanced supplementary) levels require the same standard of work as A levels but have less content. They allow students to increase the breadth of their education – for example those taking arts subjects at A level can continue to study science and technology.
GNVQs (General National Vocational Qualifications) provide a broadly based vocational qualification incorporating the core skills of communication, application of numbers and Information Technology. They are designed to develop skills and understanding in a vocational area, such as business, engineering or health and social care. They can lead to higher level study or employment.

vocational referring to a particular profession and its skills

At 16+ both academic and vocational courses are offered by a diverse range of institutions such as sixth forms in secondary schools, sixth form colleges, general further education colleges, and specialist colleges. Students can choose to attend full-time or part-time, including day release from employment, evening classes and distance learning.

Records of achievement

Check the web
Get more information about writing personal statements at:
http://www.academicadmissions.org/

Young people in compulsory education put together a National Record of Achievement (NRA) in which they keep a record of their experiences and achievements. The NRA not only includes academic and vocational qualifications and certificates, but also a personal statement giving details of hobbies, voluntary work and so on. Later, it can be used to record employment history. The NRA shows what a person has to offer when applying for a job, a training programme or for college or university. Ross Noon, a 17-year-old pupil at a state school in Birmingham included this personal statement in his NRA.

Personal statement

At present I am studying History, English Literature, Sociology and General Studies at A level. I enjoy all my A levels but find Sociology particularly interesting and challenging. This is because I enjoy reading and writing essays as well as debating issues. My History course involves two European topics: Nazi Germany and Mussolini and Fascist Italy. I find these topics give a very interesting insight into modern history. I am also looking forward to working on my personal study in History; I hope to base it on an aspect of Nazi Germany. In English Literature I have been studying *Wuthering Heights* by Emily Brontë, *Tess of the d'Urbervilles* by Thomas Hardy and *Paradise Lost* by John Milton. I have found all three texts interesting so far.

I have found that the style of study at A level is very different to my GCSE courses, and the more in-depth detail and discussions make A levels much more enjoyable. The skill of critical analysis developed in my A level subjects has been very useful in writing essays and studying sources. I have learnt how to carry out research using primary sources and how to construct an argument based on evidence.

Because of my love of History I hope to do a History degree at University. My other subjects have allowed me to develop a structured and discursive style of writing which I find extremely useful in my History studies. I also depend on the personal skills learnt as a result of the independent research undertaken in my subjects. I have learnt to work on my own, only seeking the teacher's guidance and direction occasionally.

At the end of year ten I spent one week's work experience at the school of History at Birmingham University. It was a most interesting, educational and enjoyable week. I did filing, word processing and general administrative work. I particularly enjoyed sending and receiving e-mail. During the week, I discovered that I enjoyed working with people and got a great deal of satisfaction in meeting deadlines and working under pressure. I got on with others extremely well and made good friends with the people I worked with.

As well as my Sixth Form studies, I play an active part in organizing events to raise money for charity. The most recent was a Talent Contest. I play an active part in college life, and regularly perform in concerts and revues.

As a hobby, I enjoy both playing and listening to music. I have studied the clarinet but at present I play bass guitar. I have been in a band with friends for about eighteen months now, and we have played a number of gigs at the 'Songwriter's Café', a free venue for the public every Sunday.

4 **to involve** *here:* to include
6 **insight** view
13 **indepth** well-developed
16 **to carry out research** to do a study of a subject – **primary** original – **source** [sɔːs] book, etc. which gives you information about s.th.
17 **evidence** fact that supports a belief
20 **discursive** presenting reasonable arguments that lead to a conclusion
22 **to undertake** to begin work, that requires special effort
26 **filing** ['faɪlɪŋ] sorting documents and storing them away
29 **to meet a deadline** to finish s.th. by an agreed date – **to get on with** to have a friendly relationship with
33 **charity** organization that helps people who are poor, sick, in difficulties, etc.
37 **bass** [beɪs]
39 **gig** *here:* concert – **venue** the place where an event happens

I am also an avid CD and vinyl collector, preferring all types of sixties' and seventies' music. I also enjoy reading music biographies on past bands and books on subcultures of the sixties. I enjoy going out and spending time with friends. I also enjoy travelling. My previous trips have been to Ireland, the United States and all over Europe. Through this, I have learnt about other cultures and ways of life – something which interests me greatly. I enjoy sport a lot and love to watch football and cricket and regularly go swimming to keep fit.

I enjoy Sixth Form life very much and consider myself well-suited to the way of learning at Sixth Form level. I very much hope to go to university and enjoy university life as much as I have enjoyed my A levels.

40 **avid** extremely eager or keen – **vinyl** ['vaɪnl] *here:* record

Comprehension & comparison

Use your answers to the questions below to compare your school life with Ross's.

1. a) How many subjects does Ross study?
   b) How many subjects do you study?
2. a) What makes A level studies more enjoyable than GCSE courses, according to Ross?
   b) Describe the style of study and the content of the courses you now take. Say how you find studying in Year 11 compared to in Year 10.
3. a) Which personal skills has Ross learnt as a result of his A level studies?
   b) Which of these skills have you learnt? How important are these skills for your studies and for the future? Which kind of skills would you like to learn? Which kind of skills do you think you should be taught at your current level at school?
4. a) Where, when and for how long did Ross go on work experience?
   b) Describe any work experience you have done in as much detail as possible.
5. a) Copy the table below and fill in relevant information about Ross from the text.

extra-curricular activities	*other hobbies and interests*

   b) Make a new table with the same headings and fill in comparable information about yourself.
6. What are Ross's plans for the future? What are your plans for the future?
7. Do you think you would get on with Ross (perhaps as a penfriend or an e-mail partner)? Give reasons.

Listening comprehension

All pupils in Britain spend time on work experience.
Listen to a British pupil who is talking about her placement.

Grammar

1. Look at ll. 8 to 11 *("In English Literature … interesting so far.").*
   a) Which tense or tenses does Ross use here?
   b) What does the use of these tenses tell you about what Ross was studying in his English Literature lessons at the time?
2. Rewrite the following sentences using the present perfect and the words in brackets. The first one has been done for you.
   a) Ross began his A level History studies two months ago. (study/for two months now)
   Ross has been studying A level History for two months now.
   b) Lynne and Helen started learning German three years ago. (learn/for three years)
   c) Simon joined a band last summer. (be in a band/since last summer)
   d) Celine began work experience in a retail store on Monday. (work/since Monday)

The present perfect
See *grammar file* on p.144.

Over to you

Write your own 'personal statement'. Use the material you have collected and which you have been practising in the tasks above.

Academic Report

In Britain teachers write detailed reports on all their pupils. Pupils are usually given these reports twice a year: once in February and once in July.

SIXTH FORM CENTRE — **ACADEMIC REPORT**

MID-SESSION: 1997/98 STUDENT: BALVINDER BHATTI TUTOR: Mark Poleman

Subject:	Attendance: Actual/ Possible	Assessments:	Lecturer(s) Comments: Please Initial
SOCIOLOGY	20/23	Hwk 72% Exam 41%	The exam was a little disappointing after some very encouraging work during the term. Better revision required to improve on the rather superficial knowledge shown in the exam. MP
English	22/24	64% DW 52% CG	You have made an enthusiastic start to the course. Your contributions have been valuable and show your developing understanding. Keep up your reading and prepare tests thoroughly to maintain your progress. DW
Law	100% attendance		Bal, you have shown wonderful enthusiasm for the subject. You are a bright and capable student, who is a pleasure to teach. MC

Tutor's Comments: You are a bright, enthusiastic student who is adapting well to college. Keep this up and we hope to see you do well.

Signature: Mark Poleman

tutor ['tju:tə] – **superficial** *opp. of* detailed – **thoroughly** carefully and completely – **capable** ['keɪpəbl] having the qualities to do s.th.

Comprehension & analysis

1. What are Balvinder's main strengths and main weaknesses according to the teachers?
2. Compare Balvinder's report with the type of report you get.
   a) What are the main differences in appearance and content?
   b) Which one do you like better: yours or Balvinder's? Give reasons.
   c) Which one might an employer find more useful? Give reasons.

Language

1. a) Work with a partner. Look at the style and type of comments Balvinder's teachers have made. Write down adjectives from the comments under the following headings:
   Exam results • Course work • Contributions in class • Type of student
   b) Compare your list with others in your class and make additions if necessary.
2. Find the verbs which complete these phrases:
   ___ a little disappointing • ___ on the knowledge • ___ an enthusiastic start • ___ an understanding • ___ reading • ___ tests • ___ progress • ___ enthusiasm • ___ a bright and capable student

Over to you

Design a report form, either by hand or preferably on the computer, and fill in information about yourself. Use words and phrases you have collected in the language tasks above. Your comments can be funny and they don't necessarily have to be true!

Tutor groups at single sex schools. Do you prefer to work in single-sex or mixed groups? Why?
Describe the photos in as much detail as you can. Think of words to describe what you think the atmosphere is like in each of the groups.

Single-sex education

Most state schools in Britain are co-educational, that is, for pupils of both sexes. However, there are also many single-sex schools in Britain in both the state and the independent sectors.

"Boys are like dogs, who respond to discipline from a firm leader of the pack. Girls are more like cats, who need gentle encouragement."

Your view

1. Do you agree with the above statement? Give reasons for your opinion.
2. Is this statement a valid argument in favour of or against single-sex education in your opinion? Give reasons.

Language

1. Work with a partner. Which of the words below do you associate more with cats or dogs, and which with boys or girls?
   firm • gentle • tough • quiet • noisy • clever • helpful • sensitive • confident • funny • lively • obedient • independent
2. Using words from the list (or any other suitable words you know) make a simile of your own about boys' and girls' performance or behaviour at school.

Similes
See *glossary* on p.153.

Class survey

Find out the opinion of students and teachers at your school on single-sex education.

1. Work in groups. First agree on about 10 questions to ask. These ideas might help you get started:
   subjects that could/should be taught separately • relevance of single-sex education in a vocational college • single-sex education as preparation for work and for life • possible advantages and disadvantages of single-sex classes for boys and girls.
2. Decide what type of questions you are going to ask: multiple-choice questions • graded questions • open-ended questions • Yes/No questions.
3. You will need certain personal information about interviewees (but not their names) so that you can evaluate the results. Decide which personal information (e.g. age, sex, nationality) you think is necessary and include this in your questionnaire.
4. Before you start, you could write down your group's prognosis so that you can compare it with the results you get.
5. Ask at least 15 people to complete your questionnaire and analyze the results in your group.
6. Use your results to prepare a presentation in class or write a report on your findings for your school newsletter or your home page.

Questionnaires & surveys
See *skills file* p. 140 & 141.

Presenting & reporting
See *skills files* on pp.124 & 129.

Performance and achievement

Looking at stereotypes

1. Write down things which you think are typical of boys or girls at school. Think of things like the subjects they choose/prefer, behaviour in class, performance in tests, job prospects, aims in life, etc.
2. Look at Balvinder's report on p. 26. Do you think Balvinder is a boy or a girl? Why?

Looking at charts

1. What trend in boys' and girls' academic achievement is shown in the charts below?
2. Think of possible reasons for this trend.

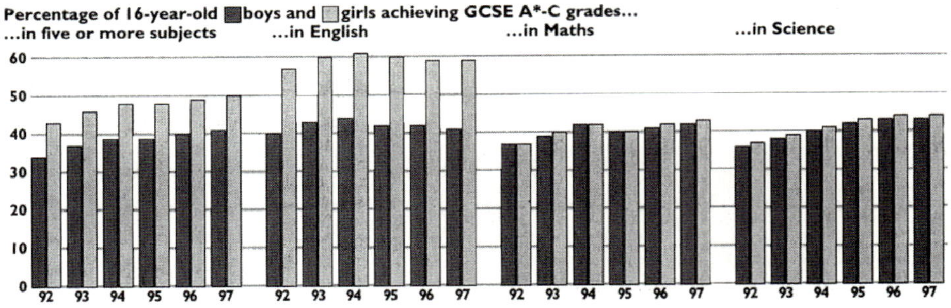

From The Observer, *January 4, 1998.*

Regardless of sex, it's cool to do well

Girls are winning the academic achievement race. Test and exam results show that they are winning at seven, they are winning at 11 and they are winning triumphantly at 16. At 18 they are catching up fast and, given time, no doubt, they will storm the last unconquered citadel where boys still do better than girls – the first-class honours degree.

Last week's 14-year-old assessment results were yet another footnote to the story of girls' onward march. The first results of national curriculum assessments carried out by teachers for subjects other than English, maths and science painted a familiar picture. Two-thirds of the girls but only half of the boys reached the expected standard in history, geography, design and technology, modern foreign languages and music.

At GCSE and A level, girls are now matching boys in the traditionally male strongholds of maths and physics.

The differences are so stark that if ministers could solve the problem of boys' under-achievement, they would be well on the way to reaching the demanding national targets they have set for the year 2002.

So what's to be done? Schools – and ministers – have to be realistic. There's nothing they can do about a crisis in male confidence that stems partly from the disappearance of many jobs which depend on muscle-power and their replacement by jobs that girls can do just as well – or better – than boys.

Some of the qualities that make girls so employable are the result of centuries of conditioning. The art of simultaneously feeding a baby, cooking the supper and doing a jigsaw with a toddler is not going to transfer to men overnight.

There is also a limit to the extent to which schools can combat the "feminine culture" that makes boys anti-reading. Research from Exeter University and part of the Leverhulme Primary Project found that boys (the minority) whose fathers or grandfathers read at home with them did better than those who read with mother.

But schools can make a difference. Research has shown that boys will read adventure, humour and sport. They won't, for the most part, read stories, though replacing *Jane Eyre* with Roald Dahl may help.

regardless not taking s.th. into account
2 **triumphantly** [traɪˈʌmfəntlɪ] very happily as a winner
4 **citadel** *(here: fig.)* strong position held by a certain group
7 **national curriculum** programme of study followed by students at state schools
8 **familiar** generally known
11 **to match** *here:* to be equally successful
12 **stronghold** *here:* referring to subjects dominated by boys
13 **stark** clearly obvious
14 **under-achievement** doing less well than one could, esp. at one's school work – **demanding** at a high level
15 **target** standard
17 **confidence** a strong belief in o.s. – **to stem from** to be caused by
21 **conditioning** process by which people or animals are trained to behave in a certain way in certain conditions
22 **jigsaw** puzzle – **toddler** child who has just learnt to walk
23 **extent** degree – **to combat** to fight against
24 **research** study of a subject to find out more about it
29 ***Jane Eyre*** 1847 novel by English novelist Charlotte Brontë (1816–1855) – ***Roald Dahl*** (1916–1990) writer of children's literature

The Qualifications and Curriculum Authority is preparing a pack of information for teachers to be sent out in the New Year to make English more boy-friendly.

It will point out the need to make allowances for boys' preference for fact over fiction in choosing books, comprehension exercises and essay titles for them. There are case studies including one in which boys compared accounts of football matches in different papers and another in which a teacher logged the books that boys borrowed from the school library. Another school paired 11-year-old boys and girls so that girls could teach boys planning and boys could teach girls a more adventurous use of language.

Yet there are dangers in all this. If schools focus simply on boys' under-achievement and the differences between boys and girls, both girls and society will be the losers. Do we really want a culture in which boys are encouraged to analyze a football match but not the relationship between Jane Eyre and Mr Rochester?

Despite their overall success, there are still plenty of under-achieving girls who drift into motherhood without the qualifications they need for employment.

Some schools have chosen to tackle the gender divide by close and regular monitoring of the performance of all pupils, irrespective of their sex. They have set short-term goals and given their slowest pupils extra help. They have also tackled discipline throughout the school – one of the keys, according to inspectors, to improving boys' achievement. Finally, they have tried to change pupils' motivation and to promote the idea that it is "cool" to achieve. That is surely the way forward.

A reminder that boys have fallen far behind girls was long overdue. But the solution lies in better teaching for both.

By Judith Judd, The Independent, *December 4, 1997.*

32 **to make allowances** to take particular factors into account

34 **case study** *see p. 21*

35 **to log** to keep a record of

39 **to focus on** to direct (one's attention) to s.th.

41 **to encourage s.o. to do s.th.** to make s.o. interested in doing s.th.

45 **to tackle** to deal with a problem

46 **to monitor** to watch carefully – **irrespective** without considering some factor

51 **reminder** s.th. that makes one remember – **overdue** late in appearing

Language

1. Rewrite the words in the following sentences from the text using your own words for the words underlined.
   a) *Girls are <u>winning the academic achievement race</u>.* (l. 1)
   b) *At GCSE and A level, girls <u>are now matching boys in the traditionally male strongholds of</u> maths and physics.* (ll. 11–12)
   c) *The Qualifications and Curriculum Authority is preparing <u>a pack of information</u> for teachers to be sent out in the New Year <u>to make English more boy-friendly</u>.* (ll. 30–31)
   d) *[…] there are still plenty of under-achieving girls who <u>drift into motherhood without the qualifications they need for employment</u>.* (ll. 43–44)
2. Find opposites for these words from the text:
   to win (l. 1) • to do better (l. 4) • realistic (l. 16) • to borrow (l. 36) • employment (l. 44).
3. Find synonyms in the text for these words:
   certainly • level • all at the same time • reports • the answer.

Synonyms and opposites
See *glossary* on page 153.

Summarizing

Writing summaries
See *skills file* on p. 125.

Tasks 1–3 below teach you step by step how to write a summary. When you have finished, look at the skills file on p. 125 and identify the steps you have taken. You can use this strategy whenever you need to write a summary.

1. Without looking at the text again write four or five sentences in your own words saying what the text is about.
2. Reread the text and write down one sentence using your own words to describe each paragraph. Do not quote statistics, numbers, figures, etc.
3. a) Put the sentences you have written in tasks 1 and 2 in a logical order.
   b) Check again that you have not copied from the text. Rewrite any sentences which you have copied.
   c) Now join your sentences using connectives from the list in the box on the right.

Connectives
to begin with • initially • firstly/secondly/thirdly • in the first/second/third place • next • for this reason • consequently • however • in conclusion
Find more connectives on p. 125.

Them & Us

Novel
See *glossary* on p. 153.

The following text is an extract from the **novel** Decline and Fall *by Evelyn Waugh in which a new teacher, Paul, meets his class for the first time. Grimes is the headmaster. While you are reading decide what kind of person you think Paul is: think about his age, appearance and character.*

1 **mob** a large, noisy crowd, esp. one which is violent
5 **to sigh** to let out a deep breath slowly
6 **to amble** to walk unhurriedly – **burst** a sudden short period of noise
7 **dumb** [dʌm] unable to speak
16 **reproach** *(formal)* criticism of s.o. in a sad way for doing s.th. wrong – **sensitive** easily-hurt emotionally
19 **uproar** confused noise caused by many people shouting
21 **grave** [eɪ] serious
25 **scrutiny** a close examination
35 **jolly well** *(BE, old)* just – **go to blazes** *(exclamation)* go to hell
36 **desperate** [ˈdesprət] hopeless
38 **instantly** at once
39 **not on the end of a barge pole** *(informal)* out of the question
42 **blow** a hard hit with a hand or an object
43 **hush** silence, esp. following a period of noise
47 **firmly** in a determined way – **form** *(BE)* class

Check the web
Get more information about Evelyn Waugh at:
http://www.e2.empirenet.com/~jahvah/waugh/

"That's your little mob in there," said Grimes. "You let them out at eleven."

"But what am I to teach them?" said Paul in panic.

"Oh, I shouldn't try to *teach* them anything, not just yet, anyway. Just keep them quiet."

"Now that's a thing I've never learned to do," sighed Mr Prendergast.

Paul watched him amble into his classroom at the end of the passage, where a burst of applause greeted his arrival. Dumb with terror he went into his own classroom.

Ten boys sat before him, their hands folded, their eyes bright with expectation.

"Good morning, sir," said the one nearest him.

"Good morning," said Paul.

"Good morning, sir," said the next.

"Good morning," said Paul.

"Good morning, sir," said the next.

"Oh shut up," said Paul.

At this the boy took out a handkerchief and began to cry quietly.

"Oh, sir," came a chorus of reproach, "you've hurt his feelings. He's very sensitive; it's his Welsh blood, you know; it makes people very emotional. Say 'Good morning' to him, sir, or he won't be happy all day. After all, it is a good morning, isn't it, sir?"

"Silence!" shouted Paul above the uproar, and for a few moments things were quieter.

"Please, sir," said a small voice – Paul turned and saw a grave-looking youth holding up his hand – "Perhaps he's been smoking cigars and doesn't feel well."

"Silence!" said Paul again.

The ten boys stopped talking and sat perfectly still staring at him. He felt himself getting hot and red under their scrutiny.

"I suppose the first thing I ought to do is to get your names clear. What is your name?" he asked, turning to the first boy.

"Tangent, sir."

"And yours?"

"Tangent, sir," said the next boy. Paul's heart sank.

"But you can't both be called Tangent."

"No, sir, I'm Tangent. He's just trying to be funny."

"I like that. *Me* trying to be funny. Please sir, I'm Tangent, sir; really I am."

"If it comes to that," said Clutterbuck from the end of the room, "there's only one Tangent here and that is me. Anyone else can jolly well go to blazes."

Paul felt desperate.

"Well, is there anyone who isn't Tangent?"

Four or five voices instantly rose.

"I'm not, sir; I'm not Tangent. I wouldn't be called Tangent, not on the end of a barge pole."

In a few seconds the room had become divided into two parties: those who were Tangent and those who were not. Blows were already being exchanged, when the door opened and Grimes came in. There was a slight hush.

"I thought you might want this," he said, handing Paul a walking-stick. "And if you take my advice, you'll set them something to do."

He went out and Paul, firmly grasping the walking-stick, faced his form.

Evelyn Waugh (1902–1966)

"Listen," he said, "I don't care a damn what any of you are called, but if there's another word from anyone I shall keep you all in this afternoon."

"You can't keep me in," said Clutterbuck. "I'm going for a walk with Captain Grimes."

"Then I shall very nearly kill you with this stick. Meanwhile you write an essay on 'Self-indulgence.' There will be a prize of half a crown for the longest essay, irrespective of any possible merit."

From then onwards all was silence until break. [...]

From Decline and Fall *by Evelyn Waugh, London: Penguin Books, 1937, pp. 38–39.*

52 **self-indulgence** allowing o.s. pleasure too easily – **half a crown** *(GB, old)* coin worth twelve-and-a-half pence
53 **irrespective of** without considering s.th. – **merit** *here:* quality of one's work

Understanding & analyzing the text

1. a) What happened when Paul went into the classroom?
   b) Why did one of the boys start to cry?
   c) What joke did the boys play on Paul?
   d) Why did the boys work hard in the end?
2. Read the following statements and decide whether they are true or false. Find a quotation in the text to support your choice. Correct the statements that are false.
   a) Mr Grimes wanted Paul to continue with the lessons from the point where the last teacher had left off.
   b) Paul was looking forward to his first lesson.
   c) When Paul started the lesson, he found it very warm in the classroom.
   d) When Grimes came in, no one took any notice.
   e) Paul promised the students money if they would start to write an essay.
3. a) Describe the pupils' behaviour at the beginning of the text and at the end.
   b) At which point in the story does the situation change?
   c) What do you think of Grimes' reaction?

Use of language

1. Look at the way Paul speaks to his pupils and find examples of inappropriate language used by him.
2. Do your teachers ever speak to you like this? How do/would you react?
3. Why is it important for teachers and pupils to use appropriate language?

appropriate correct or suitable for a particular situation or occasion

Grammar: Reported speech

A few days later Paul talks to his colleague, Prendergast, about his first lesson. This is what he says. Copy and complete the text below. You will need to use reported speech.

I went into the classroom and all the boys were sitting there staring at me. Then each of them wanted me to say good morning to them individually and in the end I told them _____ . But then one boy started to cry and the others shouted out that _____ . One serious-looking boy even suggested that _____ . When I asked _____ three boys claimed that they were Tangent. So I asked if _____ and four or five said they weren't. And then they all started fighting each other. It was terrible. Luckily Grimes arrived at that moment and gave me a stick and advised me _____ . When he had gone I told the boys that _____ . Clutterbuck said _____ . But I replied _____ and from then onwards all was silence until break.

Reported speech
See *grammar file* on p. 151.

Your view

What can and should pupils and teachers do to create a cooperative atmosphere rather than an atmosphere of confrontation in the classroom? Make a list of 'dos and don'ts' for pupils and teachers.

Text analysis

Narrator
See *glossary* on p. 152.

Define the **narrator** and the point of view used in this extract. Find two passages in the text that make this clear.

Tony Blair was at Fettes from 1966 to 1971. Many Fettesians [fet'i:dʒən] have become leading politicians and diplomats but Blair was the first old Fettesian to become Prime Minister.

Fettes ['fetɪs]
(full) boarding pupils live in school full-time during term time and only go home in the holidays
weekly boarding pupils live in school during the week in term time but go home at weekends and in the holidays
accounting course where pupils study financial accounts
fencing *Fechten*
fives *(GB)* game in which a ball is hit with the hand against three walls of a court
lacrosse [-'-] a team game; a small ball is thrown and caught with a long stick with a net on the end
archery *Bogenschießen*
Duke of Edinburgh ('s Award) *(GB)* leisure-time scheme for young people between 14 and 25
outdoor pursuits [pə'sju:t] free time activities outdoors such as hiking, etc.
pottery making of pots, etc. from clay *(Ton)*
pitch playing field

Independent schools

Many schools in the independent sector have a long and distinguished history of preparing students for higher education: most combine their academic work with a full programme of extra-curricular clubs and societies. Fettes College in Edinburgh, Scotland, is one of these schools.

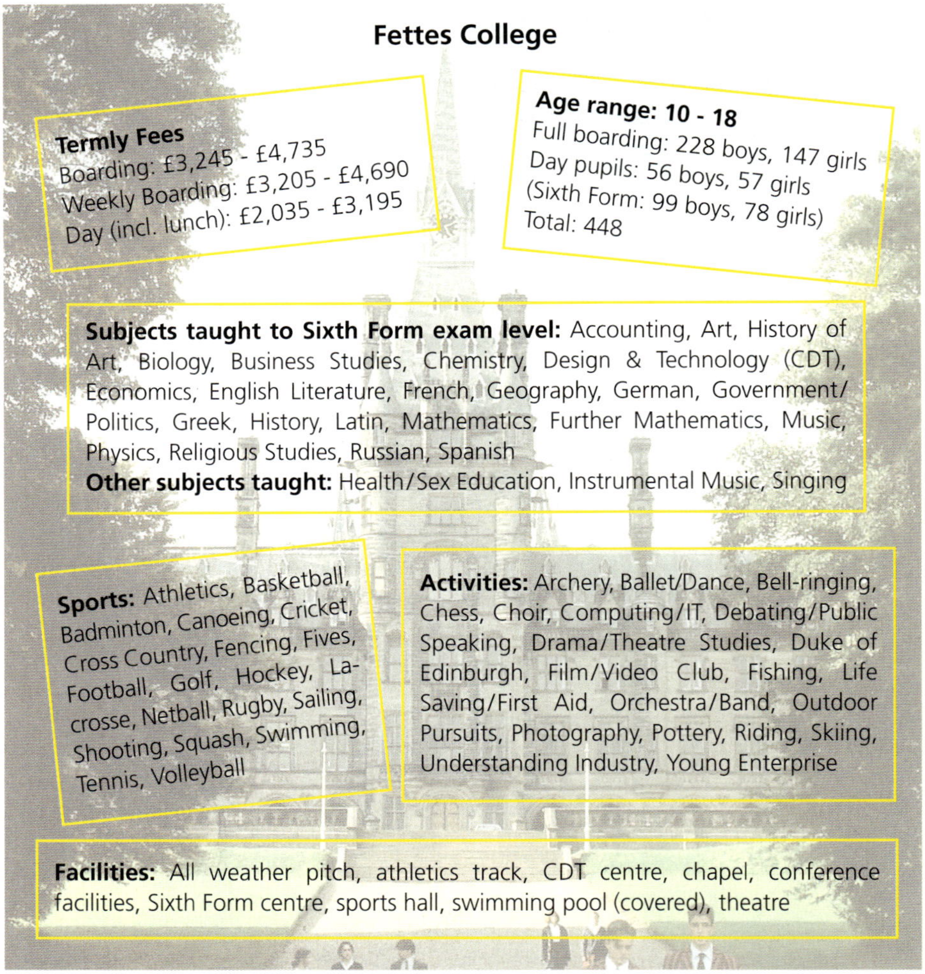

Fettes College

Termly Fees
Boarding: £3,245 - £4,735
Weekly Boarding: £3,205 - £4,690
Day (incl. lunch): £2,035 - £3,195

Age range: 10 - 18
Full boarding: 228 boys, 147 girls
Day pupils: 56 boys, 57 girls
(Sixth Form: 99 boys, 78 girls)
Total: 448

Subjects taught to Sixth Form exam level: Accounting, Art, History of Art, Biology, Business Studies, Chemistry, Design & Technology (CDT), Economics, English Literature, French, Geography, German, Government/Politics, Greek, History, Latin, Mathematics, Further Mathematics, Music, Physics, Religious Studies, Russian, Spanish
Other subjects taught: Health/Sex Education, Instrumental Music, Singing

Sports: Athletics, Basketball, Badminton, Canoeing, Cricket, Cross Country, Fencing, Fives, Football, Golf, Hockey, La-crosse, Netball, Rugby, Sailing, Shooting, Squash, Swimming, Tennis, Volleyball

Activities: Archery, Ballet/Dance, Bell-ringing, Chess, Choir, Computing/IT, Debating/Public Speaking, Drama/Theatre Studies, Duke of Edinburgh, Film/Video Club, Fishing, Life Saving/First Aid, Orchestra/Band, Outdoor Pursuits, Photography, Pottery, Riding, Skiing, Understanding Industry, Young Enterprise

Facilities: All weather pitch, athletics track, CDT centre, chapel, conference facilities, Sixth Form centre, sports hall, swimming pool (covered), theatre

Making a phone call

Telephoning
See *skills file* on pp. 126 & 127.

You ring Fettes College to get information for a school project on independent schools in Britain. Complete the following telephone conversation and then practise it with a partner.

SECRETARY: Good morning. Fettes College. Can I help you?
YOU: *State your name, where you are calling from and why you are calling.*
SECRETARY: You need to speak to Andrew Norton, our PR manager. Would you hold the line, please? I'll put you through.
ANDREW NORTON: Good morning, can I help you?
YOU: *State your name, where you are calling from and why you are calling.*
ANDREW NORTON: What exactly would you like to know?
YOU: *Ask about the fees.*
ANDREW NORTON: That depends on whether you are a full boarder, a weekly boarder or a day pupil.
YOU: *Ask about the difference between full and weekly boarders.*

Pupils at Fettes college: Note the school uniform the pupils are wearing. What is typically Scottish about it? What do you like or dislike about it?

ANDREW NORTON: As a full boarder you stay at the college all term and only go home in the holidays. Weekly boarders, on the other hand, can go home at weekends.

YOU: *Ask about the fees for full and weekly boarders.*

ANDREW NORTON: Full boarding costs ... *(give the fees)* and weekly boarding costs ... *(give the fees)*, including all meals and activities, of course.

YOU: *Ask about the number of pupils at the school.*

ANDREW NORTON: At the moment we have ... full boarders: that's ... boys and ... girls, and we have ... day pupils *(give the figures)*.

YOU: *Now you want to know the number of pupils in the sixth form.*

ANDREW NORTON: At the moment we have ... boys and ... girls in the sixth form *(give the figures)*.

YOU: *Find out if the subjects you are currently studying are taught at Fettes, too.*

ANDREW NORTON: Yes, we teach a full range of subjects including ... *(the subjects asked about)*.

or Well, we do teach ... *(give the subjects)* but I'm afraid we don't teach ... *(give the subjects)*.

or No, I'm afraid we don't teach those subjects but we do offer ... *(choose the subjects most similar to those asked about)*.

YOU: *Tell Mr Norton you are interested in the kind of sports activities which are offered at Fettes.*

ANDREW NORTON: At Fettes we are very lucky to have excellent sporting facilities. We have ... *(give examples of some of the sports facilities)* so you can really do any sports from ... to ... *(give examples of two very different kinds of sports)*.

YOU: *Tell Mr Norton that you are interested in computers and new technology and ask him what opportunities there are in this area.*

ANDREW NORTON: New technology is very important nowadays in all areas of life: at school, at work and at home. Here at Fettes we have ... *(give details of facilities)*, we run extra-curricular activities in ... *(give details)*, and of course there are courses to A level in ... *(give details)*.

YOU: *Thank Mr Norton for all his help.*

ANDREW NORTON: You're welcome. I'd be pleased to send you a school brochure if you'd like to give me your name and address.

YOU: *Give your name and address.*

ANDREW NORTON: Sorry, I didn't quite catch that. Could you spell your name for me, please?

YOU: *Give your name again and spell it, then your address again, spelling the name of your street and town.*

ANDREW NORTON: Thanks very much. And don't forget, we also have a school website. The URL is fettesedin.sch.uk

YOU: *Thank Mr Norton once again and say goodbye.*

ANDREW NORTON: Goodbye!

Fettesians playing rugby. What do you know about the game? Find out more at: ***www.rfu.com/***

Check the web

Get more information about Fettes College at: ***www.fettes.co.uk/fetthome.htm***

Get more information about independent schools at: ***www.isis.org.uk***

Your view

1. Make a list of at least three advantages and three disadvantages of private education. Then answer the following questions.
   a) If you had the choice would you prefer to go to a private or a state school? Why?
   b) Why do you think some parents in Britain are prepared to pay for their children's education when state education is free and available for all?

Having a discussion
See *skills file* on pp. 131 & 132.

2. Discuss your answers and opinions in groups.

Schools of the future

IT revolution in the classroom

The face of classrooms and the relationship between pupils and teachers is set to change rapidly in the near future. In a brochure published by the Department of Education and Science we are told that "Britain is amongst the world leaders in the development and integration of Information Technology (IT) in education. Besides being taught as a National Curriculum subject, a great deal of emphasis is placed on the use of IT in schools in all subjects and by children of all ages, abilities and aptitudes. The overall objective is to ensure that pupils are well-versed in new technologies and able to use them to enhance their learning and prepare for working life." In Britain, all schools will be linked to the National Grid for Learning. Students will be expected to take an active part in their education and not just passively download material from the Internet.

Your view →

- How important is 'IT' in education in Germany? Do you think you are offered enough opportunities to learn about new technologies at school? What is taught and, in your opinion, what is missing?

Comprehension →

Look at the illustration and describe what is meant by these key terms:

a) home-based learning
b) live links
c) paper-free learning
d) palmtop computer
e) virtual access

palmtop so small that it fits into your hand

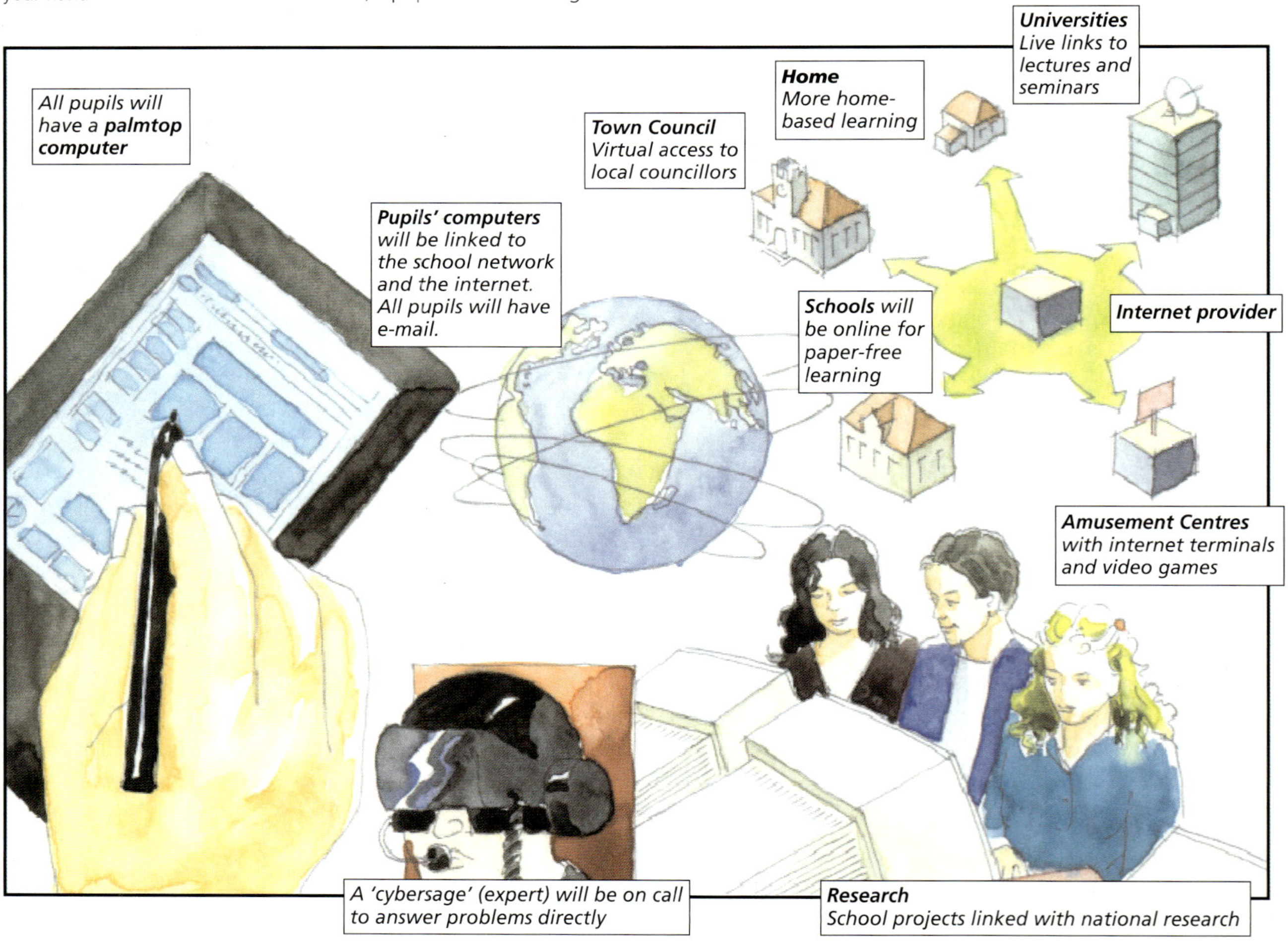

Laptop to oust books

Computer facts

- Average number of pupils per computer: 19 in primary schools. Nine pupils per computer in secondary.
- Average number of computers per school: 13 for primary, 96 for secondary.
- Average spent per pupil last year on computers: £10 in primary; £33 in secondary.
- Companies: RM; Microsoft; Apple; Acom plus a number of smaller companies fighting over the rest of the market.

There will be few books in the classroom of the future and the blackboard will become almost obsolete, *writes Vivek Chaudhary.*

Pupils in class will be linked by computer to the teacher in what is known as an "integrated learning system". This allows pupils to work at their own pace on a computer, which can mark their work.

Using the main computer, the teacher will be able to see which pupils are having difficulty and can then concentrate on pupils in difficulty, allowing others to continue learning at their own pace. Teachers will also be able to set course work using archive material on the Internet rather than having to consult a large number of reference books.

Computer companies hope that most pupils will have access to either a personal computer or laptop at home. Once homework is set, pupils can complete it and download it to the teacher's computer for marking.

Pupils will also have access to the Internet for information and any other material they may require for their schoolwork. Pupils at home because of illness will be able to take part in lessons by connecting to the class computer.

to oust [aʊ] to take the place of s.th. by force

3 **obsolete** ['ɒbsli:t] no longer used

7 **pace** speed

13 **archive** ['ɑ:kaɪv]

By Vivek Chaudhary, The Guardian, November 29, 1997.

Comprehension

According to the text, …

1. … what major difference will there be in British schools of the future?
2. … how will the work teachers do change?
3. … how will the way pupils work change?
4. … what are the main benefits of working online?

Your view

What is your opinion on this new kind of computer classroom? Start by making a list of positive and negative aspects, then state your view.

Research and report

Project: A new centre of learning

Work in a group of four. You have been given the task of setting up a new centre of learning for young people.
Consider the following points and produce a promotional leaflet explaining the aims of your centre and what is on offer for students.
Consider:

- type of students (e.g. mixed; single-sex; minimum/maximum age)
- courses of study (e.g. range of subjects; obligatory/optional courses)
- form of study (e.g. home-based/paper-free; teacher oriented)
- forms of assessment
- qualifications
- extra-curricular activities
- centre facilities
- links to business and industry
- international links and exchanges
- other aspects you consider important

Project work
See *skills file* on p.139.

Meet Britain's press

Meet the press

Introduction

- How many of the newspapers pictured below have you seen before – or even read?
- Judging by the front pages, which of the newspapers would you be most likely to buy? Why?
- a) These newspapers are all national daily newspapers. Which German national daily papers can you name?
  b) Which kind of newspapers are more widely read in Germany: national or regional? Can you think of reasons why?

Test yourself

1. Answer the multiple choice questions below on your own. If you are not sure of the correct answer, just guess.
2. Compare your choices with a partner. Discuss any differences and revise your choices, if necessary.
3. The solutions to the questions are given on p. 68. Check that your answers are correct and then write one complete sentence to go with each question.

1. In which of these countries are the most daily national and regional newspapers sold per person?
   a) Germany c) France
   b) The USA d) Britain

2. Which is the oldest national Sunday newspaper in the world?
   a) *Welt am Sonntag* (Germany)
   b) *New York Times* (USA)
   c) *The Observer* (GB)

3. *The Times* is Britain's oldest daily national newspaper. When do you think it began publication?
   a) In 1785.
   b) In 1885.
   c) In 1905.

4. Finish the sentences (a,b,c) with the correct endings (d,e,f).
   a) Nearly 60 % of people over the age of 15 in Britain read ...
   b) Over 65 % of people over the age of 15 read ...
   c) Around 90 % of people over the age of 15 read ...
   d) ... a regional or local newspaper.
   e) ... a Sunday newspaper.
   f) ... a national morning newspaper.

5. Who reads the most newspapers in Britain?
   a) Men
   b) Women
   c) No difference

6. Which of the following age groups read newspapers the most in Britain?
   a) Under 24 year olds.
   b) 25 – 44 year olds.
   c) Over 45 year olds.

7. What are the circulation figures (the number of newspapers sold) for British national newspapers on weekdays?
   a) 13 million
   b) 15 million
   c) 17 million

8. What are the circulation figures for national newspapers on Sundays in Britain?
   a) 13 million
   b) 15 million
   c) 17 million

Quality & popular press

Newspapers in Britain can generally be put into one of two categories: either 'popular' or 'quality'.

1. a) What do you think is meant by the terms 'popular' and 'quality'?
   b) Think of adjectives to describe the type of news you would expect to find in each group. Here are some to start you off:
   Popular press: *sensational, one-sided, ...* Quality press: *neutral, ...*
2. Look at the newspapers pictured on p. 56. List the names of the newspapers under the headings 'popular' and 'quality'.
3. a) Popular newspapers are also often referred to as 'tabloids'. Look up this term in a dictionary and explain it in your own words.
   b) What advantages might there be in having a tabloid newspaper?
   c) Are there any tabloid newspapers in Germany? If so, name them.
4. a) What makes the *Financial Times (FT)* stand out optically from the other newspapers?
   b) Who do you think reads the *FT*?
   c) Is there any equivalent to the *FT* in Germany? If so, name it.

Circulation & readership

The information in the tasks below refers to either The Sun *(a popular, tabloid newspaper) or* The Times *(a quality paper). Both newspapers belong to the same newspaper group owned by Rupert Murdoch.*

1. Complete the following statements using the correct tense and form of the verbs given.
   to be (x2) • to belong to • to buy • to have •to live • to print (passive form) • to write (passive form)
   a) 60 % of this newspaper's readers ___ middle and senior management and professional groups.
   b) 57 % of this newspaper's readers ___ in London and the South East.
   c) The readership of this newspaper ___ surprisingly young – 54 % of its readers being under the age of 45.
   d) Some years ago this ___ the first paper to give away a £1 million bingo prize.
   e) Since 1990 this paper ___ in London, Liverpool and Glasgow.
   f) Proprietor Rupert Murdoch ___ this newspaper for £600,000 in 1969.
   g) About 2,500 to 3,000 letters ___ to this newspaper every week.
   h) 39 % of the readers of this paper ___ a University degree or equivalent.
2. Make sentences using the following information:
   a) male readers: 55 % • female readers: 45 %
   b) MPs who read this paper: 53 % • MPs who read other papers: less than 53 %
   c) readers' ages: 15–34 years: 45 % • under 45: 61 %
3. a) Decide which statements you think refer to *The Sun* and which to *The Times*. Give reasons for your choices.
   b) Which newspaper do you think you would be most likely to read, *The Sun* or *The Times?* Why?

Tenses
See *grammar files* on pp.142–145.

Check the web
Visit *The Times* and *The Sun* at:
http://www.the-times.co.uk
http://www.the-sun.co.uk

Over to you

- Which German newspapers and/or magazines do you and your friends read?
  – Make a list of the newspapers and magazines which people in your class read.
  – Make a note of whether the readers are male or female.
  – Find out at what age people started reading them.
  – Find out how many people have ever written a letter to a newspaper or magazine.
- Make statements similar to those about *The Sun* and *The Times* using the information you have collected.

Sales figures

Mail on Sunday climbs into second position

December is a freakish month for newspaper sales figures due to the long holiday period but the jump by *The Mail on Sunday* to become the country's second biggest-selling Sunday paper has been on the cards for some time.

With the red-top tabloids in decline, it is now seen as inevitable that the *Daily Mail* will overtake sales of *The Mirror* this year.

The *Mail on Sunday* shows a year-on-year rise of more than five per cent and overtook the *Sunday Mirror* last month with a sale of 2,151,510.

The gap between *The Mirror* and the *Daily Mail* last month was just 21,000. While the *Mail* is up year-on-year by seven per cent, *The Mirror* has suffered a drop of 3.5 per cent. *The Sun* shows a drop of more than five per cent on 1996 and the *Daily Star* a fall of more than seven per cent.

The *FT* (*Financial Times*) shows the biggest year-on-year growth of the quality dailies, helped by its expansion in the US.

Despite its autumn relaunch, *The Independent* continues to struggle. Its sales dropped by 11.6 per cent in December, compared to November, to 227,060. *The Independent on Sunday* was also down by 8.4 per cent.

In contrast, *The Sunday Times* has hit its highest December sales figure for 16 years at 1,304,138.

From the article in the Press Gazette, *January 16, 1998.*

Col. 1:
1 **freakish** crazy
6 **on the cards** possible

Col. 2:
14 **relaunch** new or second start

From text to table →

Make a table to show which of the newspapers mentioned in the text increased their sales and which sold less. Do not include any figures in your table but arrange the titles clearly to show which have made the biggest gains and losses.

Language →

a) Find words in the text which mean:
strange, unusual • because of • a sudden increase • has been probable (for quite a long time) • selling less and less • to pass • an increase over the last year • the difference between two figures • a fall • increase (x2) • to have difficulties • on the other hand.

b) Decide which of the expressions in part a) can be grouped according to the categories below. Add any other expressions to each category which you know or can find in the text:
Words/phrases used to show an increase • Words/phrases used to show a decrease • Words/phrases used to make a comparison.

From table to text →

Look at the sales figures on p. 59 and write an article comparing the average six months sales figures of the following newspapers: *Daily Telegraph, The Observer, The Guardian* and *The Times.* Use the words and phrases in the box below and the vocabulary you collected in language tasks a) and b) above.

Qualifier		Comparison
about • approximately • almost • nearly • slightly • far • much • just • hardly any • no … at all	+	(twice) as high as • (three times) as low as • (four times) higher than • (three times) lower than • over • under

Giving a presentation →

Presentations
See *skills file* on p. 129.

1. Choose five newspapers from the table and draw a bar chart to show their average daily sales figures.
2. Copy your bar chart onto a flip chart or OHP transparency. Present your findings to your class. Use the language you have collected and practised in the tasks on this page.

Average sales figures of December 1997

Daily papers	Average daily sales Dec 1997	Average daily sales 6 mths to Dec 1997
The Sun	3,678,425	3,779,605
The Mirror	2,210,920	2,324,109
Daily Star	579,885	685,039
Daily Mail	2,189,907	2,237,949
Daily Telegraph	1,081,876	1,098,440
The Times	783,359	792,151
The Guardian	389,376	403,999
Financial Times	342,122	328,793
The Independent	227,060	260,223
Mail on Sunday	2,151,510	2,219,430
Sunday Times	1,304,138	1,343,324
The Observer	407,306	439,573
Independent on Sunday	266,530	287,543

From the Press Gazette, *January 16, 1998.*

mths abbreviation for months

- What are the English abbreviations for the following: day • the days of the week • year • the months of the year?

News coverage in quality and popular papers

Before you read

- How do you think news coverage differs in popular newspapers and in quality newspapers? Think about differences in content and style.
- In September 1998 a plane crashed off the Canadian coast. The front pages of *The Guardian* and *The Mirror* of Friday, September 4th 1998, the day after the crash, are pictured here. Have a close look at them and comment on:
  a) … the amount of space on the front page which is devoted to the plane crash in each of the papers.
  b) … how the headlines used differ in size, style and content.
  c) … the use of photos and text to cover the crash.

Friday September 4 1998
The Mirror
www.mirror.co.uk
30p
Liz Hurley as you've NEVER seen her
SEE PAGE 3
SMASHED TO SMITHEREENS
Six Brits among 229 killed as jet disintegrates

property, interiors, design
space
David Hare — why I took that knighthood
Friday Review
Andrew, Newcastle and sexy rugby
Sport98
45p
Friday September 4 1998
Published in London and Manchester
NEWSPAPER OF THE YEAR
The Guardian
£500m blow in Blair's backyard
600 jobs to go as factory shuts
'There is no president of the United States of America who has done more for peace in Northern Ireland than you'
Tony Blair
229 die in plane crash
He's still loved somewhere . . .
See the difference...
Inside
0800 074 0404

The Guardian and The Mirror ran reports on the crash on their inside pages. Here are extracts from both articles.

Check the web
Get more information about *The Guardian* and *The Mirror* at:
http://www.guardian.co.uk
http://www.mirror.co.uk

The Guardian
NEWSPAPER OF THE YEAR

Mystery of crash pilot's last message

Seven minutes before Swissair flight 111 plunged into the sea, the voice of captain Urs Zimmerman crackled over the radio to air traffic control.

"Pan. Pan. Pan," he cried.

"We have an emergency ..."

The call to the centre in Moncton, New Brunswick in Canada, was the last anyone heard from the McDonnell Douglas MD-11 jet, and it has perplexed investigators.

The Pan signal – short for the French panne, or breakdown – is less serious than a Mayday, and indicates that Mr Zimmerman believed the aircraft was in difficulty but not in jeopardy. [...]

There was nothing unusual about the flight when it took off from John F Kennedy airport two hours before, at 8.18 pm. Capt. Zimmerman, one of Swissair's most experienced pilots and an MD-11 instructor, headed north on the familiar route taken by flights bound for Europe.

The first sign of trouble came an hour and a quarter later, when he radioed that there was smoke in the cockpit. Although alarming, he said the flight was not in immediate danger and suggested heading to Boston's Logan airport.

Shortly afterwards he called air traffic control again. The situation had deteriorated and he needed to make an emergency landing at Halifax international airport.

The plane descended from its cruising altitude of 33,000 feet and the captain prepared to dump hundreds of tonnes of fuel into the ocean at St Margaret's Bay.

By this time the crew had ordered the passengers to put on their life vests and explained the emergency drill in the event of a difficult landing. But there was no indication of crisis on board.

"We think the plane had successfully dumped its fuel and was heading to the airport when it went down," said a Swissair spokesman. "The captain was following normal emergency procedure."

The situation, however, was about to become critical. Captain Zimmerman radioed a Pan emergency and Halifax prepared for the worst, sending all its fire engines on to the tarmac, and drafting in extra ambulances.

Flight 111 disappeared from radar screens as it descended between 10,000 and 8,000 ft.

Residents in Blandford knew something was wrong, running out of their homes because of the noise of the low flying plane. Edie Boyle said, "It sounded terrible. It was just droning."

The motors were going but it was the worst-sounding deep groan that I've ever heard," added Claudia Zinck-Gilroy.

Then they heard the crash. "It was like a clap of thunder," said Alberta Martin, of Peggy's Cove, a popular tourist destination. "There was a vibration and then everything was silent. You couldn't see flames or smoke or anything."

Locals put the point of impact as two miles off Ironbound Island.

Within the hour, scores of fishermen had put to sea on a cloudy night joining the four planes and helicopters in the search for survivors. A Canadian navy ship, the HMSC Preserver, also steamed to the site, to no avail.

Rob Gordon, a Canadian Broadcasting Corporation reporter, joined the fishermen. "It was a little after 12.30 and it was clear from the atmosphere and the way people were dealing with it that they felt they might be able to find somebody," he said.

"But as time wore on it was obvious that they weren't going to find anybody alive."

From the article by Nick Hopkins and Martin Kettle, The Guardian, *September 4, 1998.*

Col. 1:
- *2* **to plunge** to fall down abruptly
- *3* **to crackle** to make the sound of cracking wood
- *16* **jeopardy** danger of being destroyed or harmed seriously
- *32* **to deteriorate** to become worse
- *38* **dump** to drop

Col. 2:
- *8* **tarmac** black material that road surfaces are made of
- *17* **to drone** to make a constant, very low, humming sound
- *19* **groan** sound of sadness or pain
- *36* **no avail** no use

The Mirror
Friday September 4 1998
www.mirror.co.uk
30p
Liz Hurley as you've NEVER seen her
SEE PAGE 3

7 Minutes From Safety

Brave captain almost made it ... then came the plunge to disaster in the Atlantic

For 40 desperate minutes yesterday, the Swiss captain of Flight 111 fought a heroic battle to keep his crippled airliner flying.

And when the Swissair jet plunged into the cold deep waters of the Atlantic it was just seven minutes from safety.

Urs Zimmermann, 50, and his co-pilot Stephan Loew, 36, wore oxygen masks as they struggled at the controls after smoke swirled into the cockpit an hour after take-off from New York en route for Geneva. Losing power, he dumped tons of fuel.

Witnesses heard a boom like a clap of thunder as the plane went down 20 miles off the coast of Nova Scotia in Canada. There were reports of flames in one of the McDonnell Douglas M-11's three engines.

As distraught relatives gathered at New York and Geneva airports, one airport worker said: "The pilot almost made it. He was only a few minutes away – what a terrible tragedy."

Flight 111 had left New York's Kennedy airport at 8.17 pm local time.

Captain Zimmermann reported smoke in the cockpit as the jet cruised at 33,000 ft.

He asked Canadian air traffic controllers whether he should be diverted to Logan International Airport in Boston. They told him he was 192 miles from Logan and 42 miles from Halifax, Nova Scotia.

He said "Fine" and headed for Halifax. Then, as the coastline loomed, the crew declared an emergency.

A final call – "Pan, Pan, Pan" – came minutes before the crash seven miles from the fishing port of Peggy's Cove.

The call, short for the German and French word Panne, or breakdown, is one level below a May Day distress alert.

Boom

Passengers were already in their life-jackets.

About 30 miles south of Halifax, the plane disappeared from the radar screens.

His voice choking with emotion, Swissair chief Philippe Bruggisser said last night: "Seven minutes more and the aircraft would have landed."

Residents in the nearby town of Blandford said the doomed airliner screamed overhead very low, then they heard a bang.

Edie Boyle said: "All I heard was a big boom like a sonic boom."

Alberta Martin recalled: "I heard the crash and a clap of thunder shook the house."

"The engines were still going when the plane flew over but it was the worst-sounding deep groan that I've ever heard."

Darrell Fralick, 26, who lives at Peggy's Cove, said: "There was a silence for two seconds after the explosion, then my ears popped.

"At that split second, I looked at my watch and it was 10.35. I don't know why I looked at my watch, I just did."

More than 30 ambulances raced to the shore – but there were no survivors. […]

Former British Airways captain Eric Moody, who advises the pilots' union BALPA, said: "The pilot did not call a May Day alarm which suggests he thought he had the situation, though serious, under control.

Slammed

"But the crew would have been desperately trying to find the source of the smoke.

"It could have been a fire in the cargo hold which in the M-11 is under the cockpit, or it could have been electrical smoke."

The 229 on board had no chance when the big jet slammed into the water.

Captain Moody said: "I don't think the pilot was trying to land in the sea.

"Unless he was very close to land or over shallow water, he'd know his chances were non-existent.

"I don't know of any incident in which a big aircraft has successfully ditched in the sea.

"The G-forces when you hit the water are horrendous, everything disintegrates. You can't slow the plane down below 150 mph to 200 mph."

Christian Stuessi, Swissair's top MD-11 pilot, said crews were trained to issue the "pan" call only "when the situation has really become precarious."

As details of the disaster emerged, weeping relatives of passengers and crew thronged the airports at New York and Geneva.

At Geneva's Cointrin airport, an elderly couple, hearing their son's name read out, cried: "He was there, oh my God."

A Mexican woman, Lidia Picco, burst into tears as she told how her sister had been on board. "I invited her, I paid for her to come. And now she's dead," she sobbed. […]

By Mark Dowdney, The Daily Mirror, *September 4, 1998.*

Col. 1: *12* **to swirl** to move in concentric circles esp. water or air – *22* **distraught** [dɪsˈtrɔːt] extremely upset– *33* **to be diverted** to be directed or guided on a tour different from the original one – *39* **to loom** to come into sight in a threatening way
Col. 2: *5* **distress alert** emergency alarm – *7* **boom** *here:* loud sound as of thunder or storm
Col. 3: *4* **to slam** to hit hard with a bang – *21* **to ditch** *(coll.)* to make an emergency landing – *29* **precarious** dangerous – *32* **to throng** to move or gather in a crowd

Mystery of crash pilot's last message

The captain of Swissair flight 111 seems to have had no inkling of disaster. Nick Hopkins and Martin Kettle report

Mark Tran on the chequered history of a relatively new airliner

TRAGEDY OF FLIGHT 111

7 MINUTES FROM SAFETY

Brave captain almost made it.. then came the plunge to disaster in the Atlantic

Comparing styles of journalism

A **headline** is the title of a newspaper story.

A **heading** is the title you give to a piece of writing.

1. **Headlines**
   a) What effect do the headlines of each article have on the reader?
   b) Which of the headlines do you find most effective? Give reasons.
2. **Layout** (see photos above)
   a) Compare the layout of the two articles paying attention to similarities and differences in the use of photographs, sub-headings, maps and illustrations.
   b) Which newspaper do you think makes the best use of these elements?
   c) What is the function of these elements, in your opinion?
3. **Use of quotations**
   a) Under the headings *The Guardian* and *The Mirror* make a list of the people who are quoted in each article.
   b) Arrange the people in groups (eye-witnesses, officials, experts, etc.).
   c) What are the differences and similarities between the lists for each newspaper?
   d) What effect does the use of quotations have?
4. **Language and style**
   Decide which article you think is: more factual • more persuasive • more evocative • more dramatic • more serious • more vivid. Find examples to illustrate your choice.

Over to you

1. Work in pairs and devise headlines to go with the news stories outlined below. Devise one headline in the style of a popular paper and one in the style of a quality paper.
2. Compare your headlines with the headlines other pairs have written. Decide on the best headline for each type of newspaper. Give reasons for your choice.
3. Write a short article either for a quality or a popular paper to go with one of the headlines. Pay attention to the style and type of language you use!

American jeans company to shut down 7 factories for two months ... 4,000 workers affected ... workers stage hunger strike in protest at lay offs ... last year company announced plans to increase production in China

More than 600 hooligans crossed border into France ... French policeman beaten unconscious ... +/- 20 people injured ... plans for a five-year travel ban for hooligans ... more neo-Nazi groups among hooligans ... Police chief: "New hooligans show ruthless efficiency, use mobile phones to communicate and avoid alcohol."

What makes the news?

Before you read

- Which kind of stories do you think are most sucessful at an international level? Why?

Top Ten Stories

I was surprised to see that no fewer than four of the top 10 international stories in 1997 – measured in a world-wide poll by the Associated Press – were either entirely British or had a strong British content. They were Princess Diana's death (first place), the handover of Hong Kong (second), our election result (fifth) and the cloning of Dolly, the sheep (10th). The Americans came in at number 12 with the Pathfinder landing on Mars, and the only top 20 event to take place on American soil was the murder of Gianni Versace, at number 19.

I suspect that in the new global news marketplace, stories can be sold across borders as easily as oil, cameras or Tamagotchis. The British, with our strong, highly competitive media, are as good at creating slick, appealing news for international consumption as southern Germans are at cars, and West Coast Americans at software. Princess Di's death was the main world news story because we had packaged and sold her with skill, determination (and greed) for 17 years. Our election got twice as much space as the French because Tony Blair was turned into an interesting parcel of information, as desirable, in his own way, as a bottle of Remy Martin, a Spice Girl CD, or a BMW.

Col. 2:
4 **slick** quick and modern, easily done

From the article by Simon Hoggart, The Guardian, *January 3, 1998.*

Comprehension

1. According to the article why were so many top news items *"entirely British or had a strong British content"* (ll. 2–3)?
2. Make a list of the news items mentioned that were in the top twenty in 1997.
3. Write down which category of news each item belongs to.
   Example: News item: Princess Diana's death
   News category: tragedy/royal family
4. Add further news categories to your list. *Example: sport, local,…*

Over to you

Work in groups of three or four. • Make a list of all the major news items of the last year that you can remember. • Decide on a top five. Note down why each one was important. • Join another group and compare your lists. • Try to agree on a top three.

Paparazzi!

Below:
Press photographers 'at work'
What or who do you think the photographers might be taking photos of here?
Should there be any limitations on what press photographers are allowed to take pictures of? Give reasons.

Above:
On 31st August 1997 Diana, Princess of Wales, was killed in a car accident in a tunnel in Paris. Many people – including her brother at her funeral – blamed the press and particularly the paparazzi for her death. This photograph was taken shortly after Diana's death and shows photographers protesting their innocence. Find out about the circumstances leading up to Diana's death and say to what extent you think the press and the paparazzi were to blame.

Check the web
Get more information about Princess Diana's death at:
http://www.capitalismmagazine.com/1999/september/princess_diana.htm

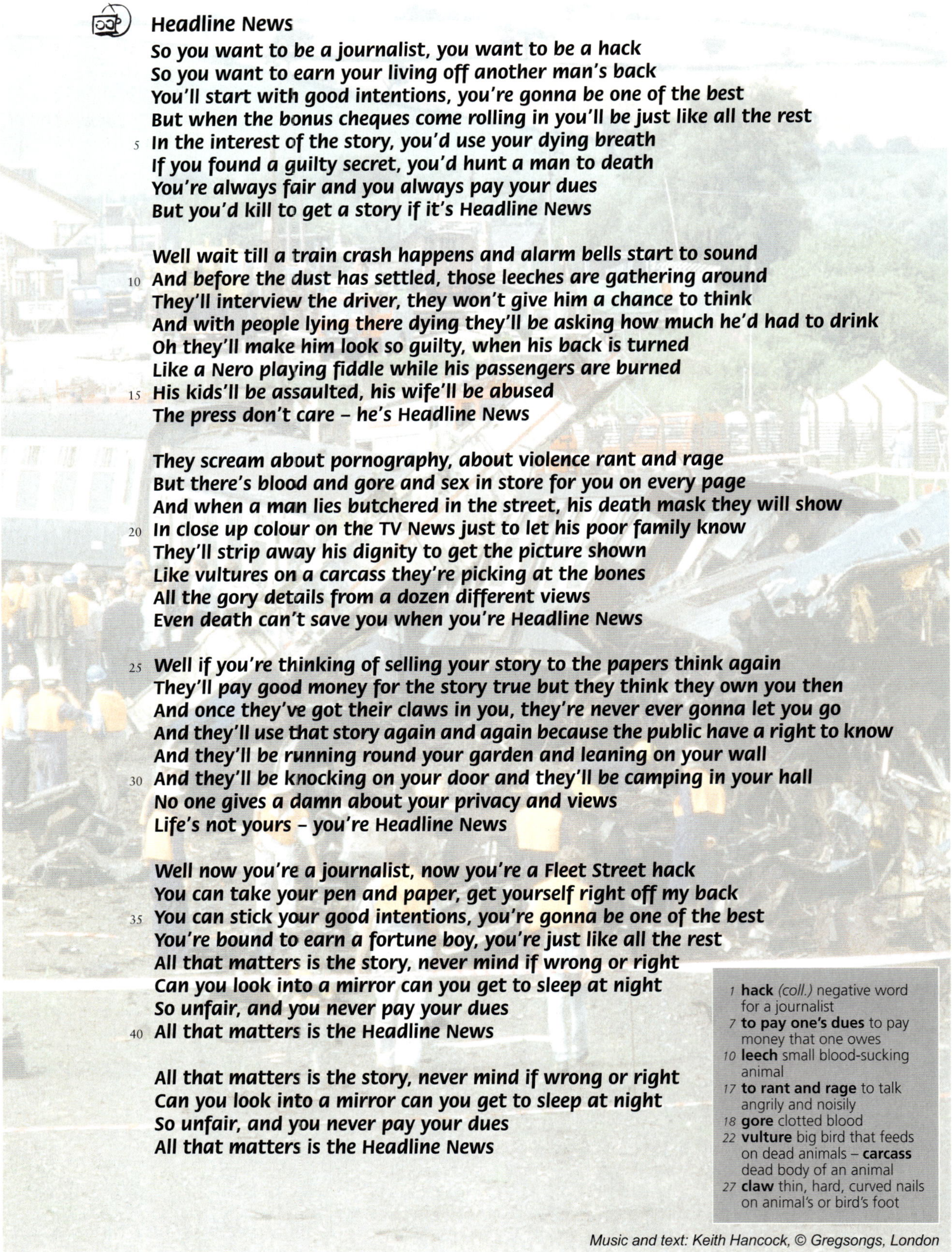

Headline News

So you want to be a journalist, you want to be a hack
So you want to earn your living off another man's back
You'll start with good intentions, you're gonna be one of the best
But when the bonus cheques come rolling in you'll be just like all the rest
In the interest of the story, you'd use your dying breath
If you found a guilty secret, you'd hunt a man to death
You're always fair and you always pay your dues
But you'd kill to get a story if it's Headline News

Well wait till a train crash happens and alarm bells start to sound
And before the dust has settled, those leeches are gathering around
They'll interview the driver, they won't give him a chance to think
And with people lying there dying they'll be asking how much he'd had to drink
Oh they'll make him look so guilty, when his back is turned
Like a Nero playing fiddle while his passengers are burned
His kids'll be assaulted, his wife'll be abused
The press don't care – he's Headline News

They scream about pornography, about violence rant and rage
But there's blood and gore and sex in store for you on every page
And when a man lies butchered in the street, his death mask they will show
In close up colour on the TV News just to let his poor family know
They'll strip away his dignity to get the picture shown
Like vultures on a carcass they're picking at the bones
All the gory details from a dozen different views
Even death can't save you when you're Headline News

Well if you're thinking of selling your story to the papers think again
They'll pay good money for the story true but they think they own you then
And once they've got their claws in you, they're never ever gonna let you go
And they'll use that story again and again because the public have a right to know
And they'll be running round your garden and leaning on your wall
And they'll be knocking on your door and they'll be camping in your hall
No one gives a damn about your privacy and views
Life's not yours – you're Headline News

Well now you're a journalist, now you're a Fleet Street hack
You can take your pen and paper, get yourself right off my back
You can stick your good intentions, you're gonna be one of the best
You're bound to earn a fortune boy, you're just like all the rest
All that matters is the story, never mind if wrong or right
Can you look into a mirror can you get to sleep at night
So unfair, and you never pay your dues
All that matters is the Headline News

All that matters is the story, never mind if wrong or right
Can you look into a mirror can you get to sleep at night
So unfair, and you never pay your dues
All that matters is the Headline News

1 **hack** *(coll.)* negative word for a journalist
7 **to pay one's dues** to pay money that one owes
10 **leech** small blood-sucking animal
17 **to rant and rage** to talk angrily and noisily
18 **gore** clotted blood
22 **vulture** big bird that feeds on dead animals – **carcass** dead body of an animal
27 **claw** thin, hard, curved nails on animal's or bird's foot

The right to know

Your view

Form groups and say what you think of the song. Give your opinion on the text and the music. Give reasons for your opinions. Comment on the opinions of others in your group.

Comprehension

1. According to the songwriter, what are journalists prepared to do in order to get a good story?
2. Describe verses two, three and four in your own words. Start by writing down a maximum of five key words to describe what the verses are about.
3. a) Compare verses one and five line for line. What has happened to the journalist according to the songwriter?
   b) What rhetorical devices are used to emphasize this?
4. What does the songwriter think of journalists?

Rhetorical devices
See *glossary* on p. 153.

Language

1. Find examples of metaphors and similes in the song and explain what they mean.
2. Why do you think the songwriter uses metaphors and similes?
3. Make up a simile of your own to describe the following:
   the way a journalist searches for news • a group of photographers trying to get a good picture • readers of newspapers when there has been a disaster.

Metaphors & Similes
See *glossary* on pp. 152 & 153.

Explaining words

1. Find the words or phrases in the text which mean:
   a) a journalist who writes quickly and does not worry about the quality of his/her work
   b) at the beginning you will try to do everything correctly
   c) in the news it will say that the man behaved wrongly: whether he did or not
   d) his partner will be treated very badly
   e) only one thing is important and that is the news report
2. Explain these words and phrases from the song using your own words:
   a) *"you always pay your dues"* (l. 7)
   b) *"alarm bells"* (l. 9)
   c) *"to sell your story to the papers"* (l. 25)
   d) *"the public have a right to know"* (l. 28)
   e) *"to earn a fortune"* (l. 36)
3. Choose two more words or expressions from the song. Paraphrase them and ask your partner to find them and vice versa.

Using a dictionary

1. How many collocations of the word 'back' do you already know? Give examples.
2. Use the dictionary entry on p. 135 to find the meaning of these phrases from the song:
   "living off another man's back" (l. 2) • *"get right off my back"* (l. 34)
3. Use phrases which include the word 'back' to say that:
   your partner has got his/her sweatshirt on incorrectly • your brother really annoyed you last night • there was a golf course behind the hotel you stayed in on holiday.
4. Find other uses of the word 'back' which are new to you and set a task similar to the one above for your partner to do.

Using a dictionary
See *skills files* on p. 134.

Role play

Hold a group discussion about the freedom of the press with the title:
"The right to know versus the right to privacy".
Work in a group of four. Decide which of the following roles you each want to play:
a journalist • a photographer • a famous TV star • a famous sports personality.
The journalist and the photographer should be completely in favour of the public's right to know and completely against any restrictions on the freedom of the press.
The TV star and the famous sports personality should be in favour of the right to privacy and would like to see restrictions on the freedom of the press.
Make a list of arguments supporting 'your' opinion before the discussion begins. (The website reference on p. 63 may be of some help to you.)

Having a discussion
See *skills files* on pp. 131 & 132.

A journalist's day

In the following text a journalist on The Daily Telegraph *talks about his daily work.*

Before you read →

- Would you like to be a journalist? What do you think a day in the life of a journalist is like?

1 **radio pager** *Piepser*

3 **Isle of Dogs** island on the River Thames, new address for many leading newspapers

31 **to cram** to squeeze

36 **charlady (= charwoman)** polite word for 'cleaner'

Check the web
Visit *The Daily Telegraph* online at:
http://www.telegraph.co.uk

The radio pager clipped to my waistband squeaked into life as I stood at Blackfriars Station waiting for the bus for the journey to *The Daily Telegraph's* offices on the Isle of Dogs. Within seconds, a colleague's device was bleeping in shrill harmony.

"Please ring newsdesk urgently," said identical messages on our small screens. After a quick call from a nearby payphone, I was bound for Oxford while my colleague headed off on some other assignment.

It was a typical enough start to a day in the lives of reporters working for Britain's leading quality newspaper, one with a jealously-guarded reputation for its comprehensive daily coverage of British and international news. [...]

Any news organisation, whether dealing with the printed or the spoken word, needs to be able to react swiftly to events. For the reporter, the unpredictable nature of news provides daily inspiration. The newspaper's ability to contact its staff almost anywhere can, ideally, satisfy both demands (though few bleep-carriers cannot produce at least one example of perverse or excessive use).

Back in the office, the decision to alert mobile members of staff has been taken by other journalists on the newsdesk, where information on what is going on streams in by telephone, computer screen and sometimes – amid all the modern technology – mailbag.

By the time I was heading west to Oxford, fellow-reporters whose journeys to work had remained uninterrupted by pager calls were arriving in the *Telegraph* newsroom. Some will spend the day gathering information by telephone about a variety of news items, one or two may dart off during the day, perhaps in the company of a photographer, in response to the first indications of significant stories.

A proportion of news coverage can be planned in advance, with reporters knowing precisely where they will be going, and when. The newsdesk team directing the operation often knows weeks ahead, for example, when a major criminal trial is due to start at the Old Bailey. There might be shorter notice of a press conference involving a person or organisation currently in the headlines. But news occurs at all hours of day and night with no respect for routines. Each reporter is ready to leave the office or abandon a less urgent assignment with a moment's warning and many keep overnight bags crammed into desk drawers.

News can be about something unusually good. It frequently concerns the unusually bad. A terrorist bombing or a train crash, a big strike or a hospital crisis will all attract the *Telegraph's* attention. But so will a boy of eight who passes mathematics at 'O' level, an unemployed charlady winning £1 million in the lottery and a survey identifying some quirky trend in human attitudes or behaviour.

The Daily Telegraph's interest, of course, is in publishing a full, accurate and well-written account of all these matters. If the reporter attends the event, he or she will dictate the story by telephone to copy-takers, or transmit it using a

laptop computer with one of an infuriating set of telephone attachments. Reporters working in the office punch their stories into computer terminals. In either case, the articles proceed through the system to other journalists, sub-editors, to be "tasted" – i.e. evaluated – and then allotted space in the edition under preparation.

Not everything the reporter does is destined for prominent front-page display. Under closer journalistic scrutiny or simply the weight of competing news items, that which seems important at 9:30 am can look a little less vital eight hours later. Even a fairly interesting article risks being squeezed out altogether if there are limits on space.

In journalism, as in most jobs, there are chores. On the *Telegraph*, these include monitoring radio and television news bulletins and compiling those short but well-read lists of clergy or Armed Forces appointments, the latest wills and the coming week's Parliamentary business. If the reporter labouring over the career moves of country parsons is also itching for some more demanding call on his skills, it is because the prospect is ever-present.

On a day off, my telephone rang at home. The foreign editor wondered whether there were any pressing reasons why I could not accept an immediate trip to the Gulf with the Royal Navy.

I looked guiltily across the room at a dinner suit, hired only an hour earlier for use at a banquet concerning my wife's work, before replying, "of course not".

48 **to infuriate** to make s.o. crazy or angry

51 **allotted** *here:* given

53 **scrutiny** careful and detailed examination

56 **chores** daily, repetitive jobs

From the article in The Daily Telegraph / The Sunday Telegraph Information Brochure, *n.d., pp. 12–13.*

Comprehension

1. Why did the author get a phone call at Blackfriars Station?
2. What is the task of the newsdesk team?
3. What are the typical tasks of a journalist as presented in this article?
4. Why does the journalist feel guilty at the end of the text?
5. What impression does the journalist give of his own paper, the *Daily Telegraph*?

Your view

If you worked as a journalist, would you prefer the long-term or the short-term work? Give reasons. Write about five sentences (60–70 words).

Vocabulary

1. Find words in the text which refer exclusively to the work of a journalist.
2. Of course, journalists are not the only people who work on newspapers. What do the people listed below do? Use the glossary on p. 69 or a dictionary if necessary.
   copy-taker • sub-editor • foreign editor • correspondent • freelance journalist • publisher

Translation

Translate ll. 56–67 *("In journalism, ... 'of course not'.")* into German, paying special attention to the way you translate the -ing forms.

Analyzing style

Style & rhetorical devices
See *glossary* on pp. 152 & 153.

The author uses different styles at different points in the text.
1. Identify subjective and objective passages in the text.
2. Which different styles are used by the author?

Listening comprehension
The Birmingham Post *is a regional newspaper published and sold in Birmingham and the West Midlands. Listen to the women's editor of* The Birmingham Post *talking about the newspaper and her work.*

The Birmingham Post
Sacked for his sins

Further assignments

Writing a feature →

- 'Teens & Twens', a British teen magazine, is doing a feature on young people in Europe. Keeping in mind appropriate text styles, write a feature for the magazine on one of the following topics:
  - A typical day at school • The most exciting thing and/or the most important thing you have ever done • A typical evening out.

Finding out about British teenagers →

- Make contact with a school in Britain and find out which papers and magazines pupils of your age read and why. You can contact British schools by e-mail. Many addresses are listed at the following website:
  http://uk.dir.yahoo.com/Education/Schools/Schools/Secondary_schools/

Looking at on-line editions →

- Find out about the on-line editions of British newspapers and magazines. Website addresses are given in the 'Check the web' boxes in this chapter and in the box on the right.
  - Find out: the name of each newspaper/magazine • whether it is a national or regional publication • whether it is a daily, weekly or Sunday publication • whether it is a quality or tabloid • whether it is a special interest publication.
  - Make notes about each on-line edition by describing and giving details of: the home page • the links • the length/types of articles covered • access to back issues • etc.
  - What advantages and disadvantages are there to having an on-line edition for the reader and for the publisher?
  - Which do you prefer, on-line editions or printed editions of newspapers and magazines? Why?

Check the web
British newspapers & magazines
www.independent.co.uk
www.standard.co.uk
www.londonstudent.org.uk
www.economist.co.uk
www.ft.com
www.sundaymirror.co.uk
www.bigissue.com
www.thisisbristol.com
www.aberdeen-indy.co.uk/
megastar.co.uk
express.linone.net/
www.cosmogirl.com
www.nme.com/
www.sundaysun.co.uk
www.theherald.co.uk
Find more publications by using a search engine, for example:
uk.dir.yahoo.com/News_and_Media/Newspapers/

Project: A comparative study of British newspapers

Prepare a dossier in which you compare:
a) a British quality and a British popular newspaper
b) the British and the German press
- ▶ Look at a current copy of both a British quality and a British popular newspaper.
- ▶ Make a survey of the topics dealt with.
- ▶ Analyze contents, lay-out, language and what kind of readership each newspaper aims at.
- ▶ Make comparisons with two similar newspapers sold in your country.

In your dossier you should include:
- a list of the addresses where you can find British newspapers in your area.
- examples of articles from British and German newspapers illustrating your findings.

- Make a similar dossier on the American press.

Projects
See *skills file* on p.139.

Solution to quiz on p. 56

1. d)	5. a)
2. c)	6. b)
3. a)	7. b)
4. a) + f)	8. c)
b) + e)	
c) + d)	

Glossary: The Press

ADVERTISING: A means of bringing products to the attention of potential buyers: paid notices stressing the advantages of and reasons for buying those products and services.
ASSIGNMENT: Instructions given to a reporter or photographer on a story to pursue and possible angles to include in it.
BACKGROUND: Information that gives a reporter further insight into a story, but does not necessarily appear in the article.
BY-LINE: The name of the reporter who wrote the story. The by-line usually appears below the headline.
CAPTION: A short explanation of the contents of a photograph, usually appearing below the picture.
CIRCULATION: The number of newspapers sold each day.
COPY: A term used in journalism to refer to written material, whether an article or an advertisement.
COPY DESK: The place in the newsroom where editors edit reporters' copy to make sure it is clear, factual and grammatically correct.
COPY TASTER: Sub-editor who "tastes" i.e. evaluates stories for inclusion in the paper.
CORRESPONDENT: A reporter stationed in another city or country, outside the headquarters of the newspaper.
CROP: To trim non-essential parts of a photograph or to change its proportions. Cropping brings out important features of a photo.
DEADLINE: The time the final version of a story is due. It is also the time when the presses begin to roll. Papers have several deadlines each day and all timing is geared to them.
DUMMY SHEET: A plan or diagram showing where each story, picture, headline and ad will be positioned on a newspaper page.
EDITION: One of several issues of a newspaper published each day (e.g. "final" edition). The purpose of editions is to allow the newspaper to change articles to keep up with the most recent news.
EDITOR: The person responsible for the contents of the newspaper.
EDITORIAL: An essay expressing the newspaper's point of view on various subjects.
EXCLUSIVE: A story that a newspaper was the first to discover and print.
FEATURES: Special interest articles.
FREELANCER: Self-employed journalist.
HARD NEWS: News that is topical, timely and important.
HEADLINE: Large, bold words appearing over all articles to summarise the story. Headlines are used to attract the attention of the reader.
HOUSE STYLE: The newspaper's rules for names, titles, grammar and punctuation so that articles are written in a consistent style.
LEAD: The news story judged most important and most prominently displayed; also the first paragraph of a story, written to catch the reader's interest and tell the highlights of the story.
MASTHEAD: Title of newspaper at the top of the front page.
NEWS AGENCY SERVICE: A network of reporters and editors who cover and prepare news and features at home and overseas.
OBITUARY: The written account of a person's life upon their death (also referred to as an obit).
OFF THE RECORD: Material and information gained during an interview that cannot be quoted directly, but may be used as background material.
PHOTO-JOURNALISM: Telling a story by means of photographs, with little or no text.
PRESS: The machine that prints the newspaper.
PUBLISHER: The owner of the newspaper, or representative of the owner, responsible for all operations of the paper.
REFERENCE LIBRARY: The newspaper's editorial library, containing files of past stories, clippings, photographs, periodicals and research books used by reporters and editors for information.
SOFT NEWS: Stories that are interesting and informative, but not necessarily timely.
SOURCE: The person or persons who supply news and information to a reporter.
SUB-EDITOR: A person who edits the copy of reporters and writes headlines, i.e. she/he "subs" copy to fit the space available, corrects spelling, checks for accuracy, etc.

A **glossary** is a collection of words all belonging to a certain topic or field. It is a useful way of collecting special vocabulary.

'Ooh, wait till the neighbours see this, you getting your name in the paper!'

Looking at the cartoon
1. Which part of the paper is the woman reading? Find the name for it in the glossary.
2. What is this type of humour called?
3. Do you think the cartoon is funny? Why or why not?

From the article in The Daily Telegraph/The Sunday Telegraph Information Brochure, *n.d., pp. 12–13.*

- Make a crossword or wordsearch using words from the glossary and give it to someone else in your class to solve.
- Make a poster for your classroom: Take a page or pages of a newspaper. (It/They need not necessarily be in English). • Identify as many of the items explained in the glossary as possible. • Highlight and label clearly the items you have identified.

← **Vocabulary**

5 Welcome to America

Photos of America

Getting started

- Which members of your class have visited the US? Find out where they've been and what they thought about it.
- Look at the photos below. Which of the places would you most like to visit? Give reasons.

Talking about the photos

Describing locations

It's/They're …

• … in the North (South/ Midwest/etc). • … on the east (west) coast. • … near the Ohio (etc.) River. • … to the north (south/etc.) of (Atlanta).

1. Match the photos with the names given below.
   the Grand Canyon • San Francisco • World Trade Center, New York • Washington D.C. • the Mississippi • southern home in Kentucky • cattle herding in Montana • Boothbay Harbor, Maine • Eskimo hunters in Alaska • Miami Beach, Florida • the Arch in St. Louis, Missouri • the Sierra Nevada mountain range

Use the map of the USA at the back of the book to do the following tasks.

2. Use the phrases in the box on the left and describe the locations of the places shown in the photos.
3. What other mountain ranges can you find on the map? Name them and say which parts of the US they are in.

Physical features and time zones

← **Describing locations & features**

Use the map of the USA at the back of the book to do the tasks on this page.

1. a) Find the name and location of the largest lake and the longest river in the US.
   b) Which river marks part of the US border with Mexico?
2. a) Measure the distances between the following cities and work out the distances in miles and/or kilometres:
   Los Angeles to Jacksonville, Florida. • Lake Ontario to Miami, Florida.
   b) Where would you be if you travelled a similar distance north, south, east or west of your home?
3. a) Choose three big cities in the US and write their names down on a piece of paper. Now describe their location to your partner and ask him/her to work out which cities you have chosen. Reverse roles and find your partner's cities.
   b) Describe the location of the place where you live as you would to an American who has never been to Germany. Refer to other cities, countries and geographical features.

Example:
"The city I have chosen is in the north of the United States. It's in the state of Minnesota and it's situated on the west bank of the Mississippi River."
"(I think) the city you have chosen is Minneapolis."

4. a) Look at the illustration on the right and compare the size of the USA with the size of:
   Germany • Britain • Europe.
   b) How many international borders does Germany have? And the USA?
   c) Bearing in mind size and international boundaries, explain what attitudes Americans and Europeans might have towards travelling long distances.

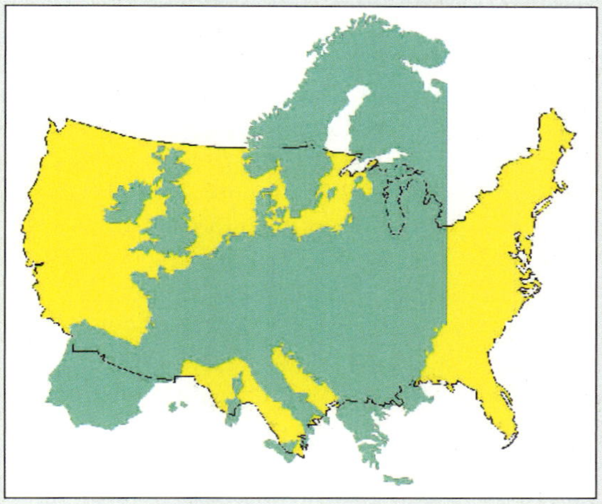

5. a) When talking about a country's borders we can talk about political borders and natural borders. What do you understand by these terms?
   b) Give an example of a political border and a natural border in Germany.
   c) Look at the map at the back of the book and define the political borders and the natural borders of the USA.

← **Looking at time zones**

1. a) How many time zones are there in the USA and what are they called?
   b) What is the difference in time from the east to the west coast of America?
   c) What time is it in Washington, Atlanta and Los Angeles when it is noon in Berlin?
2. It is 4 pm in Los Angeles, where International Advertising Inc. has its headquarters. Traci Grey, the head of the company, needs to talk to two of her colleagues immediately. As one of them is in New York and the other is in Frankfurt she decides to make a conference call.
   a) What time does the telephone ring for each of the colleagues?
   b) Which of the people in the illustration on the right is Traci Grey? Which one is the colleague in Frankfurt? Which one is in New York?

Listening comprehension
Listen to Traci Grey talking to her two colleagues.

Hunting Mr. Heartbreak

In his travelogue Hunting Mr. Heartbreak: A Discovery of America *the Englishman Jonathan Raban tells the story of a man who makes a journey of discovery through the USA.*

At only 180 miles long, I-78 was hardly an interstate at all; it was a feeder road, an overextended ramp, for a really big I, 81(40), which absorbed it just short of Harrisburg, Pennsylvania. I-81 began up in Canada, on the north bank of the St. Lawrence near the neck of Lake Ontario. It dropped due south to Scranton, Pennsylvania, then coasted along the eastern edge of the Appalachian range down as far as Knoxville, Tennessee, where it changed its number to 40 and ran west, through Tennessee, Arkansas, Oklahoma, Texas, New Mexico and Arizona to an unplace in California eighty miles northeast of Los Angeles. It was an epic road, a three-thousand-mile trans-American ribbon that tied up the subcontinent in a single wide loop. If such roads had ever been conceived in Europe, there might be one from London to Tehran, or from the French Riviera to the outer reaches of Novaya Zemlya.

I poured the Spirit into the southgoing stream. A stately, plump Winnebago with Michigan plates was doing a sedate fifty-five in the center lane, while the left lane had been commandeered by a West Virginia pickup which was idling through the landscape at fifty, and refused to give over when I flashed my lights behind it. Coming alongside West Virginia, I watched him sink a can of Michelob, crumple it in his fist and flip it out onto the median strip. By the expression on his face when he glanced back at me, I gathered that a white Dodge Spirit was not a car that inspired much respect where he came from.

For miles, I saw nothing but plates: Ohio surging past Florida ... South Carolina sinking back behind Maine ... Kentucky slipping past New York on the inside ... The states of America had all been shaken up in solution on the freeway, and there could be no image more expressive of the chronic restlessness and mobility of the nation than this race of the plates, with their jostling crests and mottos – the Puritan stovepipe hat of Massachusetts, Florida's pistol-shaped map, The Empire State, Land of Lincoln, First in Freedom, Live Free or Die, Famous Potatoes, Land of 10,000 Lakes, The Last Frontier.

Many of the cars were towing U-Haul trailers – potted, aluminum versions of the covered wagon – in which were stowed the drivers' worldly goods. Each time I passed U-Haulers, I tried to guess what had happened to them. The moth-eaten blond man in the rattletrap tan Chevy had been given the boot by his pregnant girlfriend. The elderly couple in the Mazda, closely followed by the biggest U-Haul that I'd seen, were under doctor's orders. The old man had worked all his life at Bethlehem Steel. He had a circulation problem. "You want to see another winter out? You'd better head for the Sunbelt." The wife had relatives in Houston. They were going to look around for a while, maybe rent first, then buy later. The single woman, thirtyish, whey-faced behind her tinted glasses, with a medium-sized U-Haul, was heading for a new job, in Atlanta. She looked to me like a Macy's buyer. She drove a brand-new Corsica sedan.

U-Haul's slogan promised that it made Moving an Adventure, and there was adventure in all this motion – a great deal of "chance ... hap ... luck ... speculation," as the dictionary defines the word. If you live with a road like I-81 on your doorstep, I thought, how different it must be to the world I knew. Europeans cannot move more than a few – at most a very few hundred – miles without traveling out of their own language; but Americans can, as it were, go from London to Tehran, from Marseilles to Novaya Zemlya, and still be perfectly at home, with Johnny Carson on the TV and the Burger King drive-in two blocks down the street. No wonder that people hitch U-Haul wagons to their cars and go. If the winters get too cold for old

1 **interstate** *(AE)* highway connecting major cities – **feeder road** secondary road which brings traffic to a main road
2 **overextended** *here:* longer than usual
4 **due** *here:* directly
5 **to coast** *here:* to move downhill
7 **Arkansas** ['ɑːkənsɔː]
8 **unplace** *(informal)* an unimportant place – **epic** of impressive proportions
10 **loop** curved shape which bends and crosses itself – **to conceive** to think of
11 **Novaya Zamlya** islands located in the Arctic Ocean
13 **to pour** *here:* to drive – **(Dodge) Spirit** type of car – **Winnebago** [ˌwɪnəˈbeɪgəʊ] *(AE, trademark)* vehicle used to live and travel in esp. for holidays
14 **sedate** gentle
15 **to commandeer** [ˌ--'-] to take over – **to idle** to run at a low speed
17 **to crumple** to crush
18 **median strip** *(AE)* strip separating the two sides of a motorway
21 **to surge** *(here fig.)* to come quickly afterwards
23 **shaken up in solution** *here:* separated and reorganized
25 **jostling** ['dʒɒslɪŋ] *here:* competing
29 **to tow** [əʊ] to pull along behind – **potted** *(informal)* smaller
30 **to stow** [əʊ] *here:* to store
31 **moth-eaten** *here:* wearing shabby clothes
32 **rattletrap** *(informal)* old and noisy – **tan** light brown – **given the boot** *(informal)* kicked out
38 **whey-faced** [weɪ] pale – **tinted** slightly coloured
39 **Macy's** *(US)* department store
42 **hap** *(old)* luck
49 **to hitch** *here:* to attach

bones … if the farm's foreclosed … the factory shut down … the divorce papers are served … call U-Haul and take to the road. In America, there is always someplace else where you might yet find heart's-ease, whether it's the condo in Florida or forty bucks an hour on the rig in Alaska.

Breezing south in my wicked Spirit, my eye was tuned to watching other vehicles on the road, while the landscape spooled by far too fast for me to follow the story. It came to me in totemic fragments, observed only after they were already miles behind. That bridge back there *was* the Mason-Dixon line; and it took the slick new tarmac and trim white picket fences of Maryland to make me realize that Pennsylvania had, on the whole, been like an unkempt family back yard with bald turf, a vegetable plot and the children's tricycles left out to rust in the rain. Only the sudden deterioration in the road surface as I hit West Virginia made me see Maryland, in retrospect, as a rich man's garden, with sprinklers playing on mown and rollered lawns, a pony in a paddock, rhododendrons, a bronze Pan on a stone plinth.

In West Virginia, the freeway began to twist and steepen, enclosed by darkening forest, and, unlike most of the residents of that disreputable statelet, I went legal. Down to sixty, peering anxiously into the twilight, I felt abruptly tired and thirsty. I slowed before each forthcoming exit to scan the board reading LODGINGS NEXT RIGHT by the beam of my headlights. Mac's Motel. Sunset Motel. Econo-Lodge. Howard Johnson's. Dean's Motel. Rack-rent Motel … Their scabby advertising boards were strung up in the trees, and the best recommendation they could make for themselves was that they were EZ-OFF EZ-ON, as if the true afficionado of the freeway could sleep comfortably with the breaking surf of overnight traffic in his ears.

I knew those places. They were all one. Sometimes, emptying the pockets of your trousers to take them to the cleaner's, you come across a credit card slip crumpled into a spiky ball. You carefully unfold it. It reads, bewilderingly, "Peek's Motel, Wardensburg." You do not know where Wardensburg is. You cannot remember ever having been there. It goes on: "Lodgings, one night, $18 + tax …" So you presume that you must have been alone, at least. You search in the eaves of your memory and dig out a slowly developing image.

There was … a cigarette burn in a too-thin coverlet … a cracked shower curtain gone parchment yellow … a carpet, of sorts with a quilted brown pile … an ice machine and a Coke machine in a windy open hallway … a room infected with the smell of slovenly solitude. You didn't sleep; you lay, oscillating continuously between quick, violent dreams and unhappy wakefulness. Yes, that was Peek's.

I didn't want to stay at Peek's – or Dean's – or Mac's – or Sunset – and so I kept on driving. Another fifty miles went past, another state line. I was in Virginia proper now. LODGINGS NEXT RIGHT … WAYSIDE INN. Nothing about EZ-OFF EZ-ON. I took the turning.

It was well out of earshot of the freeway. It was a real hotel. Roadshocked, I lumbered into the bar.

"And what can I do for you this evening, sir?"

I stared at the girl. She had a voice out of *Gone with the Wind*. I set to wondering stupidly if it was her own voice or if she was putting it on.

"Sir? Do you want a drink?"

From Hunting Mr. Heartbreak: A Discovery of America *by Jonathan Raban, New York: Edward Burlingame Books/HarperCollinsPublishers, 1991, pp. 108–111.*

50 **to foreclose s.th.** to lose all rights to s.th. when one cannot meet loan repayments
51 **to serve** *here:* to present
52 **heart's-ease** freedom from worry – **condo** individually-owned apartment
53 **rig** platform at sea where oil is drilled for
54 **to tune** to adapt to
55 **to spool** *(informal)* to pass like a film
56 **in totemic fragments** in particular images
57 **Mason-Dixon line** line between free and slave states before the Civil War (1861-65)
58 **tarmac** street surface made of crushed stones and tar *(Teer)* – **picket fence** wooden fence, usu. painted white
59 **unkempt** [ʌn'kemt] untidy – **bald** [ɔ:] – **turf** area where the grass has been worn away
60 **plot** *here:* small piece of land
61 **deterioration** worsening
62 **mown** cut – **rollered** smoothened
63 **Pan** mythical figure – **plinth** base
65 **disreputable** having a bad name – **statelet** *(informal)* small state – **to go legal** *here:* to stay within the speed limit
66 **to peer** to look with great effort
69 **scabby** *here:* where the paper is coming off in places
71 **EZ-OFF EZ-ON** easy off/on the highway – **afficionado** [æfɪʃɪən'ɑdəʊ] admirer
72 **surf** *(here fig.)* regular sound of cars passing
76 **bewilderingly** confusingly
79 **eaves** *here:* corners
82 **parchment** *Pergament* – **pile** *here:* surface material
84 **slovenly solitude** *here:* lonely and uncared for – **oscillating** *here:* changing
90 **earshot** hearing distance
91 **to lumber** to move clumsily and slowly
93 **to set to** *(informal)* to start
94 **to put it on** *here:* to pretend to have a particular accent

Comprehension

1. a) How many states does the route Jonathan Raban describes pass through? Use the map at the back of the book, start in Pennsylvania and follow the route through the US.
   b) How does he give a sense of the size of America?
2. Apart from the author, where do the people who are out on the road in this excerpt come from?
3. a) What does the author compare the U-Haul trailers to, and why?
   b) In your own words, say why the author thinks the U-Haulers (the elderly couple, the blond man and the single woman) might be on the road.
4. Why is travelling long distances easier for Americans than for Europeans according to the author?
5. What is the legal speed limit on the freeway according to Jonathan Raban?
6. In your own words say what impression of motels you get from this extract.

Role play: Booking a motel room

A tourist is travelling through America by car. It is 6 pm, and he/she needs a room for the night. Seeing "Peek's Motel" at a highway exit the tourist decides to spend the night there. He/She goes into the motel reception to book a room.

1. Read the phrases below and write them down in a logical order under the headings 'tourist' and 'receptionist':
   Thank you. • Do you have any vacancies/any rooms free? • Good evening, Sir/Madam. • I'd like a room for tonight. • Would you like to pay cash or by credit card? /How would you like to pay? • Just a moment, Sir/Madam. • Would you like a single or a double room? • How much will that be? • A kingsize, please. • Would you prefer smoking or non-smoking? • Here's your key, Sir/Madam. • Would you like a room with two single beds or one kingsize bed? • Certainly, Sir/Madam. • Can I help you? • Would you sign here, please? • Have a nice evening, Sir/Madam. I hope you enjoy your stay. • $39.95 plus tax.
2. Work in pairs. One of you takes on the role of the tourist and the other of the motel receptionist. Practise booking a motel room using as many of the phrases above as possible. You can add any further information and details that you think are appropriate.

Language: Synonyms, opposites and definitions

Synonyms and opposites
See *glossary* on p. 153.

1. Find words in the text with the opposite meaning to those given below. (Start at l. 41, "*U-Haul's slogan ...*".)
   similar • many • opened up • slowly • lead (vb) • accelerated /sped up • filling • intelligently
2. a) Write synonyms for the following words from the text:
   tied up (l. 9) • plump (l. 13) • flip (l. 18) • glanced (l. 19) • gathered (l. 19) • image (l. 24) • chronic (l. 24) • goods (l. 30) • head (l. 36).
   b) Rewrite the sentences from the text using your solutions to make sure that your solution has a similar meaning to the original word and also fits the sentence structure.
3. Write a definition of the compound noun 'sunbelt' (l. 36) giving as wide a meaning of the word as possible.

Grammar & use of language

The present tense
See *grammar files* on pp. 142 & 143.

1. Rewrite ll. 54–73 *("Breezing ... traffic in his ears.")* in the present tense.
2. a) In one or two sentences describe the effect of the passage on you now that it is in the present tense.
   b) Make a sentence out of the following words and then say whether you agree or disagree with the resulting statement.
   a • about • even • events • from • make • more • past • present • scene • sometimes • talking • tense • the • the • to • use • vivid • when • writers

Creative writing

- Choose one of the ideas below and write your own travel report. Include descriptions of the things you observe and experience on your 'journey'. You can use the present or the past tense.
  - Start at the place where you live and travel at least 200–300 kilometres.
  - Describe a long journey you have been on, for example, to a holiday destination.

Further activity

license plate (*AE*) number on the front and back of a car (*BE*: registration / licence plate)

1. Look at ll. 25–28 of the text.
   a) Which states do the slogans on the license plates refer to?
   b) Find the states on the map at the back of the book.
   c) What do the slogans and the crests mentioned by the author tell you about each of those states?
2. a) Which of the license plates pictured below do you prefer? Why?
   b) Design a similar license plate for your state or region. Think of a suitable slogan and illustration for your license plate.

Over to you

Most people in the US identify themselves as Americans rather than by the states they come from.

- Why do you think people in the US have this sense of belonging to one nation when they live so far apart and in such different landscapes? Brainstorm ideas in groups and then compare results as a class.
- What is most important for you in terms of identity? Put the following into your own order of importance, explain your choice and discuss your results with others in your class:
  • the town/village where you live now • the state (e.g. Brandenburg) where you live now • the country (e.g. Germany) where you live now • the town/village where you or your parents come from • the state (e.g. Bavaria) where you or your parents come from • the country (e.g. Poland) where you or your parents come from • the group of countries or states in which you live (i.e. Europe).
- Why don't more people in Europe describe themselves as Europeans? • What could be done to create a stronger European identity?

Discussions
See *skills files* on pp. 131 & 132.

Climate and weather in the USA

Temperature, rainfall and snowfall

Water freezes at:
0° Celsius (C)/32° Fahrenheit (F).

Water boils at:
100° Celsius/212° Fahrenheit.

Celsius and Fahrenheit temperatures can be converted as follows:
C = (F – 32) x 100/180
F = (C x 180/100) + 32

in. = inches
1 inch = 2.54 centimetres
ave. = average

City	*Average monthly temperature (°F)* *Jan*	*July*	*Precipitation annual (days)*	*Snowfall annual ave. (in.)*
Atlanta	41.9	78.6	115	1.9
Buffalo	23.5	70.7	169	92.2
Dallas	4.0	86.3	78	3.1
Denver	29.5	73.4	88	59.8
Fairbanks	–12.7	61.5	106	67.5
Honolulu	72.6	80.1	100	0
Las Vegas	44.5	90.2	26	1.4
Los Angeles	56.0	69.0	36	0
Miami	67.1	82.5	129	0
New Orleans	52.4	82.1	114	0.2
Portland, Ore.	38.9	67.7	154	6.8

Source: National Oceanic and Atmospheric Administration

Understanding statistics

1. Find the cities named in the table above on the map at the back of the book.
2. Convert the temperatures into degrees Celsius and the snowfall into centimetres to make the statistics more meaningful to you.
3. Which of the cities do you think the people quoted below live in?
   Mary: "I always have a pool party on New Year's Day!" • *Andy:* "You're lucky! We have the coldest winters in the USA, I think!" • *Jo:* "It gets pretty cold here, too, but there's lots of snow so at least we can have snowball fights at New Year!" • *Marcia:* "It sure never gets cold enough to snow here! I usually spend New Year on the beach!" • *Davey:* "It never gets really cold here, either, but it does rain a lot, so don't forget your umbrella if you're visiting!"
4. Based on the statistics for these cities, divide the USA into regions and write a sentence outlining the climate in each region.

Talking about statistics
See *skills file* on p. 131.

Extreme weather conditions

Before you read

- Which three natural disasters are mentioned in the headlines above?
- Which of the headlines do you think describes the scene in the photograph?
- Do extreme weather conditions like these occur in Germany? Why/why not?
- Use your geography books and find out why the USA experiences such extreme weather conditions. Give a short explanation in English.

Hurricane wreaks havoc on battered Gulf states

Hurricane Georges yesterday unleashed ferocious winds, torrential rain and flooding on the states bordering the Gulf of Mexico as thousands of people were evacuated. Gusts of 175mph were reported at Keesler Air Force Base in Biloxi, Mississippi, where the eye of the storm crossed from the Gulf of Mexico and reached shore early yesterday. Mississippi governor Kirk Fordice said he had asked President Clinton to declare an emergency, clearing the way for federal aid in rebuilding devastated areas.

"The wind is really blowing out there and things are hitting the windows," said 20-year-old Rachel Alonso, from a shelter in Gulfport, Mississippi, with her two children and about 300 other people.

So far in the southern states there has only been one storm-related death: that of a man killed in a New Orleans fire started by candles after the hurricane knocked out electricity.

Flooding posed the biggest threat. National Guardsmen waded through chest-deep water to carry people to safety from a flooded housing estate near downtown Mobile, Alabama. In the Florida panhandle, guardsmen had to rescue about 200 people from their flooded homes.

By early afternoon, Georges was virtually stationary near Gulfport, dumping heavy rain over four states – Louisiana, Mississippi, Alabama and the Florida panhandle. Georges' 105 mph winds are expected to batter this southern stretch with downpours of up to 30 inches in the next 24 hours.

At least 320 people were killed by the hurricane last week when it lashed the Caribbean and the Florida Keys. Hundreds of thousands were made homeless.

The absence of fatalities on the Gulf Coast was attributed to the evacuation of more than 1.5 million people.

New Orleans escaped serious damage when Georges veered east of the city. Relentless rain and a storm surge could have submerged the low-lying city, protected only by levees. About 10,000 people took shelter in the giant superdome, home of the New Orleans Saints, while thousands more filled seven other shelters in the city.

Hurricane centre director Jerry Jarrell said: "It's going to be causing very heavy rains for a long period of time and those winds are still continuing to blow and will probably all day. So it's just going to be a miserable situation."

Along the Gulf Coast power cuts affected more than 350,000 customers, airports and highways were closed and curfews were in effect.

By Mark Tran, first published in The Observer, *September 29, 1998.*

to wreak [riːk] *(formal)* to cause damage

Col. 1: *2* **to unleash** to let loose – *3* **torrential** [təˈrenʃl] very heavy – *6* **gust** strong rush of wind – *16* **to clear the way** *here:* to make s.th. possible – *17* **federal aid** help from central government – *18* **devastated** destroyed

Col. 2: *1* **shelter** a structure built to give protection – *9* **to knock out** *here:* to cut off – *11* **to pose** *here:* to be – *13* **to wade** to walk through water – *22* **virtually** almost – **stationary** [ˈsteɪʃnrɪ] standing still

Col. 3: *1* **to dump** to pour in great amounts – *4* **Florida panhandle** southern part of the state of Florida which sticks out in a long strip into the ocean *6* **to batter** to beat –*7* **downpour** heavy rain –*11* **to lash** to beat –*15* **fatality** [feɪˈtælɪtɪ] death in an accident *16* **to attribute** [əˈtrɪbjuːt] **to** to give s.th. as a reason for s.th. else – *21* **to veer** to change direction quickly – **relentless** *here:* never-ending – *22* **surge** sudden strengthening

Col. 4: *1* **to submerge** to cover with water – *3* **levee** high bank made to stop a river from flooding – *5* **New Orleans Saints** American football team – *22* **curfew** official regulation requiring people to be inside by a certain time – **in effect** in operation

← Comprehension

1. What kind of weather is typical of a hurricane?
2. In your own words explain why Kirk Fordice contacted President Clinton.
3. Where and why were National Guardsmen called in?
4. What happened in New Orleans?
5. How was day to day life disrupted by Hurricane Georges?

← Vocabulary

Collect all the words you can find in the text belonging to the category 'weather'. Arrange the words in logical groups giving each group a suitable heading.

← Grammar (participles) & translation

1. a) Rewrite these sentences from the text replacing the present or past participles (underlined) with relative clauses:
   - *"Hurricane Georges yesterday unleashed ferocious winds, torrential rain and flooding on the states bordering the Gulf of Mexico as thousands of people were evacuated."* (Col. 1, ll. 1 – 6)
   - *"So far in the southern states there has only been one storm-related death: that of a man killed in a New Orleans fire started by candles after the hurricane knocked out electricity."* (Col. 2, ll. 4 – 9)

   b) Find two more similar examples in the text and rewrite them in the same way.
2. Now translate the original sentences into German.

Check the web

For more information check the web at:
http://www.redcross.org/disaster/safety/hurrican.html

Population

Population trends by region from 1990 to 1997

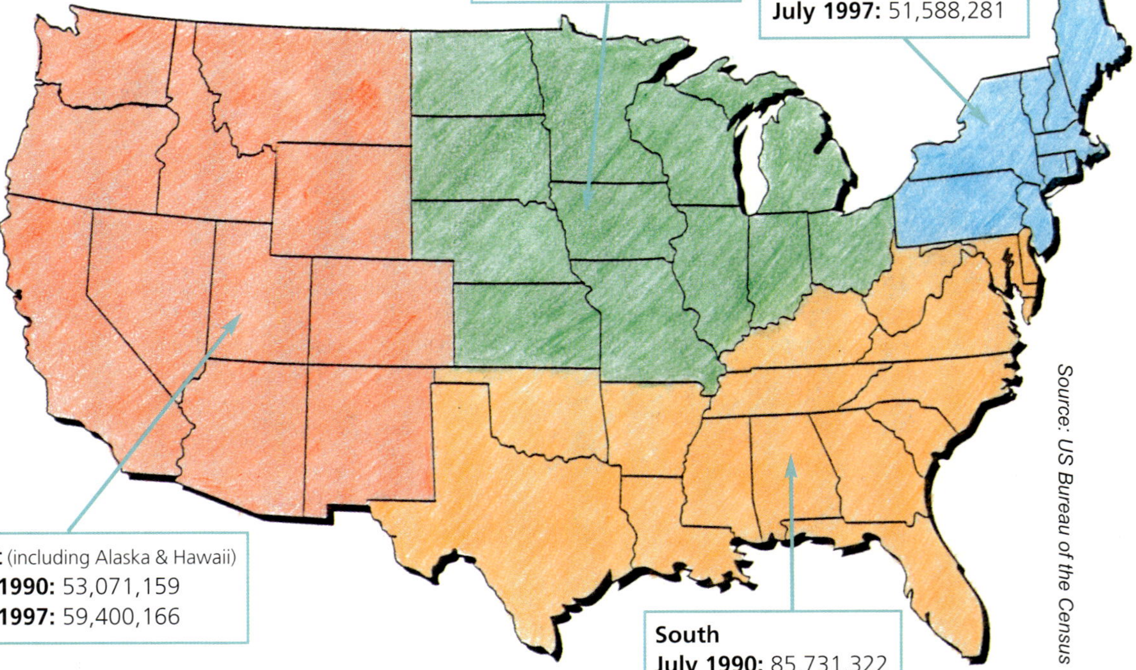

Source: US Bureau of the Census

Analyzing statistics →

1. Which US region has the highest population and which the lowest according to the 1997 statistics?
2. Calculate by how much the population in each of the regions increased over the ten years from 1990 to 1997 and then name the fastest growing region.
3. Refer to the map at the back of the book and say which states make up each region.
4. Give at least two reasons that could explain why the population is growing faster in certain regions and more slowly in others.
5. Look at the population statistics on the left which give details of the foreign-born population in some US states. The statistics are for the states with the highest and lowest percentages of foreign-born citizens.
   a) Which states have the highest and which the lowest percentages of foreign-born citizens?
   b) Find these states on the map of the US at the back of the book and try to explain why foreigners have chosen to live in some states and not in others.
6. Copy and complete the following text using the correct words from the box.

The foreign-born population is concentrated in ___ areas of the country. Old immigrant centers continue to have ___ percentages of citizens born in other countries. The ___ show that people have not been ___ geographically as much as you might expect.

spreading out • the lowest • the highest • choosing • survey • statistics • southern • traditional

Foreign-born population (%)

State	A*	B*
Alabama	0.3	1.3
California	13.1	24.9
Hawaii	10.0	18.1
Kentucky	0.4	1.2
Mississippi	0.4	2.0
New Jersey	6.2	10.1
New York	10.2	19.6
Oklahoma	0.8	2.0
Rhode Island	10.3	11.1
Tennessee	0.5	1.2

*A = US-born, both parents foreign-born
*B = Foreign-born

West, South are building more population muscle

The West and South will be stronger than ever as population trends reshape the nation's landscape. If these trends continue through 2000, nine congressional seats would be picked up by seven fast-growing Western and Southern states, according to an exclusive analysis of 1998 Census state population estimates. These states are Arizona, California, Nevada, Florida, Texas, Montana, and Georgia.

Population counts are crucial to states because they decide how many seats each will get in Congress. The more representatives a state has, the more influence it has when issues affecting the state come up for a vote.

According to the analysts, the big gainers are Arizona and Texas; each will add two seats. California, Florida, Georgia, Montana and Nevada each would gain one. The big losers are New York and Pennsylvania, each down two seats in a reflection of the continued population drain from these older industrial states.

Politics aside, the new Census numbers reveal interesting glimpses of the changes in the country's population:

– West Virginia was the first state in recent decades to have more deaths than births, pushing its population down to 1.8 million. The state never recovered from the demise of the coal mining industry.

– Kansas was the fastest-growing state in the Midwest, up 1.1 % to 2.6 million. The state's meatpacking industry attracted foreign and domestic workers.

– Georgia, up 2 % to 7.6 million, was the fastest-growing state in the South. A lot of people leaving the Midwest and the Northeast have flocked to Georgia because of its booming economy.

– The Northeast continued to be the nation's slowest-growing region. Domestic out-migration in New York had more people leave than come in. People are following jobs in the Southeast and West, regions that are less congested.

From the article by Haya El Nasser (abridged), USA Today, *January 4, 1999.*

Col. 1:
2 **to reshape** to change
4 **congressional** *(US)* referrring to the legislative body made up of the Senate and the House of Representatives (cf. Xtra File, p. 88)
5 **to pick up** *here:* to gain
8 **estimate** rough calculation
12 **crucial** ['kru:ʃl] very important
23 **in a reflection of** showing s.th. that has happened
24 **population drain** when large numbers of people leave to go elsewhere

Col. 2:
1 **… aside** apart from …
2 **glimpse** *here:* impression
8 **demise** [dɪ'maɪz] *(formal)* failure
17 **to flock** to go in large numbers
25 **congested** *here:* full of people

← ***Comprehension***

1. a) Find and copy out the sentences in the text which tell you why the population counts are so important for the individual states.
   b) Explain the reason given in these sentences in your own words.
2. a) Copy the table below and complete it with information from the text.

Name of state	*Gainer/Loser*	*Reason for gain/loss*	*Political effect*

   b) Use your table and the statistical information on the opposite page to write a short report with the title "Population trends in the USA".

Check the web
Get more information about census figures at:
http://www.census.gov
Get more information about the states at:
http://local.yahoo.com

← ***Further activities***

- A population census is carried out in the US every ten years (1990/2000/etc.). In other years estimates are made. Find the estimates or census figures for this year on the government census website and report back to your class on the current trends.
- Go to the website of one of the states described in the text as a gainer. Try to find out what makes it so attractive geographically, economically, culturally, historically, etc. Then go to the website of one of the states described as a loser and try to find out why this is the case. Be prepared to present your findings to your class.

Giving a talk or presentation
See *skills file* on p. 129.

Focus on the South

Population statistics show that the South is by far the fastest growing region in the US. And perhaps more than any other region in the US, the South has a culture and 'flavour' of its own.

Getting started →

- What do you know about each of the items in the illustration below?

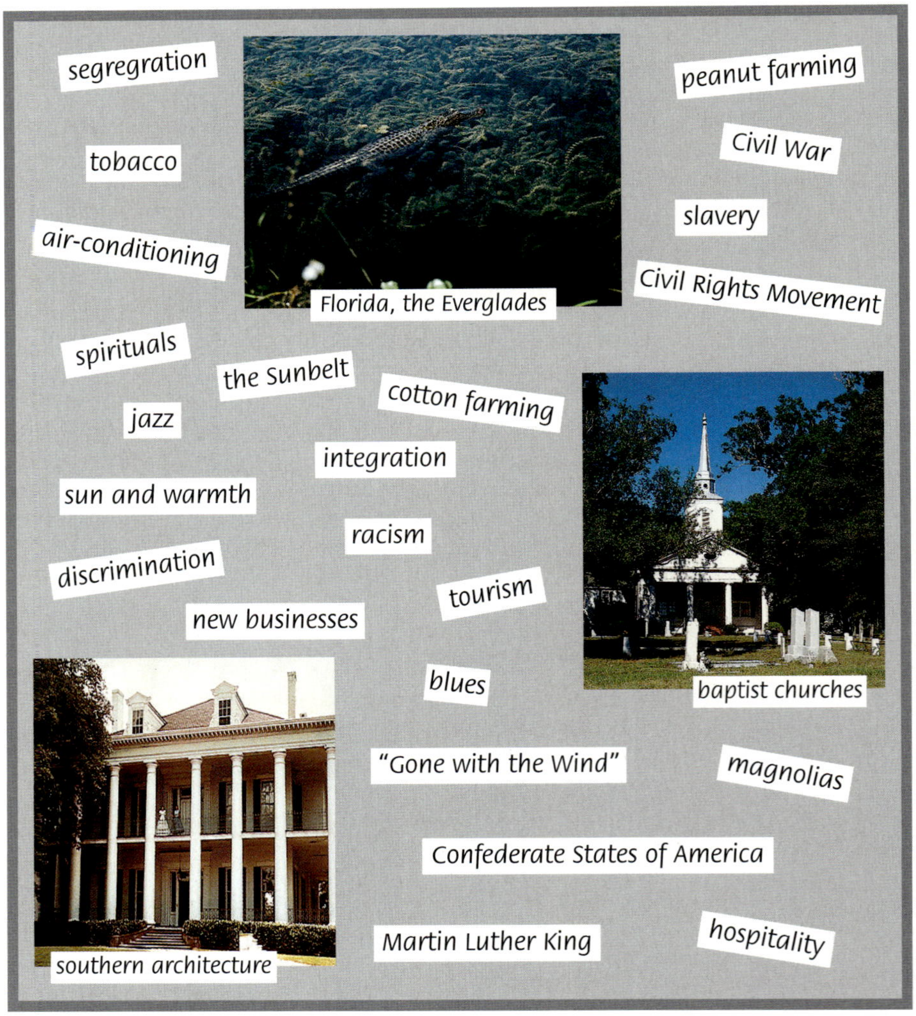

Collecting information in a mind map →

Mind maps
See *skills file* on p. 121.

Complete the mind map below by adding the words, names and terms from the illustration.

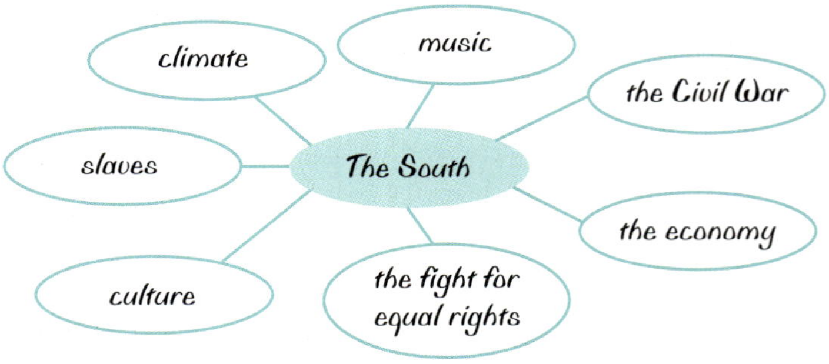

The southernisation of America

The following text looks at what makes the South so special, at how the South has been influenced by the rest of the United States and at the influence the South is now having on the rest of the USA.

Don't be put off by the length of the text. And don't worry if you don't understand every single word especially when you are reading the text for the first time. Understanding the gist (the main points of the text) is important at this stage!

Surviving without a dictionary
See *skills file* on p. 134.

While you read

- Read one paragraph at a time and then write a heading or a short sentence in your own words as a reminder of the main point made in it. This will help you understand the text better and help you concentrate on the most important points.

There has always been a special feel about southern life, quite apart from its poverty, its racism and its peculiar politics. One part of it is a reluctance to move. Partly thanks to their strong belief in the family, southerners have a strong attachment to place. With the exception of Florida, southern states still have remarkably few inhabitants born outside the region. In the Deep South states of South Carolina, Georgia, Alabama, Mississippi and Louisiana, less than 10 % of the people are not native southerners. Compare that with California or New York, where 54 % and 32 % of the population respectively were born outside the state.

The attachment to family and place is especially strong in rural areas. Drive into a small town or village anywhere in the Deep South, and you will quickly sense a changelessness – a party of crew-cut "good ol' boys" going out hunting, with full gunracks in the back of their pick-ups, who look like extras from a 1950s television show; or a black family in a shotgun shack that might have featured in "Huckleberry Finn." And since the South remains more rural than the rest of the country – farming was the biggest industry as recently as 1960 – even urban southerners still feel the tug of their old rural roots.

Then there are the famous "southern" attitudes: conservatism, the love of church and family, the fondness for violence, the hostility to the federal government even when (as in the New Deal) it was pouring money into the region. For a long time the rest of America laughed at all this; it called southerners rednecks, it accused them of lacking sophistication or being uncivilised, it assumed that such primitive views were bound up with racism. But laughed at or not, these attitudes have helped to differentiate the South, to lend it a special character that set it apart from other regions. […]

Now all this has changed, in two hugely significant ways. One is that the South has become more like the rest of America than at any time in its history. Consider its geography and climate. Before the air conditioner and jet aircraft, these were forbidding to outsiders. The summer is still as steamy as in any Tennessee Williams play; the swamps of Louisiana and south Florida as exotic and full of alligators, egrets and armadillos; the azaleas and rhododendrons of Georgia and the Carolinas, or the magnolias of Mississippi, just as gorgeous. But a business trip to Atlanta or Charlotte or Dallas is now much like a business trip to any American city – the same air-conditioned airport, the same views of suburbs clustered like centipedes around the roads on the city's edges, the same tower blocks downtown.

In its economy, politics and society, too, the South is losing its isolation. Retail outlets and fast food joints look the same in the 11 confederate states as elsewhere. Employment patterns too. There are still more farmers than elsewhere; states such as Tennessee and North and South Carolina have a higher proportion of their

2 **peculiar** *here:* unusual – **reluctance** unwillingness
3 **attachment** emotional link
7 **native** by birth
8 **respectively** in the order given
10 **to sense** *here:* to feel
11 **party** a group – **crew-cut** very short 'army-style' haircut – **"good ol' boys"** *(AE, informal)* local young men
12 **gunrack** a frame for holding guns – **pick-up** small truck with no roof and low sides at the back
13 **shotgun shack** *(AE)* a small wooden house where the rooms are built in a line away from the front door – **featured** appeared
16 **tug** [ʌ] strong pull
18 **fondness** strong liking – **hostility** *here:* opposition
19 **New Deal** domestic policies for economic and social reform after the Depression (1933–1941)
20 **redneck** *(AE)* uneducated white farm worker esp. from the South
21 **to lack** not to have **sophistication** opp. of primitiveness – **to assume** *here:* to think, possibly incorrectly
22 **bound up** closely linked to
23 **to lend** *here:* to give
30 **egret** ['i:grət] *Wasservogel der Reiherfamilie* – **armadillo** *Gürteltier*
31 **gorgeous** ['gɔ:dʒəs] extremely beautiful
33 **clustered** arranged – **centipede** *Tausendfüßler*
35 **retail outlet** a shop
36 **joint** *(AE, informal)* place
37 **pattern** trend

41 **engaged** employed

45 **hospitality** being friendly to visitors – **all-embracing** including everyone – **drawling** speaking with long vowels

46 **onrushing tide** strong forward movement

51 **to sneer at** *(negative)* to laugh at, to make fun of

53 **to converge** *here:* to become similar

55 **to deplore** to criticize strongly

57 **emergence** *here:* development

58 **distinctiveness** quality of being different

59 **sheer** absolute

63 **to afflict** to trouble

65 **perpetually** permanently

66 **inexorably** in a way which cannot be stopped

67 **to crumble** to fall apart

71 **on an economic roll** *(informal)* booming

74 **oppressed** *here:* being made to pay

76 **upbeat** optimistic

77 **edgy** *(informal)* uncertain

84 **poised** ready – **to occupy** *here:* to hold

workforce in manufacturing than most (North Carolina is the most industrialised state in the country). Yet a large majority of southerners are, like a large majority of all Americans, engaged in service jobs such as health care, professional services, teaching or government.

And yet. It is hard to visit the South even for a short time and come away with the feeling that it is just another part of America. The burden of history is too great; southern hospitality too all-embracing; even the drawling accent too different. It will be many years before these things can be swept away by the onrushing tide of conformity.

That brings in the second big change, which is not to the South but to the rest of the country. Charles Wilson of the Centre for the Study of Southern Culture calls it the southernisation of America. The [1994] mid-term elections confirmed that the "primitive" attitudes that east-coast liberals used to sneer at are now those of America. It is the liberals who are now the obvious minority. As the South and the rest of America converge, it is at least as much thanks to the rest of the country joining the South, as to the South rejoining the Union.

Many traditionalists regret this. They deplore the harsher tone to American life that reflects the southern influence. They hate the religious right. Yet in many other ways America is gaining from the emergence of a triumphant new South that retains so much of its distinctiveness. This is not for the usual reason, that variety is enriching; for that could have excused the injustice, poverty and sheer inefficiency that for too many years characterised the South. The case for applauding the South's combination of continuing distinctiveness with success now is that it may be showing the rest of the country a way forward: an escape from the doubting, gloomy mood that afflicts it.

For some years middle-class Americans have feared that the American dream – perpetually rising living standards, with each generation living better than its parents – is over. Crime seems to be rising inexorably. Wages and living standards are under pressure. Roads and bridges are crumbling. Politicians are worse than ever.

The mood is different in the South. There, people who were poor for decades are at long last living the American dream. Few southerners worry, as do so many northerners, about whether they can afford the houses, college education and other luxuries of their fathers. Instead they are on an economic roll; such a strong one, indeed, that they are pulling the rest of the country with them. As for the hated politicians, southern businessmen still work with, not against, city halls and state governments; and the middle classes do not feel so oppressed by high taxes. Southern Republicans are, understandably enough, especially upbeat. […]

Black-white relations remain edgy; but they are better than elsewhere in America. The South still has plenty of problems: rural poverty, bad schools, crime. But these are no longer southern problems; they affect the whole country. And in other respects the South is poised to occupy an unusual position in America: leadership. It makes a nice change from most of its history.

Southerners are on an economic roll: magnolia trees in bloom and the modern skyline of Atlanta.

From the article in The Economist, *London, December 10, 1994.*

Collecting information from the text

Use the sentences and headings you wrote while reading the text to make notes about the following changes. Add further information from the text which you consider important. Write in note form, not in full sentences.

a) Economic changes
b) Political changes
c) Changes in technology
d) Changes in attitudes

Comprehension

Answer the following questions in your own words:

1. Which three key terms were used to characterize the South in the past?
2. How did the jet aircraft and the air conditioner help change the South?
3. In what ways has the US as a whole become more like the South in recent years?
4. Why is the American dream not dead in the South?
5. Which southern problems are also relevant to the US as a whole? Which are relevant in other countries of the world?

Vocabulary: definitions & word families

1. Explain these words from the text in your own words:
   rural (l. 9) • urban (l. 15) • suburbs (l. 33) • majority (l. 40) • service jobs (l. 41) • southernisation (l. 50) • traditionalists (l. 55).
2. Copy and complete the table below with the words given in the box. Write each word under the correct heading and then supply the additional forms.

noun	*verb*	*adjective*
life (l. 1)	*to live*	*living/live*

life (l. 1) • attachment (l. 3) • inhabitants (l. 5) • population (l. 8) • to accuse (l. 20) • significant (l. 25) • isolation (l. 35) • distinctive (l. 58) • economic (l. 71)

Grammar: relative clauses

Relative clauses
See *grammar file* on p.148.

1. Copy and complete the sentences below with 'who' or 'which'.
   a) There has always been a special feel about southern life, ___ is not only marked by poverty and racism.
   b) Southern states still have remarkably few inhabitants ___ are born outside the region.
   c) The attachment to family and place, ___ is strong in the South, is especially strong in rural areas.
   d) You can still see young men ___ look like extras from a 50s television show, with crew-cuts and driving their pick-ups.
   e) Attitudes like conservatism and love of church and family, ___ are famous southern attitudes, give the South a special character and set it apart from other regions.
   f) In a state like North Carolina, ___ is the most industrialized state in the country, a high percentage of the work force is in manufacturing.
2. Explain these terms in your own words using relative clauses:
   Example: A pick-up truck is a vehicle ___
   Solution: A pick-up truck is a vehicle *which can transport few people but a lot of goods.*
   a) Armadillos, egrets and alligators are animals ___
   b) Liberals are people ___
   c) Fast food joints are restaurants ___
   d) A minority is a group ___
   e) Southerners are people ___
   f) A retail outlet is a store or group of stores ___

Southern rock

The South is most famous for jazz, blues and spiritual music, but rock music from the south has also proved popular around the world. Sweet Home Alabama *by Lynyrd Skynyrd was the first of the band's songs to get into the Top 40 in the USA back in 1974. However, more than 25 years later, the song is still frequently played today.*

Sweet Home Alabama

Big wheels keep on turning
Carry me home to see my kin
Singing songs about the Southland
I miss Alabamy once again
And I think it's a sin – Yes

Well, I heard Mr Young sing about her
Well, I heard ol' Neil put her down
Well, I hope Neil Young will remember
A Southern Man don't need him around, anyhow

Chorus:
Sweet Home Alabama
Where the skies are so blue
Sweet Home Alabama
Lord, I'm coming home to you

In Birmingham they love the guv'ner
Now we all did what we could do
Now Watergate does not bother me
Does your conscience bother you?
Tell the truth

Chorus

Now Muscle Shoals has got the Swampers
And they've been known to pick a song or two,
Lord they get me off so much
They pick me up when I'm feeling blue
Now how about you?

Chorus

Sweet Home Alabama,
Oh sweet home baby
Where the skies are so blue
And the guv'ner's true
Sweet Home Alabama
Lordy, Lord, I'm coming home to you
Yea, yea, Montgomery's got the answer

2 **kin** family
24 **to pick one up** *here:* to make one feel better – **to feel blue** *(informal)* to feel sad

Think of a suitable caption to go with this photograph of the band Lynyrd Skynyrd.

Working with the song

1. What does the song title tell you about how the song writer feels about Alabama?
2. Have you ever felt, or do you feel, this way about your home town/state/country? Why or why not?
3. a) Give grades of 1 (like it very much) to 5 (don't like it at all) to say what you like or don't like about the song in terms of:
   the tune (melody) • the singer's voice • the chorus • the words.
   b) Give reasons for your choice.
4. What or who do you think "her" (ll. 6 & 7) in verse two refers to?
5. Decide which verse these statements refer to and answer the questions.
   a) This verse refers to another pop song about the south: What was the singer's name and what was the song, which was critical of the south, called?
   b) This verse mentions a big political scandal in the US: What was the scandal known as? What do you know about it? Try to find out more.
   c) This verse is about the recording studios where the song was recorded. What was the name of the town? What was the recording team called?
   d) In this verse we hear that the singer is going home to visit his family. What is he doing and how does he feel on the journey?

Check the web
Get more information about the song at ***http://members.xoom.com/south_talkin/docs/skynyrd1.htm***

Project: Planning a trip to the US

At the end of a successful season, the basketball team you play for decides to go on a trip to the USA together. A local travel company makes a donation of 250 Euros per person to go towards the cost of the flight and your club has given you free tickets for a basketball match at the home of the Bulls in Chicago.
Work in groups and plan your trip keeping to a maximum budget of no more than 1,750 Euros per person.

Decide:
- which regions and/or cities you want to visit (including Chicago).
- when you want to travel.
- where you want to fly to and from.
- how you want to travel when you are in the US.
- where you want to stay (hotels, campsites, etc.)

Collect the following information about the places you want to visit:
- Cultural attractions/special sights
- Climate and weather
- Natural features (mountains, lakes, etc.)
- Local specialities (food)
- Sports and leisure acitvties

Define:
- transportation costs.
- accommodation costs.
- other costs (entrance fees to shows, museums, etc.).
- dates and times of travel, events, etc.

Plan your trip in detail making a comprehensive day-to-day itinerary which includes times, dates, addresses and costs.

Collect all the information in a folder which you can present to the other groups in your class.

Over to you

Project work
See *skills file* on p. 139.

Finding information
- Ask for information at travel agencies in your area.
- Contact tourist information centers in the places you want to visit.
- Look up the places you want to visit on the Internet using a search engine. Try using the following key words in your search:
US • tourism • name of state of your choice • name of town/area of your choice • AAA (American Automobile Association) • sports events • US airports

The American political system

Checks and Balances

At some schools in the US, students have to take an American government examination, which tests their knowledge of the American political system. They must pass the examination before they can graduate. In the following short play two seniors are just about to take the examination.

(It's 7:45 am and the warning bell has rung at Ballway High School. Today the dreaded yearly American government examination is to take place. If the students don't pass, they won't be allowed to graduate.)

SCOTT: Hey Jill! Bet you know everything for the test today! Could you help me with a few things?

JILL *(looking at her watch)*: In ten minutes you want to learn what you haven't learned the last three weeks!

SCOTT: But I've studied hard!

JILL: Yeah, maybe during a few commercial breaks. You're hopeless.

SCOTT: Hey! I know a lot, there are just a few things I'm not sure of. It must have been hard for the people to write the Constitution in 1887...

JILL *(laughing)*: It was written in 1787 not 1887. Back then some Americans realized that the states were looking out more for their own interests than for those of the country as a whole. It was becoming clear that a big change was needed in how the United States of America should be run. A Constitutional Convention was planned in 1787– did you hear that? 1787 – so that these problems could be discussed, and delegates from most of the states went to Philadelphia to take part. Finally the group of delegates, also called framers, agreed upon a Constitution.

SCOTT: I see!

JILL: Some states were worried about losing some of their independence and about how much power the federal government would have over them and over the people. But all the states finally accepted the Constitution by 1790 and it was agreed that a Bill of Rights would be included.

SCOTT *(writing notes furiously)*: Hang on a minute ... by 1790 all states had accepted the Constitution. But who has the real power? The American people?

JILL: Not exactly! The people do influence their government and its powers ...

SCOTT: Wait, I think I remember: the branches of government act as watchdogs over each other! That's why the system is called the system of checks and balances! And I know that there's a legislative branch, an executive branch, and a judicial branch ...

JILL: Right, and the legislative branch is made up of Congress. Congress is made up of the House of Representatives and the Senate. The House has 435 members who are elected every two years directly by the people in their constituencies. In the Senate there are 100 Senators who serve six-year terms. The number of representatives a state has depends on its population, whereas the number of senators is the same for every state ...

SCOTT: ... because otherwise the small states were worried about being unfairly represented.

JILL: Exactly! Senators are also elected every two years, and nowadays they are also elected directly by the people. But no more than one-third of them can be up for election at any one time ...

to graduate to receive a degree or diploma

2 **dreaded** which causes great fear

4 **Bet...** *(informal) here:* I'm sure

15 **Convention** a formal assembly

21 **federal** referring to a central government separate from the state governments

23 **Bill of Rights** the first ten amendments (additional laws) to the US Constitution, added in 1791, which guarantee the liberty of the individual

27 **branch** part

29 **judicial** [dʒu:ˈdɪʃl]

33 **constituency** an area which has an elected representative in government

35 **whereas** on the other hand

SCOTT: Why not?

JILL: So that there is always some continuity in the system. In other words, there are some experienced people around to help the newcomers.

SCOTT: And what about the president. Now he – or she – really is the boss, right?

JILL: Well, he – or she – is head of the executive branch. Anyway, the president serves a four-year term and can only serve for two terms – so a maximum of eight years. And remember: the president isn't chosen directly by the people: the people elect state electors who then vote for presidential candidates.

SCOTT: Geez, it's all so complicated! And what about the whatsit – the judicial branch?

JILL: The judicial branch is made up of a system of federal courts, the main part of which is the Supreme Court.

(The last warning bell rings.)

JILL: Only five more minutes. Now listen! This is how a bill becomes a law. The bill, which is a proposal for a law, starts off being debated in various committees of either the House of Representatives or the Senate. Both have to agree to the same version of the bill. If and when they do, the bill goes on to the president, who either gives it a thumbs up and signs it, or a thumbs down and vetoes it.

SCOTT: Okay, got it. So that's how Congress is checked by the president.

JILL: Yep and if the president vetoes a bill, Congress can still decide that it wants to try to make it a law. A vote is held, and if two-thirds of both the Senate and the House are in favor of the bill, it becomes a law without the president's agreement.

SCOTT: So the president's power can be checked too!

JILL: Right! But that's not the end of it. If there is any doubt whether a new law follows the principles of the Constitution – or in other words if it's thought to be "unconstitutional", the Supreme Court can decide to consider the case. If the Supreme Court decides that the law is unconstitutional, the law is thrown out. Congress could then try to change the law, so that the Supreme Court accepts it, or Congress could, of course, try to amend the Constitution to make the law fit!

SCOTT: Does anyone check the judicial branch?

JILL: Yep, the president appoints judges to the federal courts, and the Senate has to approve these appointments, for example.

SCOTT: Great! Now I know everything!

JILL: That wasn't even half of it! I haven't even mentioned how the president can suggest legislation to Congress, or how Congress must approve the president's budget plans …

SCOTT: Stop it! It's too much to keep in my head! I do know a bit about impeachment, where presidents …

JILL: … and judges …

SCOTT: … can be thrown out of office if they've done something really bad like a crime.

JILL: … and if two-thirds of the Senate think that the president – or judge – is guilty!

(The final bell rings.)

SCOTT: I guess I really should have studied more.

JILL: Good luck, Scott. See you at graduation – if you pass!

43 **continuity** [ˌ--ˈ---]

50 **Geez** [dʒi:z] *(informal, exclam.) Jesus* – **whatsit** *(informal)* term for s.th. you have temporarily forgotten the name of

59 **to give s.th. a thumbs up/down** *(informal)* to show approval or accept s.th./to show disapproval or reject s.th.

61 **Yep** *(informal)* yes

71 **to amend** to change

74 **to approve** to accept

86 **to guess** to suppose

87 **graduation** ceremony at which students receive their leaving degrees or diplomas

★ **Listening comprehension**

Each week the President of the United States addresses the nation by radio. Listen to one of President Clinton's radio addresses.

Bill Clinton was President of the United States from 1993 to 2001.

The US political system: 'checks and balances'

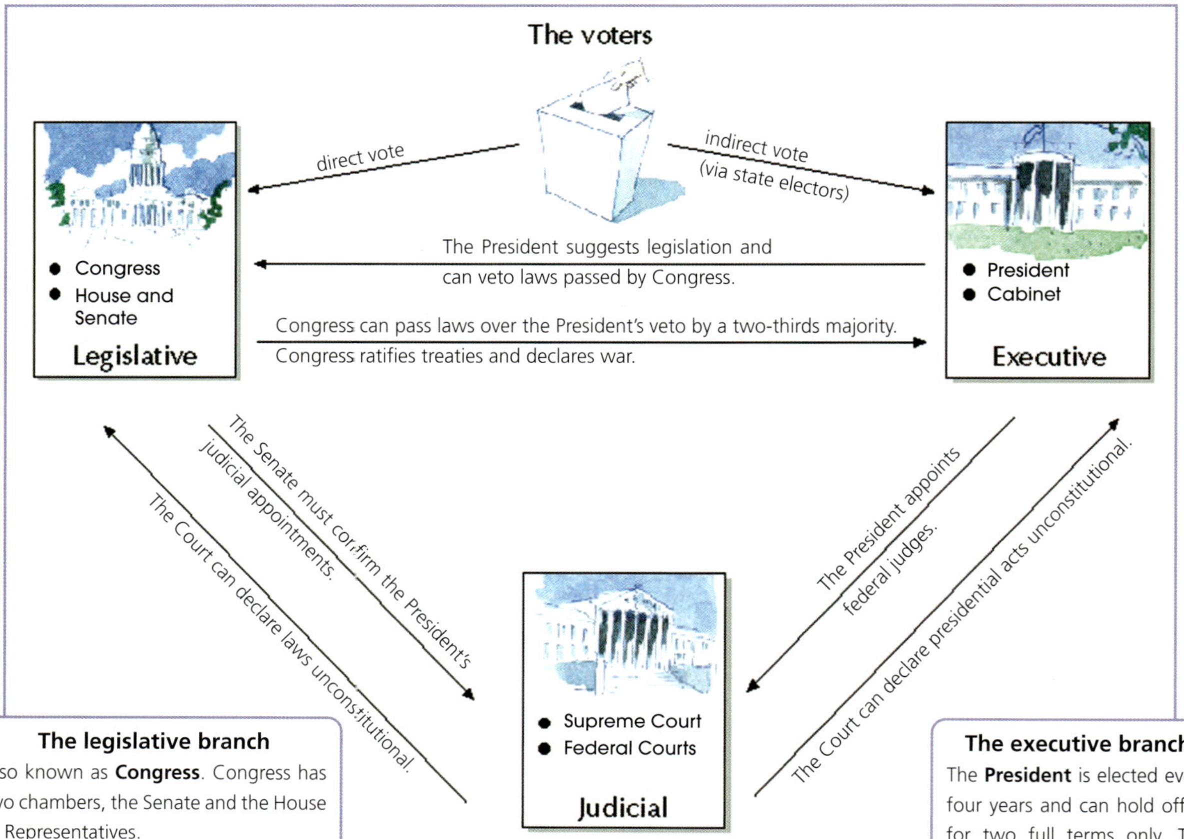

The legislative branch

Also known as **Congress**. Congress has two chambers, the Senate and the House of Representatives.

Senate:
100 Senators, elected for a 6-year term, one third are elected every two years.

House of Representatives:
435 members, elected every two years. States with a high population have more Representatives than states with a low population.

The House and the Senate can reject each other's bills.

Congress decides on the federal budget (how federal money is spent).

The judicial branch

The **Supreme Court** has nine judges. They are appointed for life. The Supreme Court is responsible for seeing that the Constitution is upheld and that laws that are made are allowed under the Constitution.

There are 11 US **Courts of Appeals** and 90 US **District Courts**.

The executive branch

The **President** is elected every four years and can hold office for two full terms only. The President is Head of State and Commander-in-Chief of the armed forces. The President appoints a **cabinet** and the cabinet is approved by the Senate. Cabinet members need not be members of Congress.

The Political Parties

Members of Congress are elected as individuals and not as members of a political party. However, in practice there are two main parties in Congress: the Republicans and the Democrats. Both parties cover a wide range of opinion from conservative to liberal and unlike most European parties cannot be defined as being strictly left or right of centre. Even within each party there are significant regional differences in party politics. The Republicans are often associated with business and industry. They generally oppose a strong federal (central) government. People in rural and suburban areas and small cities are more likely to vote Republican (except in the South where the Democratic Party has traditionally been strong in all areas). The Republican emblem is the elephant. The Democrats are often associated with labour and are generally in favour of a strong federal government especially where social issues are concerned. Large urban centres are more likely to vote Democrat. Their emblem is the donkey.

The electoral process

The American electoral process is basically a winner-takes-all system, in which one person wins and all the others lose. Each state has its own voting laws and practices. US citizens over the age of 18 who are registered to vote can do so. (Voters must register themselves: there is no automatic registration.)
There are basically two levels of elections: primary and general.
Each party holds its own **primaries**. At the primaries voters affiliated to a party decide which of their party's candidates should be chosen to run for election.
At a **general election** all registered voters vote for the candidate of their choice and the candidate who gets the most votes is the winner (winner-takes-all). In some elections, like the presidential elections, voters do not vote directly for the candidate but for an 'elector' who supports that candidate. The candidate who gets the most votes from the electors wins the post.

6 **affiliated to** to be in close connection with *(nahe stehen)*

Check the web
Get more information about voting at:
http://www.sos.state.tx.us/function/projectv/pvote/index.htm

How the President is elected

The presidential elections are the most important elections in the USA. They are held every four years. There are six basic stages to the presidential elections.

Stage 1: Individuals decide to stand for President
Individuals (US born-citizens over the age of 35) decide to run for the post of President. Usually there are a number of candidates from each of the main parties as well as some independent candidates.

Stage 2: Primaries
The parties hold primaries (or in some states a process known as a caucus) between February and June of election year. Often, to vote in a party's primaries, a voter must first register with the party. At the primaries the delegates who will attend the national party conventions are selected (see Stage 3). Essentially at the primaries the party's grass roots indicate which of their party's candidates they would prefer to run for President.

Stage 3: National conventions
Republican and Democratic national conventions are held in July or August of election year. Here the delegates from the states (elected at the primaries) choose one of their party's candidates to stand for president. The number of delegates a state can send to each of the national conventions depends on the size of the population in that state. The presidential candidate for each of the parties is officially announced at the conventions.

Stage 4: General elections
A general election is always held on the Tuesday following the first Monday in November. The general election decides which electors from each state will become members of the electoral college (see Stage 5). At the general election all registered voters can cast their vote for one of the presidential candidates. Votes are added together in each state. The candidate who wins the most votes is declared the winner in that state. The electors who support the winning candidate become members of the college for that state (winner-takes-all).

Stage 5: Electoral college
The electoral college is made up of the electors from each state. The number of electors a state has in the electoral college depends on the number of members it has in Congress. This can be as many as 47 (California) but as few as three (District of Columbia). Each elector has one vote. In December the electors each cast their vote for the presidential candidate who won the general election in their state. The candidate who wins most of the electoral college votes becomes president (winner-takes-all).

Stage 6: Inauguration
The results are declared on January 6 and the president is sworn in on January 20 at what is known as the Inauguration Ceremony.

11 **grass roots** the ordinary people affiliated to a party or organisation

22 **to cast** to give

35 **to be sworn in** *vereidigt werden*

36 **inauguration** the action of placing in office formally and ceremonially

6 Life in the city: Atlanta

Facts and figures

Atlanta
Estimated population:
(city) 400,000
(metropolitan area) 3,500,000
Median age of population: 31.5
City land area: 136 square miles
(352,2 sq km)
Average daily temperature:
January 41.9°F; July 78.6°F
Number of churches: 1,500
Number of radio stations: 27
Number of TV stations: 10

Atlanta – capital of the New South and shining example of a growing city

Getting started →

1. Find Atlanta on the map at the back of the book and describe its location.
2. a) Think of adjectives to describe Atlanta as shown in the photograph above.
   b) Describe the buildings in as much detail as possible. Say what you think the function of some of them might be.
3. Do any of the figures about Atlanta given on the left surprise you? Find similar figures for the area where you live and make comparisons.
4. Write a paragraph about your first impression of Atlanta based on the figures and the photograph above.

a)

b)

c)

d)

Atlanta Timeline

1773 The English soldier James Oglethorpe secures a charter for the colony of Georgia.
1843 Terminus, the end of the railroad line which connects Georgia and the Tennessee River, is renamed Marthaville and then Atlanta.
1865 The Civil War ends and Atlanta's reconstruction period begins.
1868 The "Atlanta Constitution" publishes its first daily morning newspaper.
1885 Georgia Institute of Technology is founded.
1892 The Coca-Cola Company is established in Atlanta by Asa Candler.
1936 Margaret Mitchell's tale of the American South, Gone With The Wind, is published.
1964 Dr. Martin Luther King, Jr. is awarded the Nobel Peace Prize.
1974 Baseball's Hank Aaron of the Atlanta Braves breaks Babe Ruth's lifetime home run record.
1976 Jimmy Carter, governor of Georgia, is elected the 39th president of the United States.
1979 Atlanta's advanced mass transportation system, MARTA (Metropolitan Atlanta Rapid Transit Authority), begins operation.
1980 Cable News Network (CNN) is established in Atlanta, the first television station to broadcast 24-hour news around the world.
1988 Atlanta hosts the Democratic National Convention.
1994 Superbowl XXVIII is held in Atlanta.
1996 Atlanta hosts the biggest sports event in its history, the Summer Olympics.
1999 SUPERCOMM presents the latest innovations in the world of communications.

reconstruction rebuilding of a damaged area – **home run** a hit which allows the batter to make a complete circuit of the bases – **to host** *here:* to hold an event – **convention** large official meeting – **SUPERCOMM** name of an annual conference and exhibition

1. Find the entries in the timeline which match the photographs a) – f) and construct sentences using relative clauses starting with 'who' or 'which'.
   Example: *Photograph x) is of the Democratic National Convention, which took place in Atlanta in 1988.*
2. The present tense is used in the timeline but the past tense would be used to talk about the events.
   Work with a partner. Ask each other questions about the timeline using the past tense. Begin your questions:
   When did/was … ? • What happened in … ? • Who/What was … ?
   Example: Q: When did James Oglethorpe secure a charter for the colony of Georgia? A: He secured the charter in 1773.
3. a) Identify the use of the passive voice in the timeline.
   b) Rewrite the facts about the years 1868, 1892, 1974, 1976, 1980, 1996 and 1999 substituting the passive for the active voice and vice versa.

← ***Language & grammar***

Relative clauses
See *grammar file* on p. 148.

Tenses
See *grammar files* on pp. 142–145.

The passive voice
See *grammar file* on p. 147.

Introducing Atlanta

Before you read →

- Where can you find information in English about a city, such as Atlanta, which you know very little about? What kind of information would interest you most?

While you read →

- The following text is taken from the beginning of a guide to Atlanta. While you read make a note of the four "alternative" names for Atlanta which are given in the text and try to explain briefly why Atlanta is known by these names.

They call it the Big A, the capital of the New South, and the International Gateway City – all names evocative of Atlanta's dynamism, dash and spirit. This ever-expanding city – the 13th largest metropolitan area in the United States – teems with energy. Its architecturally innovative downtown area is a sleek showplace of glittering glass skyscrapers, a setting worthy of the city's role of the South's major marketplace and its hub of finance, communications, and transportation.

This is the home of the world's largest airport. It's one of the nation's top meeting and convention cities and is headquarters for hundreds of businesses, including Delta Air Lines, Lockheed, Days Inns, Ritz-Carlton, Holiday Inn, Georgia-Pacific, Coca-Cola (never ask for a Pepsi here), Turner Broadcasting System, and Scientific Atlanta. Atlanta hosted the Democratic National Convention in 1988, [...] the Super Bowl XXVIII in 1994 and the Summer Olympics in 1996. It is the major shopping center of the Southeast region; home to 29 colleges and universities; and a southern crossroads where three interstate highways converge.

Atlanta is also called the Dogwood City, and this name evokes another of its alluring aspects. Coexisting with the bustling metropolis is a very southern city of magnolias and colonnaded white mansions. Every spring (and spring here can begin in February), the city blossoms with delicate pink dogwood buds, fragrant honeysuckle and yellow jasmine, and beautiful pink, white and red azaleas. Drive a few miles out of the metropolitan area and you'll find yourself in verdant countryside.

Big-city Atlanta celebrates holidays with small-town exuberance. Annual events include chili and barbecue cookoffs, traditional Fourth of July picnics and parades, and Christmas chestnut roasts. The city's patron saint is *Gone With The Wind* author Margaret Mitchell (the book comes up almost on a daily basis), and history – especially Civil War history – is venerated. And while it's extremely dynamic, this is also a leisurely city where people are never in so much of a rush that they dispense with southern graciousness and hospitality. Atlanta is consistently ranked as one of the best places in the country to live – a sentiment that any resident will enthusiastically confirm.

To this appealing mix of urban sophistication and southern gentility add a vibrant cultural scene, with a growing theater community; major art and science museums; prestigious symphony, ballet, and opera companies; big-league sports; a culinary spectrum that ranges from fried chicken 'n' biscuits to beluga caviar; hot nightlife; and a delightfully temperate climate.

2 **evocative** that gives a strong image – **dynamism** ['daɪ-] energy – **dash** energy, style
3 **metropolitan** referring to a large city – **to teem with** to be full of
4 **architecturally** related to building design and construction – **innovative** new, original – **sleek** shiny
5 **worthy** which is good enough
6 **hub** centre around which things rotate
8 **convention** large official meeting
11 **to host** to hold an event
14 **to converge** to meet
15 **dogwood** type of tree with white flowers – **to evoke** to create a strong image
16 **alluring** attractive – **bustling** ['bʌslɪŋ] lively, full of people
17 **colonnaded** with rows of evenly spaced columns (= *Säulen)*
18 **bud** *Knospe* – **fragrant** ['freɪgrənt] pleasant smelling – **honeysuckle** *Geißblatt*
19 **azalea** [ə'zeɪlɪə]
20 **verdant** fresh and green
21 **exuberance** [ɪg'zju:bərəns] excitement
22 **cookoff** *(AE)* cooking competition
23 **chestnut** ['tʃesnʌt] *Kastanie*
27 **to venerate s.th.** *(formal)* to show respect to s.th.
30 **to dispense with** *here:* not to show these qualities – **graciousness** ['greɪʃəsnəs] *(formal)* politeness
31 **hospitality** friendliness towards strangers – **consistently** never changing
34 **to confirm** *here:* to agree with
35 **sophistication** knowing about culture, new ideas, etc.
36 **gentility** politeness, respectability
37 **vibrant** [aɪ] lively
39 **prestigious** much admired
40 **league** [li:g]
41 **culinary** [ʌ] – **spectrum** a wide range
43 **temperate** mild

Add further a clean and safe state-of-the-art urban mass-transportation system and visitor attractions that run the gamut from legacies of the Confederacy to black heritage sites (Martin Luther King, Jr., was born and is buried here), from historic homes to the futuristic SciTrek Museum, and from a newly refurbished zoo to tours of the high-tech CNN Center studios. And that's not to mention theme parks, a presidential library (Jimmy Carter's, of course), a magnificent botanical garden and conservatory, a winery that's a replica of a 16th-century French château, and Georgia's Stone Mountain Park, one of the nation's most gorgeous parks and Atlanta's third-largest tourist attraction. [...]

It is most fitting that Atlanta in the 1990s is an international gateway/transportation hub. The city was conceived as a rail crossroads for travel north, south, east, and west, and its role as a strategic junction has always figured largely in its destiny. It all began with a peach tree. [...]

Atlanta in the nineties remains a forward-looking city that is constantly renewing itself – a dynamic metropolis where the past is honored and the present enthusiastically embraced. The city's motto is "Resurgens". The phoenix has risen from the ashes and taken wing.

From Frommer's Atlanta *by Rena Bulkin, New York: Simon & Schuster/Macmillan, 1993, pp. 1, 3, 11.*

45 **state-of-the-art** using the most modern technology
46 **to run the gamut** to offer a whole variety of things – **legacy** s.th. that is passed down to later generations
48 **refurbished** renovated
50 **botanical** relating to the study of plants
51 **conservatory** a glass construction in which plants are kept – **replica** ['replɪkə] an accurate copy of s.th.
52 **gorgeous** ['gɔːdʒəs] extremely beautiful
54 **gateway** *here:* entry
55 **to conceive** *here:* to plan
56 **junction** *(AE) here:* crossing – **to figure largely** *here:* to be a very important aspect
57 **destiny** fate
60 **to embrace** *here:* to welcome – **resurgens** rising again (*Latin:* resurgent)
61 **to take wing** to fly away

Comprehension

1. What do you find out about Atlanta in the text in terms of:
   architecture • infrastructure • business • sport • culture • history • people and lifestyle?
2. Describe the style of the text and say who you think it is aimed at (type/age of people, etc.). Find examples in the text to support your answer.
3. What do you find most interesting about Atlanta? Give reasons.

Language: adjectives

1. The following adjectives are used to describe Atlanta in the text. Copy and complete the table giving a definition and a synonym to go with each adjective.
   ever-expanding (l. 2) • innovative (l. 4) • glittering (l. 4) • bustling (l. 16) • state-of-the-art (l. 45) • historic (l. 47) • forward-looking (l. 58)

Word	Definition	Synonym
ever-expanding	getting bigger all the time	constantly growing

2. a) Add five more adjectives with definitions and synonyms to your table to describe the area where you live.
   b) Compare and contrast the area where you live with Atlanta on the basis of the adjectives in your table. Use the phrases below:
   Similarly ... • In the same way ... • By contrast ... • By comparison ...

Adjectives
See *grammar file* on p.149.
Synonyms
See *glossary* on p.153.

Over to you

Write a text promoting the area where you live. Consider the categories you looked at in comprehension task one above and make use of the adjectives you found in language task two.

Listening comprehension
In this interview Karen McNeely, Public Relations Manager at the Atlanta Convention and Visitors Bureau, talks enthusiastically about Atlanta.

Check the web
Get more information about Atlanta at:
http://www.ci.atlanta.ga.us/

World's busiest airport

Atlanta's airport, known as William B. Hartsfield International airport, has played a major role in the development of Atlanta as the new capital of the south. In 1999 the airport was officially named "World's Busiest Airport" by the Airport Council International.

Before you read →

- Why do you think it is important for a modern city to have an international airport nearby? Make a list of reasons and add to it – if necessary – as you read the text.

Atlanta flying high, via world's No. 1 airport

ATLANTA – Somewhere, William B. Hartsfield must be smiling.

The six-term mayor, whose name graces this city's airport, weighed the future 75 years ago and guessed that air traffic would supplant rail travel. He led efforts to transform a dirt racetrack on 300 acres south of the city into an airfield.

Last year, William B. Hartsfield International Airport, a 24-hour-a-day beehive sprawling across 3,800 acres, overtook Chicago's O'Hare as the airport with the most passengers in the world. Tuesday, a trade group that tracks world airport traffic made it official in a report that said airports the world over handled more than 2.8 billion passengers last year, an increase of 2.9 % from 1997.

The designation as "World's Busiest Airport" – from the Geneva-based Airports Council International (AIC) – is a coup for this New South capital with historic ambitions of becoming an international city.

In as much as Atlanta has realized those dreams, it has done so largely because of its airport. The story of the airport is the story of the modern Atlanta.

"To understand what the airport means to Atlanta, you have to turn the clock back to the mid-1920s," says University of Georgia political scientist Charles Bullock. "At that point, there wasn't that much difference between Atlanta and Birmingham (Ala)."

In the '20s, the federal government was about to institute an airmail service between New York and Miami, and was to choose one of the two Southern cities as an intermediate stop. Atlanta, even then a hustling self promoter, invited a top postal official to town, greeting him with dignitaries and a motorcade. It won the route. "The acquiring of the airport and all that goes with it has made Atlanta the dominant city in the Southeast," Bullock says.

Officially, the designation as "World's Busiest Airport" means nothing. But it confers certain bragging rights, and officials here were eagerly awaiting the coronation. After all, this city boasted as early as the 1960s that its airport was the world's busiest – on weekdays, between 11 a.m. and 2 p.m.

"We're very proud of our airport," Mayor Bill Campbell says. "First and foremost, it's the engine that drives the economic train. The population is exploding throughout metro Atlanta, and all that's because of the airport. I think the airport was the most important factor in the Olympic Games coming to Atlanta."

Already, Hartsfield is an economic gem with an annual direct financial impact of nearly $15 billion on the Georgia economy. With 42,300 employees, the airport and its tenants form the state's largest employment center.

Hartsfield's four runways serve carriers that take people to 195 cities, including destinations in 20 foreign countries. Dominant among them is Delta Air Lines, which began flying passengers into Atlanta in 1930 and whose growth into the nation's third-largest airline helped fuel Hartfield's growth. […]

From the article by Larry Copeland, USA Today, *April 7, 1999.*

Col. 1:
- 5 **whose name graces …** i.e. the airport is named after him
- 6 **to weigh** *here:* to consider
- 9 **to supplant** to take the place of
- 16 **beehive** *here:* a busy place
- 17 **to sprawl** to cover a large area in a disorganized way
- 25 **to handle** *here:* to deal with
- 29 **designation** giving s.th. a particular title
- 33 **coup** [ku:] a great achievement

Col. 2:
- 14 **Ala** *short for* Alabama
- 17 **to institute** *(formal)* to start up
- 21 **intermediate** in between
- 23 **hustling self promoter** s.o. who aggressively makes him-/herself popular
- 26 **dignitary** *(formal)* s.o. of a high rank – **motorcade** [-keɪd] procession of cars carrying important people
- 36 **to confer** *(formal)* to give – **to brag** *(negative)* to say all that one has achieved
- 38 **eagerly** ['i:gəlɪ] anxiously
- 39 **coronation** *here:* ceremony giving the airport official status

Col. 3:
- 1 **to boast** [əʊ] to talk too proudly about what one has done
- 8 **first and foremost** most importantly
- 20 **gem** [dʒem] jewel; *here:* having a high value
- 25 **tenant** s.o. who pays rent to use rooms
- 29 **carrier** *here:* aeroplane
- 38 **to fuel** *here:* to increase

Comprehension

1. Who was William B. Hartsfield and why was the airport named after him?
2. Find the following facts in the text:
   a) What are Hartsfield airport's opening hours?
   b) How big is the airport?
   c) How many people work at Hartsfield airport?
   d) How many runways has the airport got?
   e) How many cities and how many foreign countries can you fly to from Atlanta?
   f) Which is the most important airline in Atlanta?
3. a) Make notes to go with each of the following key items.
   "World's Busiest Airport" • New York to Miami airmail service • Olympic Games • economy and employment
   b) Use your notes to write a short text describing the development of Hartsfield airport.

Grammar: Conditional sentences

The story of Atlanta's airport is a success story, but things could have gone differently.

1. Rewrite the facts below using 'if-clauses' to say what would have happened if things had gone differently.
   a) William Hartfield realised that air traffic would soon be more important than rail travel so he had the racetrack turned into an airfield.
   If William Hartfield ___ he ___ .
   b) In the 1920s a top postal official was treated like a VIP in Atlanta and as a result Atlanta won the postal service route from New York to Miami.
   If a top postal official ___ then Atlanta ___ .
   c) One of the reasons why the Olympic games came to Atlanta in 1996 was because Atlanta had such a good airport.
   The Olympic games ___ if the Atlanta ___ .
2. a) Now complete the following sentences saying what you did and what would have happened otherwise:
   Today: remember my mum's birthday – mum not be upset with me
   Last night: arrive early at the cinema – not have a problem getting a good seat
   Last Saturday: go to Josie's party – meet Toby and Simon
   b) Describe three further 'real-life situations' in a similar way.

Example:
If Atlanta hadn't been named "World's busiest airport", the mayor would have been very disappointed.

If-clauses & the conditional
See *grammar file* on p. 146.

Vocabulary

1. Make a list of the language used in the text specifically related to air travel.
2. a) What do the symbols on the right stand for?
   b) Describe the symbol commonly used for:
   lift/elevator • cash point/cash dispenser • post office.
   c) Think of other symbols which you often see in public places such as airports, stations, restaurants, etc. Describe the symbols to your partner and ask your partner to say what the symbol stands for.

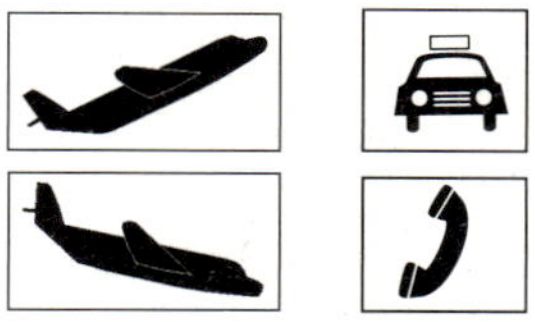

Translation

Translation
See *skills file* on p. 122.

Translate l. 29, column 1 to l. 14, column 2 *"The designation as … between Atlanta and Birmingham (Ala)."* into German. Before you begin your translation identify the main difficulties in the extract in terms of translation.

Creative writing

Choose <u>one</u> of the following topics and write a text of about 250 words on it.

- The town where you live has recently been named "World's …est town". Decide which superlative best suits your area and write an essay explaining how/why your town came to win this title.
- An international airport is to be built within 10 kilometres of your home. Write an essay giving your opinion on whether this development is positive or negative.
- Write a text based on either a true-life or an imaginary experience which takes place at an international airport. You can write a dialogue or a story. It can be humorous, serious, realistic or fictitious.

Writing essays
See *skills file* on p. 124.

What's on the minds of Atlantans?

Before you read →

- What are the three main problems facing the area where you live?
- What are the three main problems facing major cities around the world in your opinion?

The Atlanta Business Journal *asked influential Atlantans for their opinion on the three biggest problems facing the city. Here are some of the responses the* Journal *received.*

James Soutouras, Senior partner, Smith James Group Inc.

Traffic, education, quality of life

As an executive search firm, we recruit for client companies throughout the United States. One of the first questions we are always asked by candidates: "Where is the company located?". The problem: we now hear that same question on a routine basis when we are recruiting people for positions in the Atlanta area.

Our choices are simple. We either deal with the traffic problem on a serious basis or we will pay an ever-increasing price in the quality of life and our ability to attract a skilled/educated work force. If you don't think traffic is going to be a bigger issue in the future than it has been in the past, you haven't been recruiting Generation X candidates.

When recruiting out-of-town executives with children for a move to the Atlanta metro area, they almost always ask about private schools. Atlanta's reputation in education is improving, but we still have a long way to go.

The most important reason for the decline in the quality of life continues to be the Atlanta metro commuting experience. People are starting to ask whether it is worth living in the Atlanta area.

Chris Coleman, President, Folio Z

Why look for three when the first two – "improving our schools and our traffic mess" are so huge? Fix those and a whole bunch of other problems will get better or go away.

Technology-related industry generates the biggest chunk of our national domestic product, and there's no place to hide in this business if you're semi-literate or semi-skilled. We love to think of Atlanta as a techno-mecca, but nothing's going to burst that bubble quicker than a lame educational system.

I lived in Seattle and Portland, Ore., for 20 years prior to coming to Atlanta in 1982, and I'm still astonished at how cavalier we are in Atlanta about felling trees, laying asphalt and squabbling over who gets rapid transit. The only way to solve traffic problems is to put fewer cars on the road.

Neal Reynolds, Chairman, The Ad Shop

The three biggest problems facing the metro region are traffic, inner-city crime and school busing. If the traffic problems are addressed, businesses will start moving further out of town.

The inner-city crime has already caused Underground Atlanta to fail and has sent other entertainment establishments to the suburbs.

The busing of our schoolchildren from majority to minority has caused a deterioration of "neighborhoods" in some areas. When the children don't go to the same schools, there is no common thread to hold a neighborhood together.

The traffic problems can be improved by raising the parking prices and giving incentives to businesses to promote public transportation. Crime on and around MARTA also needs to be stopped. The killing of a businessman getting off at the Lenox MARTA Station several weeks ago sure doesn't help. Crime has been around for thousands of years, and we're not going to stop it overnight. We can start by promoting the family and church.

3 **executive search firm** a firm which finds employees at management level to fill vacancies in other companies – **to recruit** [rɪˈkruːt] to employ

10 **Generation X** term which refers to young people between 15–35; they are typically cynical, selfish and question authority

18 **Folio Z** IT marketing firm in Atlanta

20 **bunch** group

22 **chunk** large amount of s.th.

23 **semi-literate** not being able to read or write well

24 **techno-mecca** *here:* an ideal place for people interested in technology

25 **lame** [eɪ] *here:* poor, weak

26 **Ore.** *short for* Oregon

27 **cavalier** not taking other people's feelings into consideration – **to fell** to chop down

28 **to squabble** to quarrel noisily about s.th. unimportant

32 **to address** *here:* to deal with

37 **deterioration** worsening of conditions

40 **incentive** s.th. which encourages you to do s.th. – **to promote** *here:* to encourage the use of

Chuck Martin, Mayor, City of Alpharetta
We must do a better [job] managing and conserving our natural resources – air, water and land.

We need to continue to put more emphasis on our educational system.

Business leaders need to be involved with our youth, "on the ground" and face to face.

I think leaders in our region should promote within each of their organizations a sense of urgency about these problems.

[...] I am concerned that we only address issues when the cameras are on. ... Our region's issues are full-time and cannot be corrected with part-time attention.

46 **to conserve** to keep s.th. in its original, natural state

Staff report, Atlanta Business Chronicle, *July 26, 1999.*

Comprehension

1. Copy and complete the table below with information from the interviews. It may not always be possible to fill in all three columns!

Problem	*Effect on city life*	*Possible solution*

2. a) What do each of the people interviewed do for a living?
   b) Identify links between the interviewees' jobs and the importance they attach to particular problems.

Working with words

Mind maps
See *skills file* on p. 121.

1. Find words in the text to go with each of the following headings. Use each heading as the starting point of a mind map. Add any more relevant words that you know.
   • education • environment • work • transport & travel • crime
2. What do these phrases from the text mean?
   • to deal with (l. 7) • to have a long way to go (l. 14) • to promote (l. 40) • to put more emphasis on (l. 48) • to be concerned that (l. 53) • to address an issue (l. 53)
3. Using the words you found in tasks one and two write a short text outlining Atlanta's main problems.

Grammar: participles & subordinate clauses

Participles & subordinate clauses
See *grammar file* on pp. 148 & 150.

1. Rewrite the following sentences replacing the participles with subordinate clauses.
   a) *"When recruiting out-of-town executives with children for a move to the Atlanta metro area, they almost always ask about private schools."* (ll.12 – 13)
   b) *"The three biggest problems facing the metro region are traffic, inner-city crime and school busing."* (ll. 31 – 32)
   c) *"The killing of a businessman getting off at the Lenox MARTA Station several weeks ago sure doesn't help."* (ll. 41 – 42)
2. Rewrite the following sentences by shortening the subordinate clauses (<u>underlined</u>).
   a) *"One of the first questions <u>we are always asked by candidates</u>: "Where is the company located?"."* (ll. 4 – 5)
   b) *"The problem: we now hear that same question on a routine basis <u>when we are recruiting people for positions in the Atlanta area.</u>"* (ll. 5 – 6)

Over to you

• Before reading the statements you were asked to identify the three main problems facing your own area. Write a statement of your own about the three problems you identified. Choose at least one phrase from each of the Atlantan statements to use in your own statement. Use a similar style to the style of the Atlantan statements and structure your statement in a similar way by following the guidelines below.
  • Name the main problems.
  • Give a short outline of the effect of the problems on life in your region (with examples).
  • Briefly point out what will happen if the issues are not addressed.
  • Suggest solutions.

Congestion, urban sprawl and quality of life

In the following interview Gary Sumner, a writer for the Atlanta Business Chronicle, *talks to John A. Williams, about congestion, urban sprawl and quality of life in Atlanta.*

Before you read →

- What do you think the connection is between congestion, urban sprawl and quality of life?

John A. Williams is CEO (Chief Executive Officer) of a property company which owns, operates and develops apartment complexes in 14 cities in America. In 1998 he was a member of the Metro Atlanta Transportation Initiative (MATI), and in 1999, he took over as chairman of the Metro Atlanta Chamber of Commerce.

Chronicle: What is the traffic situation around metro Atlanta?

Williams: We have the longest average commute in the nation, 34 miles a day. It's the longest in miles and in time, and that's basically the result of a fairly extensive amount of low-density development that's been sprawled out to the outer reaches of the metro area. Consequently, although in some cases our traffic problem may not be worse than other cities, the length of our commute and the fact that we have experienced a substantial amount of urban sprawl has created a situation that is not acceptable. […]

Chronicle: The Texas Transportation Institute reported that traffic congestion costs the Atlanta region about $1.5 billion a year in lost time and wasted gas.

Williams: I'm not a traffic engineer and can't comment on whether that's accurate or not, but, obviously, you have very unproductive time when you're sitting in traffic. I think there are substantial costs, both to our productivity and to our health. And to our mental health.

Chronicle: Does the transportation infrastructure create other problems for quality of life?

Williams: Urban sprawl tends to be ugly. Sometimes, we haven't been as thoughtful as we should have been as we've gone to the suburbs. Many of the areas do not have sidewalks. Many have cul-de-sac streets that really don't create neighborhoods and don't allow for interaction between sections of the community. One of the initiatives of the chamber is that we've partnered with the Urban Land Institute to try to determine how we can change the patterns of our growth. We emphasize an environment where you can live, walk and work – mixed-use neighborhoods where people can live close to where they work. […]

Chronicle: Previously, you were asked if you sought the chairman job, and you were quoted as replying, "Hell, no." Is that accurate?

Williams: I stand by it. I didn't seek the job. But it's a great honor to be chairman of the Metro Atlanta Chamber. I was vice chairman of the Cobb County Chamber twice, and I've been chairman of the Regional Business Coalition. As a developer, I've been active in both urban and suburban counties, so I have a roughly unique perspective. I'm delighted to serve a community I grew up in and love and want to spend the rest of my life in.

Chronicle: How can you find the time?

Williams: I'm organized, and I have some wonderful people working for me.

Atlanta Business Chronicle, *February 8, 1999*

4 **low-density** *here:* a low level of
4 **to sprawl** to spread out in a disorganized way
4 **outer reaches** *here:* the edge of the metropolitan area
7 **substantial** large
13 **productivity** rate at which goods are produced
15 **infrastructure** *here:* road systems which are necessary for traffic to flow
19 **cul-de-sac** a short road which is closed at one end
20 **interaction** communicating and working with one another
25 **to seek, sought, sought** *here:* to try to get
25 **chairman** head of a group
30 **roughly** *here:* approximately

Comprehension

1. In your own words say why Atlantans have the nation's longest average commute.
2. In what ways do the traffic problems affect people's lives, according to John Williams?
3. What is the difference between the neighborhoods that have been developed in the past and the neighborhoods John Williams now prefers?
4. a) Why do you think John Williams was chosen as chairman of the Metro Atlanta Chamber?
   b) Why was he so pleased to be offered the position?
5. What can you now say about the connection between congestion, urban sprawl and quality of life? Refer back to what you wrote before reading the text and make additions to your answer as necessary.

Grammar: adverbs

Adverbs
See *grammar file* on p. 149.

1. Find examples of the adverbs in the text which mean:
   … fundamentally … • … a quite large amount of … • As a result …• … clearly … • Some time ago … • … a viewpoint, which almost no-one else has.
2. Make sentences about city life using the adverbs given below. If necessary, look up any of the words you don't understand in a dictionary!
   above all • basically • for example • similarly • however • in fact • consequently • recently • fortunately • of course • probably • usually • generally
   Example: *There are many things I like about living in the city, but above all I enjoy the nightlife.*

A step further

1. Think of a suitable two or three-word heading for each of the statements below.
2. In your own words sum up what is said about Atlanta in the statements in terms of:
   in-town living costs and conditions • positive aspects of urban sprawl • Atlanta's unique geographical position • a person's freedom to choose where they want to live.

"More people are choosing to live in-town these days. But it's not a choice everyone should, or can, make. City schools still are wanting, and the cost of housing in town is high and being driven higher by increasing demand."

"With no oceans, mountains or other natural boundaries to contain it, metro Atlanta continues to grow outward. If we drew a growth boundary around us, as some cities have done, the result would be higher housing costs, people and homes pushed closer together, and less choice. That's not what Atlanta is about."

"What the anti-suburbanites consider 'sprawl' is an unprecedented growth wave that has made Atlanta prosperous. If that growth suddenly stopped, it would mean economic disaster for real estate agents, home builders, commercial construction companies, architects, furniture stores and many more metro Atlantans whose livelihoods depend on a growing economy."

Role play: an interview

- Work with a partner. Make a radio interview.

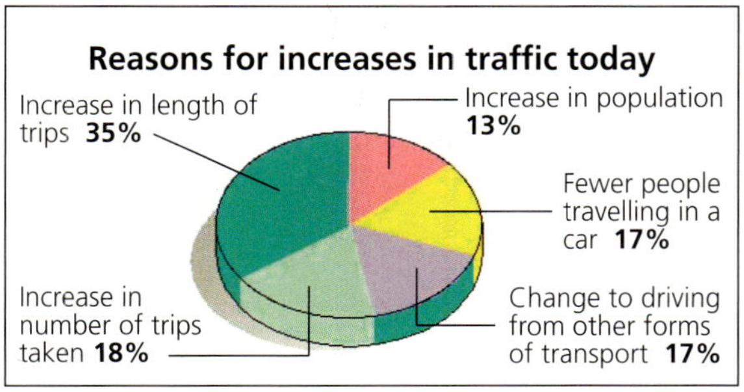

- Devise questions and answers based on the information in the pie chart.
- Produce cue cards based on your questions and answers listing key words only.
- Use your cue cards to perform an interview. One of you is a journalist (the interviewer), and the other is a spokesperson from the Department of Transportation (the interviewee).
- Record your interview onto a cassette, making sure you speak very clearly and slowly. Be prepared to play your cassette to your class.

The best place to live?

Before you read →

- You have accepted a job in a town 200 kilometres away and are looking for a place to live. How important are the following things for you in deciding where to live? Put them in your own order of importance:
  close enough to be able to walk to place of work • low rent • garden • good views • good public transport • small community • large community • good shopping facilities.
- What other things are important for you in terms of where you live?
- In what ways might your choice change later in life, for example, if you have a family or when you get old?

The following text looks at why people have chosen to live in particular areas of Atlanta and the advantages and disadvantages of living in a large metropolitan area.

Surviving without a dictionary
See *skills file* on p. 134.

There are no annotations with this short text. Concentrate on understanding the text as a whole, without necessarily understanding every single word. Try to understand new words by their context, their word families and/or their relation to similar words in German or other foreign languages you know.

A sense of community

Peachtree Street, downtown Atlanta. Would you like to live here? Why?/Why not?

"Where do you live?" is one of the first questions people ask at cocktail parties. The decision isn't to be undertaken lightly. [...]

Perhaps more than cars, clothes or clubs, where we choose to live is the ultimate statement of who we are. When Sandy Hill and her husband moved to Atlanta from Los Angeles, a shorter commute was at the top of her wish list. She chose one of Gwinnett's newest developments, Forest Plantation, in Suwanee, for a 10-minute drive to work, clean air and the relatively low cost of living – nearly an acre and a 2,700-square-foot house at about $200,000.

On the other hand, John Burrison, who has lived in downtown Atlanta in a Peachtree Towers condo for 15 years, wanted in-town ambience. He likes being able to walk to work as a professor of English at Georgia State University, and he enjoys the sight from the height of his apartment windows of neo-Gothic buildings glowing in the night skyline. He does not own a car, so to maintain his urban lifestyle, public transportation is a necessity.

The communities and the neighborhoods of Atlanta include something for everyone – new developments, a 137-year-old town, historic homes in funky settings, a planned community, places in the country, a city cooperative. If there's one common feature, it's that they have a sense of community; they're places where people go for walks in the evening, stop to chat, where everybody knows your name.

Why is community so important? "Atlanta is a huge metropolitan area, and when you think about living in a city of 3 million, it's frightening," said Thomas D'Alesandro, a developer with Mobil Land Development Georgia. "But when you break it down to a neighborhood of a few hundred or thousand people, where you live becomes something comforting, reassuring, and that helps you deal with life in a big city."

From "The Best Places to Live" *by Linda Couch and Rebecca Poynor Burns,* Atlanta Magazine, *November 1996.*

Vocabulary

1. Explain the following words from the text:
   a commute (l. 5) • cost of living (l. 7) • in-town ambience (l. 10) • urban lifestyle (l. 13) • public transportation (l. 13) • common feature (l. 17) • sense of community (l. 18).
2. Look in the text for the American English (AE) for these British English (BE) terms:
   town centre • block of flats • flat

Comprehension

1. a) In your own words explain why the Hills chose to live in Suwanee and why John Burrison chose to live in downtown Atlanta.
   b) Would you be more likely to choose to live in the suburbs or in downtown Atlanta? Give reasons.
2. What different kinds of neighborhood are there in Atlanta, according to the text?

Language

1. a) Look at the last paragraph of the text and find the adjectives used to describe life in a big city and life in a community.
   b) Think of other adjectives which you think describe city life and life in a smaller community. (Your choices need not reflect the opinion expressed in the text!)
2. Work in pairs and consider the community you live in. Think of positive and/or negative adjectives to describe your community. Start by finding adjectives to finish the following sentences:
   Life in our community is ___ • People in our community are ___ • Housing in our community is ___ • Schools in our community are ___ • Public transport in our community is ___ • Shopping facilities in our community are ___ • etc.

Over to you

- Would you like to live in a city like Atlanta? Why or why not?

Changing communities – multi-cultural communities

Before you read

- What causes a community to change? Think of three things that would make the community you live in change for the better in your opinion and three that would make it change for the worse.
- What does the term "multi-cultural community" mean to you? Note down positive and negative aspects of living in a multi-cultural community.

Atlanta's new main street: Buford Highway

From the parking lot, the Buford Highway Farmers Market in Doraville looks like many other grocery stores in metro Atlanta. But step inside and you're in another world.

Here you can get live eel, dried sea cucumber and peeled mung beans. Seasoned squid sits next to ice cream in the frozen food aisle. Coconut juice from Thailand, bitter leaves from Africa and ginger cakes from Jamaica are a few rows down.

Over in produce, behind a display of Asian cabbage, Mexican employees are bagging bok choy to the rhythmic pulse of salsa music.

A typical weekend finds the Korean-owned market packed with a unique mix of shoppers, all speaking their native tongue.

Eddy Suantio, a vendor handing out tiny paper cups of instant coffee, cappuccino and ginseng cereal from his native Indonesia, pauses to enjoy the moment.

"Take a glance around me right now. That man is Chinese. There is an American. I see people from Russia, Poland and Jamaica. Everywhere you look, you see people from somewhere else," he says.

2 **grocery store** shop which sells food and small household goods
4 **eel** *Aal* – **peeled** where the skin has been taken away – **seasoned squid** *gewürzter Tintenfisch*
5 **aisle** [aɪl] area between shelves where you can walk
6 **ginger** ['dʒɪndʒə] *Ingwer*
7 **produce** ['--] farm products (fruit and vegetables)
8 **bok choy** Asian vegetable
9 **unique** [juː'niːk] very unusual
11 **vendor** person who sells s.th. – **tiny** very small
12 **cereal** ['sɪərɪəl] mixture of grains, usu. eaten for breakfast
13 **glance** a quick look

In a suburban landscape once populated largely by working class whites, ethnic businesses have changed the face and character of Buford Highway.

No master plan dictated the change. The corridor became international because of the individual decisions of hundreds of entrepreneurs who often work 14-hour days with no time off, borrowing from relatives and friends to expand their small businesses.

Consider some of the merchants. Kim Phuong is a Vietnamese refugee who came here with nothing 11 years ago but saved enough money to open two bridal shops after she learned to speak English. Lily Lee is a Chinese immigrant from San Francisco who was one of the first Asians to open a business on Buford Highway 12 years ago. Jesus Brito fled desperate poverty in Mexico and now owns a shopping center and will soon open a grocery.

"I was lucky that people who came from other countries under very adverse circumstances were willing to make an investment here," said Paige Perkins, development director in Chamblee along the Buford Highway corridor. "The old Americans, they left us and they moved to whatever the promise was up Ga. 400 or up in Gwinnett County. And they decided that this was not good enough anymore."

Perkins shudders when she thinks about what Buford Highway might look like today without the immigrant influx.

"There'd be an abandoned KFC on the corner. There would be an abandoned furniture store across the street from it. There'd be a burned out IHOP where Don Taco is now. There'd be a church that nobody wanted to go to where the International Medical Center is. I'd have apartments that I don't know who would live in them," she said.

Asians and Hispanics now live in large numbers along the Buford Highway corridor, census figures show. The census tract that contains DeKalb-Peachtree Airport, for instance, had more than 40 percent Asian and Hispanic residents in 1990. Vietnamese are the largest Asian group along the road, growing by more than 700 percent from 1980 to 1990. In Chamblee, 59 percent of children under age 14 belong to an ethnic minority, said development director Perkins.

19 **entrepreneur** s.o. who starts a business
22 **merchant** s.o. who buys and sells things – **refugee** s.o. who has to leave his/her homeland for political reasons
23 **bridal shop** shop which sells wedding clothes
26 **desperate** *here:* terrible
28 **adverse** negative
30 **Chamblee** community to the north of Atlanta
31 **Ga. 400 (Georgia)** an interstate
33 **to shudder** to shake because you have thought of s.th. bad
35 **abandoned** deserted – **KFC** Kentucky Fried Chicken
36 **IHOP** International House of Pancakes
41 **census** an official counting of the population

From "The Real International Boulevard" by Elizabeth Kurylo, The Atlanta Journal-Constitution, *March 2, 1998.*

Comprehension →

1. Explain why Buford Highway can truly be called multi-cultural.
2. Copy and complete the table below with information from the text.

Name	Country of origin	Reason for coming to Atlanta	Current employment
Eddy Suantio			
Kim Phuong			
Lily Lee			
Jesus Brito			
Paige Perkins			

3. a) Who were *"the old Americans"* (ll. 30–31) and why did many of them leave Buford Highway?
   b) What do many of the new residents and entrepreneurs in Buford Highway have in common?

4. In your own words say what would have happened to Buford Highway if the new entrepreneurs had not moved there.
5. a) Is the change in the face and character of Buford Highway viewed positively or negatively in the article? Give reasons.
   b) Refer back to the notes you made before reading the article. Add any further positive or negative aspects about multi-cultural communities that you can find in the text.
6. Do you think Buford Highway is typical of multi-cultural communities in most big cities? Give reasons for your opinion.

Working with words

1. a) Make a table of the countries and corresponding nationalities mentioned in the text. Use a dictionary if necessary.
   Example:

Country	Nationality
Thailand	Thai

   b) Find out the nationalities and countries of origin of members of your class and add them to your table.
2. Find the words in the text which mean:
   to talk in the language of the country of your birth • to have a quick look around • a choice a person makes for themselves • time when you are not at work • a person who has left their country, for example, for political reasons • for example • people who live in a particular area or building.

Over to you

A group of American college students are on an exchange visit to your college. You take them on a tour of your town.
- Choose a particular area or street which has changed considerably in the last few years, either in terms of population, infrastructure and/or facilities and land-use.
- Write a short guide to the area you have chosen.
  - Describe positive (and negative) aspects of the area today.
  - Describe how the area used to be.
  - Explain the reasons for the changes that have occurred.
  - Say how you think the area would be if things hadn't changed.

From Terminus to Atlanta

No profile of Atlanta would be complete without a reference to Margaret Mitchell's famous historically-based novel Gone with the Wind. *The following text is an extract from the novel.*

As the train carried Scarlett northward that May morning in 1862, she thought that Atlanta couldn't possibly be so boring as Charleston and Savannah had been and, in spite of her distaste for Miss Pittypat and Melanie, she looked forward with some curiosity toward seeing how the town had fared since her last visit, in the winter before the war began.

Atlanta had always interested her more than any other town because when she was a child Gerald had told her that she and Atlanta were exactly the same age. She discovered when she grew older that Gerald had stretched the truth somewhat, as was his habit when a little stretching would improve a story; but Atlanta was only nine years older than she was, and that still left the place amazingly young by comparison with any other town she had ever heard of. Savannah and Charleston had the dignity of their years, one being well along in its second century and the other entering its third, and in her young eyes they had always seemed like aged grandmothers fanning themselves placidly in the sun. But Atlanta was of her own

3 **distaste** dislike

4 **curiosity** [ˌkjʊərɪˈɒsətɪ] desire to find out s.th. – **to fare** *here:* to change

8 **to stretch the truth** to lie in order to sound more interesting

12 **dignity** quality held by s.o. who should be given respect (*Würde*) – **well along** a long way

14 **to fan** to wave a flat object to cool o.s. – **placidly** calmly

15 **crude** basic, rough – **headstrong** determined to do what one wants, despite what others may think – **impetuous** acting quickly without thinking

22 **semblance** outward appearance

24 **Cherokees** a tribe of North American Indians – **to cede s.th.** *(formal)* to give up one's rights to s.th.

26 **to drive** *here:* to push with force

27 **stake** a pointed wooden post

34 **Macon** ['meɪkn]

42 **to leap to life, leaped / leapt** *here:* to quickly become very busy

44 **thriving** doing well financially

46 **wont to** *(old)* having a tendency to do s.th.

47 **to hatch** to produce a young bird

49 **to recommend** *here:* to make s.th. seem attractive – **mighty** *(informal)* extremely – **pushy** *(informal)* trying to draw attention to o.s.

50 **successively** coming one after another

54 **depot** ['depəʊ] place where you keep large amounts of products

61 **to condemn** [kən'dem] to criticize strongly

63 **vigorous** having a lot of energy

generation, crude with the crudities of youth and as headstrong and impetuous as herself.

The story Gerald had told her was based on the fact that she and Atlanta were christened in the same year. In the nine years before Scarlett was born, the town had been called, first, Terminus and then Marthasville, and not until the year of Scarlett's birth had it become Atlanta.

When Gerald first moved to north Georgia, there had been no Atlanta at all, not even the semblance of a village, and wilderness rolled over the site. But the next year, in 1836, the State had authorized the building of a railroad northwestward through the territory which the Cherokees had recently ceded. The destination of the proposed railroad, Tennessee and the West, was clear and definite, but its beginning point in Georgia was somewhat uncertain until, a year later, an engineer drove a stake in the red clay to mark the southern end of the line, and Atlanta, born Terminus, had begun.

There were no railroads then in north Georgia, and very few anywhere else. But during the years before Gerald married Ellen, the tiny settlement, twenty-five miles north of Tara, slowly grew into a village and the tracks slowly pushed northward. Then the railroad building era really began. From the old city of Augusta, a second railroad was extended westward across the state to connect with the new road to Tennessee. From the old city of Savannah, a third railroad was built first to Macon, in the heart of Georgia, and then north through Gerald's own county to Atlanta, to link up with the other two roads and give Savannah's harbor a highway to the West. From the same junction point, the young Atlanta, a fourth railroad was constructed southwestward to Montgomery and Mobile.

Born of a railroad, Atlanta grew as its railroads grew. With the completion of the four lines, Atlanta was now connected with the West, with the South, with the Coast and, through Augusta, with the North and East. It had become the crossroads of travel north and south and east and west, and the little village leaped to life.

In a space of time but little longer than Scarlett's seventeen years, Atlanta had grown from a single stake driven in the ground into a thriving small city of ten thousand that was the center of attention for the whole state. The older, quieter cities were wont to look upon the bustling new town with the sensations of a hen which has hatched a duckling. Why was the place so different from the other Georgia towns? Why did it grow so fast? After all, they thought, it had nothing whatever to recommend it – only its railroads and a bunch of mighty pushy people.

The people who settled the town called successively Terminus, Marthasville and Atlanta, were a pushy people. Restless, energetic people from the older sections of Georgia and from more distant states were drawn to this town that sprawled itself around the junction of the railroads in its center. They came with enthusiasm. They built their stores around the five muddy red roads that crossed near the depot. They built their fine homes on Whitehall and Washington streets and along the high ridge of land on which countless generations of moccasined Indian feet had beaten a path called the Peachtree Trail. They were proud of the place, proud of its growth, proud of themselves for making it grow. Let the older towns call Atlanta anything they pleased. Atlanta did not care.

Scarlett had always liked Atlanta for the very same reasons that made Savannah, Augusta and Macon condemn it. Like herself, the town was a mixture of the old and new in Georgia, in which the old often came off second best in its conflicts with the self-willed and vigorous new. Moreover, there was something personal, exciting about a town that was born – or at least christened – the same year she was christened.

From Gone with the Wind *by Margaret Mitchell, New York: Avon, 1973 (first published by Macmillan Publishing Company, 1936), pp. 140–142.*

The old and the new: the newly restored Margaret Mitchell house in downtown Atlanta

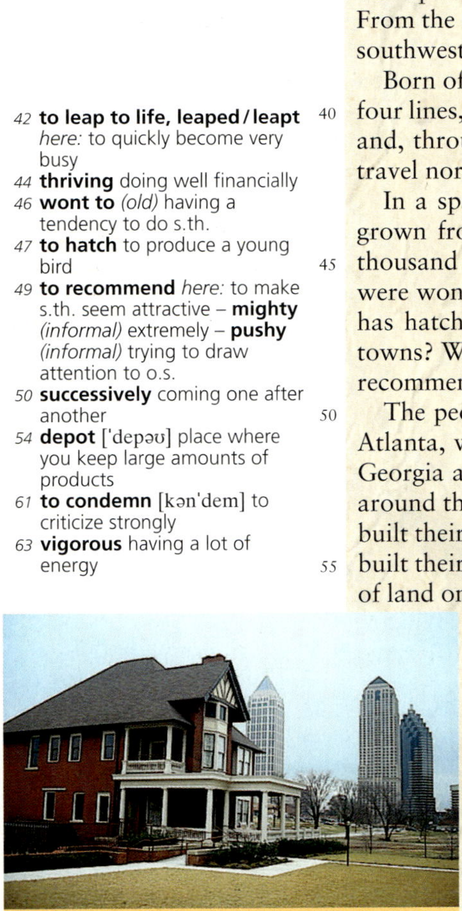**Comprehension**

1. Why was Scarlett so interested in Atlanta?
2. In your own words say …
   a) … why Scarlett and Atlanta were similar.
   b) … what you learn about the origins of Atlanta in the extract.
   c) … what you find out about the people who settled in Atlanta.
3. Consider what you have learnt about modern Atlanta in this chapter. Compare Atlanta today to Atlanta as described in *Gone With the Wind.* To what extent would you say that the character of Atlanta has remained the same? Find words and expressions in this text to support your conclusion.

Use the *grammar & skills files* on pp. 121 – 151 to help you with the tasks on this page. There is an index of all files on p. 159.

Looking at style

1. In this extract the author frequently writes about Atlanta as if the town were a person. Find examples of this use of 'personification' in the text.
2. In other parts of the extract the author adopts a factual style when describing the town. Find examples in the text which illustrate this.
3. When does Margaret Mitchell choose these different styles and why in your opinion?

Grammar : relative clauses

Rewrite the following sentence replacing the words underlined with suitable relative clauses:
"Savannah and Charleston had the dignity of their years, <u>one being</u> well along in its second century and <u>the other entering</u> its third, and in her young eyes they had always seemed like aged grandmothers <u>fanning</u> themselves placidly in the sun." (ll. 11–14)

Translation

Translate ll. 39–49 of the text. *("Born of a railroad, … mighty pushy people.")*

Project

Project: A talk on improving your town

You have applied for a work placement in an international urban planning company. As part of the application process you have been asked to prepare a talk in English about ways of improving the quality of life in your town/city in terms of economy, infrastructure and living standards.
Follow the guidelines below:

- Consider what makes a town or city an ideal place to live. What is the current situation in your town/city? Copy and complete the table below.

	ideal situation	*situation in own town/city*
schools	*small schools, …*	
bus services		
shopping facilities		
…		

- Which two areas from your table do you consider to be most in need of improvement in your town/city? Note down your reasons. Concentrate on these two areas in your talk.
- Brainstorm ideas of how improvements could be made in each area.
- Make cue cards listing key words and phrases.
- Collect and/or devise visual material to illustrate your talk. For example:
  • an OHP transparency listing the main points of your talk • a chart with relevant facts and statistics • a map or photographs showing the current situation • an illustration showing the difference the improvements would make.

Projects
See *skills file* on p. 139.
Giving a talk
See *skills file* on p. 129

7 Glued to the tube

The influence of television

Are you glued to the tube?

Note down your answers to these questions.

1. How many hours a day do you watch TV?
   a) None.
   b) 1 hour
   c) 2–3 hours
   d) More than 3 hours.

2. When you get home from school:
   a) TV is the last thing you think of – you have so many other things to do.
   b) you check to see if there's anything worth watching on TV later, but you don't switch the TV on straightaway.
   c) you switch the TV on straightaway, but you don't watch all the time. It's just background noise.
   d) you switch the TV on and sit down and watch everything.

3. When do you do your homework?
   a) Before you watch TV.
   b) After you watch TV.
   c) While you are watching TV.
   d) You don't do homework because you are too busy watching TV.

4. How many TV sets have you got in your home?
   a) We haven't got a TV set.
   b) 1
   c) 2
   d) 3 or more

5. How often do you eat meals in front of the television?
   a) Never.
   b) Very occasionally (not more than once a week).
   c) Regularly (almost every day).
   d) Whenever you're at home.

6. What do you do when the commercials are on?
   a) Switch off the TV: you never watch the commercials.
   b) Leave the room, read a book, look through a magazine.
   c) Zap through the other TV channels until the commercials are over.
   d) Watch them, of course. Commercials are really entertaining!

7. How many of these types of programmes do you watch regularly?
   a) Documentaries and news
   b) Drama and crime programmes
   c) Soap operas, serials & sitcoms
   d) Game shows
   e) Music videos
   f) Cartoons
   g) Films

Work out your score
Questions 1–6:
a) = 0 points b) = 1 point
c) = 2 points d) = 3 points
Question 7: 1 point per choice
Now turn to p. 119 to find out what kind of TV viewer you are!

Growing up on television

In her book entitled Growing Up On Television *Kate Moody writes:*

"(Children) say that they go to school 'after Huckleberry Hound,' eat a TV dinner 'during Gilligan's Island,' and go to bed 'after Charlie's Angels,' [...] Each year children read less and less and watch television more and more. In fact, Americans of all ages watch more television each year. The typical child sits in front of the television about four hours a day – and for children in lower socio-economic families the amount of time thus spent is even greater. In either case, the child spends more time with TV than he or she spends talking to parents, playing with peers, attending school, or reading books. TV time usurps family time, playtime, and the reading time that could promote language development."

From Growing Up On Television: The TV Effect *by Kate Moody, New York: The New York Times Book Co., 1980.*

6 **thus** *(formal)* in this way
7 **peer** s.o. the same age as you
8 **to usurp** [ju:'zɜ:p] *(formal)* *here:* to take up more time than it should

Finding arguments →

1. In your own words say how watching television has a negative effect on children, according to Kate Moody.
2. Work with a partner and together find counter arguments to show that watching television can also be a positive experience.
3. Which of the arguments do you find most convincing? Why?

to beat s.o. to a pulp to hit s.o. brutally and repeatedly

Looking at cartoons
See *skills file* on p. 130.

← *Looking at the cartoon*

1. What point is the cartoonist making?
2. Would you say that the cartoonist is exaggerating a) a little b) a lot c) not at all? Give a reason for your choice.
3. Think of a suitable title for the cartoon.

Did you know? American viewing habits

Hours per day that TV is on in average US household: 7 hours, 21 minutes
Number of hours of TV watched annually by Americans: 250 billion
Chances that an American falls asleep with the TV on at least three nights a week: 1 in 4
Number of 30-second TV commercials seen in a year by an average child: 20,000
Number of TV commercials seen by the average person by age 65: 2 million
Hours per year the average American youth spends at school: 900
Hours per year the average American youth spends watching television: 1500
Chance that an American parent requires that children do their homework before watching TV: 1 in 12
Percentage of local TV news broadcasting time devoted to advertising: 30
Number of murders seen on TV by the time an average American child finishes elementary school (aged approx. 12): 8,000
Number of violent acts seen on TV by age 18: 200,000
Percentage of US households that have at least one TV: 99
Number of TV sets in the average US household: 2.24
US homes with three or more TV sets: 66 %
Percentage of American children who have a TV set in their bedroom: 54
Americans who regularly watch television while eating dinner: 66 %
Total spending on TV advertising aimed at children in 1995: $550 million

9 **to require** *(formal) here:* to have as a rule

← *Small talk*

Work with a partner. Chat about the facts and statistics given in the box above.
- Start each of your comments: "Did you know (that) ...?" • Pay attention to the new word order in your sentences. • Respond to the facts you are given by repeating the statistical information and adding a suitable comment or exclamation. (Some responses are given in the box on the right to start you off.)

Example: *"Did you know that in the average US household the TV is on for seven hours and twenty-one minutes every day?"*
"Seven hours and twenty-one minutes? That's unbelievable! When do Americans find time to do anything else?"

Responses
That's incredible! • That's unbelievable! • That doesn't surprise me at all! • Actually, I'm surprised it isn't more! • That sounds just like at my place! • I wish I lived there! • I'm glad I don't live there!

← *Writing a comment*

Essay writing
See *skills file* on p. 124.

Keeping in mind the text extract on p.106 and the cartoon and statistics on this page, write your own comment of between 100–120 words (the length of the extract on p. 106) with the title 'The influence of TV'.

What's on?

Quick survey

Questionnaires & surveys
See *skills file* on p.140.

1. Carry out a quick survey in your class to find out …:
   a) … how many different channels students in your class have on their TV at home.
   b) … how many students have cable, satellite or only terrestrial TV.
   c) … how students decide what to watch. Do they zap from channel to channel/look at a TV guide/discuss what to watch with other members of their family/etc.? Why?
   d) … which channels and which kind or kinds of programmes students like most and least.
   e) … how many hours per day students in your class watch TV.
   f) … when students most often watch TV.
2. Use your results to make statements like those on p. 107. Put your results on display in your classroom.

Finding & comparing information

Look at the extracts from an American TV guide on the opposite page.

1. a) What category of programme are:
      This Morning (7 am) • The Price is Right (11 am) • All my Children (1 pm) • D.C. Cab (8 pm)?
   b) Find examples of other programme categories given in the guide and make a list of them. Think of more categories of your own and add these to your list.
   c) Explain 'sitcom' and 'soap' in your own words? (Look the words up in a dictionary if necessary.)
   c) Explain all the categories you have listed in your own words.
2. a) Which kinds of programmes are broadcast most often at each time of day?
   b) What does this tell you about the types of viewers at different times of day?
3. a) Which programmes (if any) in the TV guide do you recognize? (For example, can you find any shows which are also broadcast on German TV?)
   b) Look at a German TV guide and compare it with the American guide. Look for differences and similarities in the programmes and the programming and try to explain them.

Looking at the cartoon

1. Do you recognize the show featured in the cartoon? What is it called in German?
2. The show is called 'Blind Date' in English. What is a 'blind date'? Do you prefer the English or the German name for the show? Why?
3. Explain in English what happens in the show.

Over to you

Work with a partner or in a group. Imagine you are the programme planners for a new TV channel aimed at teenagers.

1. What kind of programmes would you choose to broadcast? Make a list of the categories you would like to include (but not of actual programmes you know).
2. Your channel will be broadcasting for ten hours a day. Decide:
   a) when you would choose to broadcast.
   b) when you would choose to broadcast particular types of programmes.
   Give reasons for your choices.

TV Guide

7 AM
- 2 **Today**
- 4 **This Morning**–Local News
- 5 **CBC News**
- 7 **Good Morning America**
- 17 **Lilias, Yoga and You**
- 29 **BeetleBorgsMetallx** TV Y7
- 49 **Tiny Toon Adventures**
- A&E **Classroom**
- AMC ***A Bill of Divorcement***–Drama TV PG
- CNN **News**
- CSP **Washington Journal**
- DIS **Aladdin**–Cartoon TV Y
- E! **E! Daily News**
- ESN **SportsCenter**
- HBO **Animated Hero Classics**–Cartoon TV Y
- HIS **Year by Year** TV G
- MTV **Jams**
- SCI **Voyage to the bottom of the Sea**–Adventure TV G
- TNT **Bugs Bunny**–Cartoon TV Y
- USA **Mighty Max**–Cartoon TV Y

11 AM
- 2 **Leeza**–Discussion TV PG
- 4 11 **The Price is Right**–Game TV G
- 5 **Wimzie**–Puppets
- 7 **Geraldo Rivera**–Discussion
- 17 **Magic School Bus** TV Y
- 29 **Newlywed/Dating Hour**
- 49 **Jerry Springer** TV 14
- A&E **Quincy**–Crime Drama TV G
- DIS **Chip 'n Dale**–Cartoon TV Y
- E! **'Starship Troopers' Behind the Scenes**–Profile TV G
- EMP **Victoria's Body Shoppe**–Fitness
- ESN **SportsCenter**
- ES2 **Fitness Beach**
- FX **Picket Fences**–Drama
- LIF **Our Home** TV G
- MAX ***The War Between the Tates***–Comedy Drama TV PG
- MSN **Homepage**–Magazine
- NIK **Dr. Seuss** TV Y
- SCI **Man & Machine**
- TLC **Elementary School** TV G
- TNN **Dallas**–Drama TV PG
- TNT **Spenser: For Hire** TV PG
- USA **Wings**–Comedy

1 PM
- 2 **Days of Our Lives** TV 14
- 5 7 **All My Children**–Serial TV PG
- 9 **Canadian Living TV**–Discussion
- 11 **Neon Rider**–Drama
- 17 **Mystery!** TV PG L
- 29 **700 Club**–Religion
- 49 **Dr. Quinn**–Drama
- A&E **Law & Order** TV PG
- CNN **News**–Crime Drama
- DIS **Jungle Clubs**–Cartoon TV Y
- DSC **Home Matters** TV G
- E! **E! News Daily**
- ESN **Bodybuilding**
- ES2 **NBA 2Night**–Basketball
- FAM **Home & Family** TV G
- FNC **News**
- FX **SuperCollectors**–Drama TV G
- HBO **Making of 'The Phantom'**–Documentary TV PG
- HIS **As It Happened** TV G
- LIF **Commish** TV PG
- MSN **News**
- MTV **Videos**
- NIK **Allegra's Window**–Children TV Y
- SCI **Mysteries, Magic & Miracles**–Speculation TV PG
- TLC **Great Country Inns** TV G
- TNN **Wildhorse Saloon** TV G

8 PM
- 2 11 **Players** TV PG
- 4 **Candid Camera** TV PG
- 7 **Sabrina**–Comedy TV G
- 9 **Figure Skating**
- 11 **Jag**–Drama TV PG V
- 17 **Washington Week**
- 23 **Out of Ireland**–Magazine
- 29 **The Visitor** TV PG
- 49 ***Cocoon***–Fantasy
- A&E **Biography** TV G
- CNN **News**
- DSC **Queen of the Beasts** TV G
- EMP **Hardcore Football**
- ENC ***D.C. Cab***–Comedy
- FAM **Ed Sullivan All-Star Comedy Special**
- FX **X-Files**–Drama
- HBO **Space Jam**–Fantasy
- HIS **In Search of History** TV G
- MAX ***Stephen King's 'Thinner'***–Horror
- MSG **Paul Hornung's Sports Showcase**–Interview
- MSN **Big Show**–Interview
- MTV **Sports and Music Festival**
- NIK **Kablam!**–Cartoon TV Y
- SCI ***Puppet Master II***–Thriller
- TNT **NBA Basketball**
- USA **Walker, Texas Ranger**–Crime Drama TV PG

Typical TV: Game shows and soap operas

Before you read →

- Which game shows (German and/or American) do you know?
- What makes game shows so popular in your opinion?

The longest running daytime game show in the USA: The Price is Right!

Frantic music blares as a ring of bright flashing lights frames the edge of your television. Inside the lights is an entire studio filled with spastic hordes of people jumping, clapping, and screaming at the tops of their lungs, all hoping their name will be called. Everyone in the studio is as lively as possible, to the point of absurdity, because of an unspoken understanding that excited, active audience members have a better chance of being chosen to compete. Bright colors are everywhere in the studio and after the first round of contestants are called down to the front, the show's host finally steps onto the stage. He is Bob Barker, an ever-present fixture of television for the past twenty-five years, holding court over the last remaining and longest running daytime game show on network television, *The Price is Right*. The object of the many games in the show is to be the best consumer. Each player places a bid on an item presented trying to be closest to the suggested retail price without going over.

Each item is wheeled before the audience by identically dressed models/hostesses who caress and demonstrate it as a quick explanation of its features are read. Even the manufacturer's logo is placed on the screen. All ranges of items for bid are presented throughout the show, from cleaning products to sports cars, from frozen dinners to chandeliers, implying to the viewer that even people who buy chandeliers and sail boats are watching the show.

Source: UltimateTV.com

1 **frantic** wildly excited
2 **entire** [ɪnˈtaɪə] complete
3 **at the top of their lungs** as loudly as possible
5 **understanding** a rule that is known yet is not written down anywhere
8 **fixture** s.o. who is always seen in a certain place
11 **consumer** *Verbraucher* – **to place a bid** *here:* to suggest a price
12 **retail price** price one pays in a shop
14 **to caress** to touch lovingly
17 **chandelier** [ˌʃændəˈlɪə] *Kronleuchter* – **to imply** to suggest

Comprehension →

1. Describe the scene at the beginning of the show in your own words.
2. Why do the members of the audience behave so excitedly?
3. Who is Bob Barker?

Grammar: → adjectives & adverbs

Adjectives & adverbs
See *grammar file* on p. 149.

1. Adjectives and adverbs are used in the text to make it more vivid. Make separate lists of all the adjectives and all the adverbs used in the text.
2. a) Decide whether you can add an adjective or an adverb at each of the points marked ______ in the following short text:

   Yesterday as I was driving 1. ______ *along Main Street I saw a* 2. ______ *woman waving* 3. ______ *for me to stop. I stopped* 4. ______ *and* 5. ______ *opened the window. "Thank goodness," the woman said* 6. ______. *"Can you take me to the* 7. ______ *TV studios? I have to be on stage in 15 minutes."*
   "On stage?" I repeated 8. ______. *Then I took a* 9. ______ *look at her. "You're Annabel Chance, aren't you? You host that* 10. ______ *game show."*

   b) Copy and complete the text adding suitable adjectives and adverbs at the points marked.

   c) Continue the story. Write another five or six sentences using adjectives and adverbs to make your text more interesting.

Over to you →

Choose a popular game show or talk show and write a description of it in the style of the text above. Read out your text to your class and see if the other students can name the show you are describing.

← **Dialogue (small talk)**

Small talk
See *skills file* on p. 128.

1. Write out the dialogue below in the correct order by matching the answers to the questions.
   Questions: What kind of show is 'The Price is Right'? • So why is it called 'The Price is Right'? • And who takes part in the game? • I see. And what exactly do the contestants have to do? • Just a second. What kind of things are they? • Wow, that's incredible. Why don't we go along and try and win a new TV set?
   Answers: All kinds of things: from washing powder and window cleaning liquid to sail boats and cars! • Funny you should mention it, because I just happen to have two tickets for the show next week! • Because the aim of the show is to guess how much things cost in the shops: in other words to get the price right. • Well, there's the host, Bob Barker, and the contestants who are chosen from the audience. • It's a game show. • It's quite simple. All kinds of things are brought on stage and the contestants guess what the retail price of the things is.
2. a) Practise the dialogue with a partner.
   b) Continue the dialogue making arrangements for when and where to meet, how to travel to the show, what to wear, etc.

The following text is a description of an episode of the soap opera All my Children.

Check the web
Find out more about American soaps at:
http://www.ultimatetv.com/soaps

All My Children: One of the longest running soaps in history

An injured woman lies dying, lost somewhere in the woods. The only man who knows her location is unconscious in the hospital and might not wake up in time to save her. Elsewhere, two recently divorced parents prepare a birthday party for their teenage daughter. The mother, whose career pulls her away, laments not spending more time with her daughter and bickers with her ex-husband. Soon he reveals a dark secret from his past: His mother died on one of his childhood birthdays and he has never been able to enjoy one since. Nearby in a coffee shop, a mysterious woman talks to a young girl, and gets directions to an old cabin the girl once played in with her brother. After her departure, the young girl's brother follows the mysterious woman to the cabin where he learns that she is actually their long-lost mother.

Source: UltimateTV.com

4 **to lament** *(formal) here:* to say one is very sorry not to have done s.th.
5 **to bicker** to argue about unimportant things
7 **coffee shop** café where you can usu. also buy coffee

← **Comprehension**

1. How many different storylines can you identify in the description of this episode?
2. Identify the elements in the episode described which are typical of all soap operas.
3. You can find out what happened in past episodes of most American soaps and dramas on the internet. Write a website entry for the above episode of *All My Children*. You will need to give the characters names. Remember to use the past tense.

← **Your view**

Essay writing
See *skills file* on p. 124.
Connectives
See *skills file* on p. 125.

What makes soap operas so popular? Follow these steps and write a comment:
- Explain the two statements below in your own words. (Translate them if necessary.)
- Think of at least two more reasons of your own and write your own two statements.
- Collect all the statements in your class on a transparency or flip chart.
- a) Choose the five statements you find most convincing.
  b) Arrange them in a logical order.
  c) Join them using connectives.

"Soap operas offer a reference point for shared experience with others, where they can compare notes and interact with those who also watch."

"The viewer's own personal life may never match those of the characters they watch, but the viewer can live that life through the soap, and for many viewers, missing a day of their favorite soap is like having slept through a day of their own lives."

to match to be like s.th. else
reference point type of connection

Ratings and guidelines

Before you read →

rating 1. (*here:*) classification of a programme in terms of its content; 2. popularity of a TV programme in terms of the number of people who watch it (see p. 115)

- You work for a TV company and have to devise a rating system which shows the suitability of programs for specific age groups. Decide which age groups to include in your system and draw up symbols and explanations. Remember to make your system and symbols easily understandable for the viewers.

Licensing

All TV stations in the US must be licensed by the Federal Communications Commission (FCC). Licenses are given for a few years only and if stations do not conform to FCC regulations, their licenses can be taken away. One of the things the FCC does is to make sure that no single group has too much influence and that there is a wide range of choices in all areas. For example, a newspaper cannot own a TV station and a TV station cannot own a radio station in one area. And no company or group can own more than 12 TV stations nationwide.

Censorship and parental guidance ratings

There is no governmental censorship or reviewing of TV programmes. However, in 1990, Congress passed the Children's Television Act, which prohibits indecent broadcasts outside of "safe harbor" hours (10 pm to 6 am), the hours when it is least likely that children will be watching unsupervised. Also, according to this Act, the FCC must "consider to what extent the licensee [...] has served the educational and informational needs of children" when considering TV license renewals.

With the Telecommunications Act of 1996 Congress requires television manufacturers to install "V-chips" into new sets. With a rating system designed by the networks themselves (see below), the chip would block out violent programming. The age-based parental guidance system has been introduced on a voluntary basis by most TV networks in America except NBC (who sees the system as a form of censorship and therefore against the principles of the First Amendment). The aim of the system is to help parents decide which programmes they think are suitable for their children to watch, especially during 'prime time' (between 7.30 pm and 9.30 pm).

The rating system

TV Y
These programmes are designed to be appropriate for all children, including children aged 2–6.

TV Y7
These programmes are designed for children over 7 years old. The programmes may have mild fantasy violence or comedic violence. Programmes in this category with the rating TV Y7 FV have more fantasy violence.

TV G General audience. These are not children's programmes but most parents would find them suitable for children of all ages and children could watch them on their own. The programmes should have little or no violence, no strong language and little or no sexual dialogue.

TV PG
Parental guidance suggested. These programmes have material that parents may find unsuitable for younger children. Additional codes may be added to show moderate violence (V), some sexual situations (S), occasional bad language (L) or suggestive/sexual dialogue (D).

TV 14
These programmes contain material that many parents would find unsuitable for children under 14. Children under 14 should not be allowed to watch these programmes without an adult if at all. These programmes can contain violence (V), sexual situations (S), strong language (L), very sexual dialogue (D).

V MA
Mature audience only. These programmes are made specifically for adults and are unsuitable for children under the age of 17. The programmes can contain graphic violence (V), explicit sexual activity (S), very coarse language (L).

Col. 1
1 **to license** (*BE* **to licence**) to give permission to operate
20 **parental** [pə'rentl]
23 **Congress** *(US)* the part of the government (House of Representatives and the Senate) that makes laws – **to pass** *here:* to agree on a law
25 **to prohibit** to make s.th. illegal
36 **to require** to make s.th. obligatory

Col. 2
11 **First Amendment** part of the US Constitution which protects a citizen's right to freedom of speech
29 **comedic** [kə'mi:dɪk] funny

Col. 3
30 **mature** [mə'tjʊə] grown-up

Comprehension

1. Copy and complete the table below with information from the text.

FCC	*Children's Television Act*	*Telecommunications Act*	*Parental guidance system*

2. What does the letter 'V' in V-chip stand for?
3. Which elements of programmes is the parental guidance system most concerned with?
4. Why is NBC opposed to the parental guidance rating system?
5. You are staying with an American family and you look after the 7-year-old daughter one evening while your hosts go out. At 8 pm she wants to watch TV.
   a) Look at the TV guide on page 109 and decide which of the programmes listed you would allow her to watch and which you wouldn't, using the ratings symbols as your guide. Explain your choice.
   b) To what extent were the symbols useful to you? How could the system be improved in your opinion?

Grammar: passive & active

1. Find examples of the passive voice in the text. Rewrite them in the active voice, if possible.
2. Write the following sentences in the passive voice:
   a) TV broadcast networks can often dub out foul language.
   b) Someone told me that the US government established the FCC in 1934.
   c) Parents must watch the first fifteen seconds of a show in order to see the rating icon.
   d) Pressure groups objected strongly to the violence shown in the TV film.
   e) The network only aired the show after a team of editors had given it a rating.
   f) The Advertising Complaints Board has to deal with all complaints against advertisements.
   g) If the TV stations want the FCC to renew their license they must take notice of the guidelines.

Passive & active
See *grammar file* on p. 147.

'The only time I dare turn my back on them is when they're plunked in front of the TV.'

There's a spelling mistake on the TV screen! Can you find and correct it?

Your view

1. In what ways is the rating system used by the networks similar or different to the one you designed? Which do you think is better? Why?
2. What disadvantages or dangers of a rating system can you think of? List them and then in a group discuss the pros and cons of having a rating system. Try to come to a conclusion and be prepared to explain your conclusion to the rest of your class.

Discussions
See *skills files* on pp. 131 & 132.

Looking at the cartoon

1. Describe the cartoon in as much detail as possible. Describe the setting, say who you can see and what each person is doing.
2. What is the cartoonist making fun of in your opinion?
3. In what way(s) would a V-chip make a difference in situations like this?

Talking about cartoons
See *skills file* on page 130.

TV stations and networks in the USA

3 **commercial station** sponsored or paid for by advertisers

11 **affiliated** [əˈfɪlieɪtɪd] *here:* connected to a particular network

13 **donation** money given without expecting s.th. in return – **foundation** [-ˈ--] institution which provides money to charities, for research, etc.

35 **competing** offering similar services

Too much, too many?

The problem of describing American television is quite simply that there is so much of it! In 1998 there were over 1,500 commercial and non-commercial TV stations in the US! And although there are similar types of stations, no one station is exactly the same as another. Over 90 % of all American homes can receive at least 6 different TV stations and more than 60 % can receive 10 or more – without cable and without paying any fee or charge! The majority of stations are commercial stations and buy their programmes from the networks. There are around 530 independents (non-network affiliated) and around 350 non-commercial stations. Non-commercial stations allow no advertising or commercials and are supported by individual donations, grants from foundations and private organisations and funds from city, state, and federal sources.

The networks

The networks are not television stations and they are not licensed to broadcast. They produce programmes which individual TV stations then choose to buy and broadcast. There are four major commercial networks: ABC (American Broadcasting Company), CBS (Columbia Broadcasting System), NBC (National Broadcasting Company) and Fox. Then there are various cable networks such as CNN (Cable News Network), which features only news and news stories, ESPN, the all-sports cable network, and MTV, the music network. Cable has also led to a wide variety of new minority interest networks, such as Black Entertainment Television (BET) which appeals to African-American viewers. The leading network in terms of viewing figures is NBC with 11 % of viewers, but the biggest network is not a commercial network, it is PBS (Public Broadcasting System) which shares its programmes with over 250 non-profit, non-commercial stations. PBS only attracts about 2 % of viewers, but public television is growing, which is remarkable when you consider that public television has very limited financial resources.

Cable and pay-TV

In the US there is no single cable system. Each local community can choose from competing cable companies and decide what price to ask for (if any). There are now over 11,600 cable systems operating in the US and cable is reached by over 56 million people. The top pay-cable services are Home Box Office with 17 million subscribers, Disney Channel with 5.6 million and Playboy (!) with 4 million.

Glued to the tube?

According to Nielsen Media Research in 1998 TV was watched daily in the average American home for 7 hours and 21 minutes! But there is a difference between the TV being on and the amount of TV actually being watched. TV sets in America are turned on like radio sets: for background noise and music. In particular, people view morning and daytime shows only intermittently while they are doing other things. Life goes on alongside the TV, and TV is only watched when something interesting is happening! And of course there is probably the "odd" American, who doesn't watch any TV at all!

Vocabulary

1. Make an alphabetical word list of all the words in the text opposite which belong to the semantic field 'television'.
2. Explain in your own words what each of the words means.

Comprehension

Explain the difference between …:
a) … commercial and non-commercial stations
b) … TV stations and TV networks
c) … PBS and NBC
d) … the time a TV is on in an American household and the time Americans watch TV.

Translation

Translation
See *skills file* on p. 122.

Translate ll. 40 – 49 of the text on p. 114 into German. Remember to translate the heading "Glued to the tube?".

Media Research

Audience figures are researched and published on a regular basis by Nielsen Media. A programme's Nielsen Media rating is a definitive sign of its success or failure.

Asking for information

1. Work with a partner. One of you looks at the Nielsen Media research information for the week of May 31–June 6, 1999 below. The other looks at the information on page 116. Ask each other questions and make a note of the information missing in your table.

Programme Name	Network	Day/Time	Audience
20/20 – WED	ABC	Wed, 10 pm	9,846,000
WILL & GRACE	NBC		
		Thurs, 9 pm	10,107,000
DATELINE	NBC	Tue, 10 pm	9,366,000
LAW AND ORDER		Wed, 10 pm	
	NBC	Thurs, 10 pm	
TOUCHED BY AN ANGEL	CBS	Sun, 8 pm	9,538,000
60 MINUTES			
20/20 – FRI	ABC	Fri, 10 pm	8,895,000
FRIENDS	NBC		

Source: Nielsen Media Research

! **rating** 1. (*here:*) popularity of a TV programme in terms of the number of people who watch it; 2. classification of a programme in terms of its content (see p. 112)

Possible questions
What was on at (8 pm) on (Thursday)?
Which network was (Friends) broadcast on?
How many people watched (ER)?
What day/time was (ER) on?

2. Make a new table ranking the top ten programmes from 1 to 10.
3. Who do you think has a special interest in the audience rating system and why?
4. Make a short written analysis of the figures. You should refer to the number of viewers, the networks, the time/day of broadcast and the rankings in your analysis.
5. Look up the latest Nielsen ratings on the internet. Find out which programmes and which networks have been most popular in the last few weeks. Make comparisons with the information given above.

Check the web
Check out the latest Nielsen ratings at:
http://ytv.yahoo.com/nielsen

Over to you

- What were the top ten programmes watched by students in your class in the last week? Carry out a class survey and make a summary of your results in table and written form.

Media Research (see p. 115)

Work with a partner. One of you should look at the Nielsen Media research information for the week of May 31–June 6, 1999 below. The other looks at the information on p. 115. Ask each other questions and make a note of the information missing in your table.

When you have finished turn back to p. 115.

Possible questions
What was on at (8 pm) on (Thursday)?
Which network was (Friends) broadcast on?
How many people watched (ER)?
What day/time was (ER) on?

Program Name	Network	Day/Time	Audience
20/20-WED	ABC		
WILL & GRACE	NBC	Thurs, 9.30 pm	9,727,000
	NBC		
DATELINE	NBC	Tue, 10 pm	9,366,000
	NBC	Wed, 10 pm	
E.R.	NBC	Thurs, 10 pm	9,998,000
TOUCHED BY AN ANGEL			
60 MINUTES	CBS	Sun, 7 pm	9,887,000
20/20-FRI	ABC		
FRIENDS	NBC	Thurs, 8 pm	9,913,000

Source: Nielsen Media Research

Talking TV!

Looking at the cartoon
1. How do you think the dialogue continues? With a partner write the conversation the couple has, and then act out your dialogue to your class.
2. a) What point is the cartoonist making?
   b) Do you agree or disagree that "television destroys the art of conversation"? Give reasons.

Over to you

- You plan to spend an evening watching TV at home when, quite unexpectedly, there is a power cut in your area, so there is no electricity and you cannot watch TV. What do you decide to do instead? Work in a group of two to four students and plan your evening.

Listening comprehension
Listen to this short story by Art Buchwald called 'The Shock of Recognition'.

Blame the couch potatoes …

The following text is an extract from the novel Popcorn *by Ben Elton.*
The story so far: Bruce Delamitri, a film-maker, who makes sexist and extremely violent films receives an Oscar for the best film director. When Bruce arrives home after the Oscar ceremony his house has been broken into by Wayne and Scout, two heavily-armed psychopathic killers. Wayne and Scout have killed Bruce's security guard and his agent and have seriously injured a young actress who came home with Bruce. They take Bruce, his ex-wife Farrah and his daughter, Velvet, hostage. Wayne and Scout face the electric chair if they are caught, and knowing this, Wayne plans to use the media to prove that they are innocent even though they have committed numerous murders. He wants Bruce to make a statement on TV. Bruce is to say that because of watching his films Wayne and Scout have become killers. Wayne calls the TV networks and tells them to send in two camera people (Bill and Kirsten) to televise the scene. He also demands a direct link to the ratings computer so that he can see how many people are watching. Bruce suggests that instead of making a statement, he and Wayne could debate the topic on TV. Bruce could then deny that he is responsible for the killings (and so save his reputation), but Wayne would still have the chance to put forward his arguments. Wayne agrees and the debate is broadcast live. As this extract begins, the debate has been going on for several minutes.

"Excuse me," Kirsten said nervously, looking up from her equipment. "Um, this is all very interesting, of course, and the producers are delighted, they're very happy in control … it's just that the ratings are beginning to drop – see here, it's all displayed on my monitor. The chief wants to know if it would be OK to record this and then edit it for the evening news?"

"No need for that, Kirsten. I have an idea. Hey, America!" Wayne shouted at the camera. "Listen, phone your friends, tell them all to tune in, because in ninety seconds I'm going to shoot Farrah Delamitri. In one minute and one half, the wife of the guy who just got the Oscar gets shot dead live!"

* * * *

Farrah screamed. Velvet screamed. Even Kirsten thought about protesting, but then she remembered the sacred duty of the news-gatherer: never intervene, not even if the news is being created for your benefit.

"Please, Wayne, don't," Bruce said.

"She's my Mom!" Velvet sobbed.

Outside, in the command truck, Chief Cornell was in agony. Should he send his SWAT teams in now? If he did, there would certainly be bloodshed. If he didn't, likewise.

Oh, how he wished that somebody else would take responsibility.

Inside the mansion, Wayne had got up and was studying the ratings on Kirsten's computer screen.

"They're climbing, aren't they?"

"Yes they are," Kirsten replied, "but none the less my producer is saying please don't kill the woman."

Farrah sobbed, pulling pathetically at her manacled hand.

In the control truck a lively debate was in progress.

"We have to terminate the broadcast," some were saying. "He's feeding off it. It's creating his crimes."

"He killed plenty of people before there were any cameras to play to," others contended. "We can't turn off. We don't choose the news. We don't have a right to censor national events just because they're unattractive."

"But if he's creating the news for us?"

"We can't take responsibility for his actions."

"Can we take responsibility for our own?"

Popcorn is available as a paperback and has also been performed as a theatre play.
Why do you think Ben Elton chose the title *Popcorn*?

couch potato *(slang)* lazy person whose main pastime is watching television and videos
3 **control (truck)** mobile unit linking the journalists to the TV station
5 **to edit s.th.** to cut and prepare material
11 **sacred duty** most important job – **to intervene** to stop a course of action
14 **to sob** to cry *(weinen)* so much that one's breath comes irregularly
15 **agony** [ˈæɡənɪ] pain
16 **SWAT** (Special Weapons And Tactics) name for law enforcement officers specially trained to deal with violent situations, esp. the taking of hostages
24 **manacled** [ˈmænəkld] chained

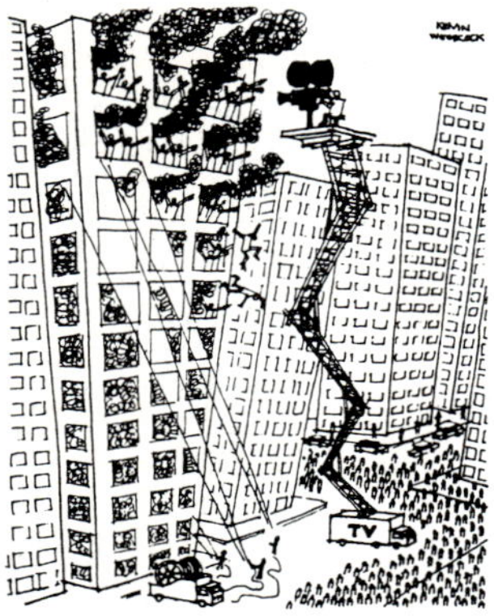

1. Write a caption for the cartoon.
2. Write the TV presenter's commentary.

The cameras stayed on, as no one had doubted for a moment that they would, and the ratings continued to climb.

Inside the lounge Wayne showed off his guns to the camera. "Hurry up now, y'all," he said. "You don't want to miss it, do ya?"

When the ninety seconds ran out, Wayne shot Farrah dead.

* * * *

"OK, hit it," said Chief Cornell, and silently, through the doors, the windows and even the roof, the SWAT teams began to enter Bruce's house.

In the siege room the shot still resonated.

"You bastard! When will this end!" Bruce had rushed over and was holding Velvet, who sobbed hysterically, still handcuffed to the lampstand beside her dead mother.

"You saw the ratings, man. They went up. Blame the couch potatoes."

"You hypocritical swine!" Bruce shouted "You killed her – no one else did! What is it you're saying? That the media, the public, is responsible for the fact that you're a murdering lunatic?"

"I'm just saying I wouldn'ta shot her if people had switched to The Simpsons."

"You are responsible!"

"Yes. I'm responsible for me, but you are responsible for you and they are responsible for them. I don't see anyone doing much about that. I've got an excuse, I'm a psycho. What's your get-out?"

Kirsten received a message from the producer. She turned to Bill. "Get down! There's a SWAT team coming in!"

"No!" Wayne shouted into the camera.

Above them they could hear the sound of the roof being breached. Wayne grabbed Scout by the hand, and addressed the camera. "Wait! Hold it. I'll give myself up, Scout too, I swear. Stop the attack. Keep the cameras rolling. We'll give up."

Outside Chief Cornell signalled that his forces should pause. Was it possible that they could get out of this nightmare without further bloodshed?

Wayne continued to shout at the camera. "But we give ourselves up to the people. The people are responsible. They decide our fate, the fate of everybody in this room." He had hold of the ratings computer now. "It's up to you, the people out there … the lives of us all are in your hands. Here's how it is. When I've finished talking, if everybody watching switches off their TV, I swear me and Scout will walk out of here with our hands up … But if you keep watching, I will kill every last mutha in this room, including myself and Scout. Not a bad show, huh? Exciting, right? And to see it, all you have to do is stay tuned in for another few seconds. Well, you're responsible. Are you gonna turn off your TV?'

From Popcorn *by Ben Elton, London: Pocket Books, 1997, pp. 286 – 290.*

42 **siege** [si:dʒ] being surrounded by police, with no way out for the kidnappers
44 **handcuffed** chained to s.th. with handcuffs *(Handschellen)*
57 **to breach** to break through
63 **fate** [feɪt]
67 **mutha** *(vulgar, negative)* stupid person

Considering the text →

1. Why does Wayne announce that he is going to kill Farrah?
2. How – if at all – could Farrah's life have been saved?
3. Why is Kirsten in such a difficult position?
4. If you had been watching the live broadcast, would you have turned off your TV? Why? Why not?
5. a) Describe how the following groups and characters behave in the extract:
   the TV networks • the police • Wayne and Scout • Bruce • the public.
   b) Under the same headings write down to what extent each of the groups or characters can be held responsible for Wayne and Scout's actions.

Your view →

Who do you think is most responsible for the killings? Write a comment of about 100 words giving your reasons.

1. Responsibility is one of the key words in this extract.
   a) Find examples of the use of the words 'responsibility' and 'responsible' in the text.
   b) What is the opposite of responsibility and responsible?
   c) Find a synonym in the text for the noun 'responsibility' and for the verb form 'to be responsible'.
2. Find all the words in the text which belong to the semantic field 'television' and list them in the following categories: people • actions (verbs) • equipment.

← **Vocabulary & language**

Refer to the *skills files* to help you with the tasks on this page. There is an index of all files on p. 159.

Project: A panel discussion

TV talk show: Guilty or innocent? Who is really to blame?
Work in groups of eight. You are going to produce a TV talk show.

- Each of you must take on the role of one of the following characters:
  Wayne • Bruce • Chief Cornell • the TV network controller • a young person whose brother was murdered by Bruce and Scout • a fan of Bruce's films • a chairperson.
- Prepare an opening statement of about 100 words putting forward your point of view. The chairperson should decide how to introduce the debate to the 'audience' and in which order he/she is going to ask the characters to speak.
- Arrange yourselves so that you are sitting in a half circle. (Decide together where each person should sit.)
- The chairperson should open the debate and then call upon each person to make their statement in the order he/she has decided. (At this point there should be no discussion or interruptions.) Each character should make notes of the arguments put forward by the other characters so that they can make counter-arguments.
- Once everyone has made their statements, the debate should continue in as lively a manner as possible. (It is the chairperson's responsiblity to keep the debate going!)
- After an agreed length of time (e.g. 10 minutes), the chairperson should ask each speaker to make a final statement.
- Practise your debate in your group.
- Finally have your debate in class. The rest of your class is the audience. They should applaud, etc. as they think appropriate. The chairperson can also ask members of the audience for their opinion, if he/she wishes! If possible, make a video recording of your debate.

Are you glued to the tube? (see p. 90)

Read below to find out what kind of TV viewer you are!

0 – 5 points: Anti-TV-ite
Either your parents are strong anti-TV-ites and don't allow you to watch TV, or you belong to an increasingly rare group of non-TV viewing teenagers. So long as you don't mind not being able to take part in conversations about TV programmes with your friends, that's fine. But remember, TV is not all bad: you can learn a lot from some programmes. And talking about TV programmes can be a good way of starting a conversation with someone you want to get to know!

6 – 12 points: Choosy viewer
You have a very sensible attitude towards TV. You choose carefully what to watch and when, and have plenty of other hobbies and interests as well. You know enough about what is going on on TV to join in conversations at school, but there are many other topics which you find equally if not more interesting. You prefer to spend your time doing other things, but you can also enjoy a quiet evening at home watching TV. You are a shining example to your classmates and family! Congratulations!

12 – 18 points: TV addict
TV is never far from your thoughts. You often talk about TV programmes with your friends, you can sing nearly all the soap opera theme tunes by heart and can always say what is on without looking in a TV guide. However, although the TV is nearly always on when you are at home, you don't spend all your time watching it: it is often just a kind of background noise. Be warned: TV addicts run a high risk of becoming total 'couch potatoes'!

over 18 points: Couch potato
You are the ultimate couch potato! All you do, all you think about and all you talk about in your free time is TV. You wake up to TV, talk about it in school and can't wait to get home and watch it again in the afternoons. By the time you are twenty-one you will probably have terrible eyesight from staring at the TV for so long every day and you will probably be very unfit and overweight because you don't get any exercise. Start trying to change your TV viewing habit now: before it's too late!

Song text: *N'oubliez jamais*

N'OUBLIEZ JAMAIS

by Joe Cocker

Papa, why do you play all the same old songs?
Why do you sing with the melody?
'Cause down on the street something's going on,
There's a brand new beat and a brand new song.

He said:
In my life there was so much anger,
Still I have no regrets,
Just like you I was such a rebel,
So dance your own dance and never forget …

N'oubliez jamais,
I heard my father say,
Every generation has its way,
A need to disobey.
N'oubliez jamais,
It's in your destiny,
A need to disagree,
The rules get in the way,
N'oubliez jamais

Mama, why do you dance to the same old songs?
Why do you sing with the harmony?
'Cause down on the street something's going on,
There's a brand new beat and a brand new song.

She said:
In my heart there's a young girl's passion
For a lifelong duet,
And some day soon someone's smile will haunt you,
So sing your own song and never forget ...

N'oubliez jamais,
I heard my father say,
Every generation has its way,
A need to disobey.
N'oubliez jamais,
It's in your destiny,
A need to disagree,
The rules get in the way,
N'oubliez jamais

What is this game?
Searching for love or fame,
It's all the same.
One of these days you'll say
That love will be the cure.
I'm not so sure …

N'oubliez jamais,
I heard my father say,
Every generation has its way,
A need to disobey.
N'oubliez jamais,
It's in your destiny,
A need to disagree,
The rules get in the way,
N'oubliez jamais

Don't you ever forget …
Our love …
Every generation … every generation …
'Ain't it so … ?
N'oubliez jamais …
N'oubliez jamais …

n'oubliez jamais *(French)* never forget
4 **brand new** completely new
7 **to have no regrets** not to feel sorry about anything
15 **destiny** the force that some people believe controls what happens to them in their lifetime
24 **passion** very strong often sexual feeling
26 **to haunt** [hɔ:nt] to keep coming back even after a long time has passed
41 **cure** medical treatment needed to recover from an illness
55 **ain't** *(slang)* isn't

Mind maps

Mind maps are useful for collecting and organizing a large amount of information about a certain topic. You can make a mind map for yourself or as a group. The basic structure of a mind map is always the same.

How to make a mind map

Use a pencil so that you can easily delete things or change their position, if necessary.

1. Write your main topic in the middle of a page and draw a circle around the word or phrase. (Fig. 1)
2. Think of important things directly related to the main topic. Write each idea (subtopic) in a circle around the outside of your first circle. Draw lines connecting the subtopics to the main topic. (Fig. 2)
3. Now add more circles with related ideas around the subtopics. (Fig. 3)

Instead of drawing circles you can use lines with 'branches' for subtopics. (Fig. 4)

Ways of using mind maps

- To brainstorm ideas on a given topic:
  Write the topic heading in the centre circle and add all new and related aspects.

- To organize information from a text (or other source):
  Start with the most important point in the text, add the main subtopics, then add relevant detailed information or quotations from the text.

- To develop word fields:
  Start with the generic term and add all related words.

- To organize arguments:
  Start with the topic of discussion. Add a branch or circle: 'for' and another one 'against'. Continue by adding further branches/circles with arguments 'for' and 'against'.

Fig. 1

Fig. 2

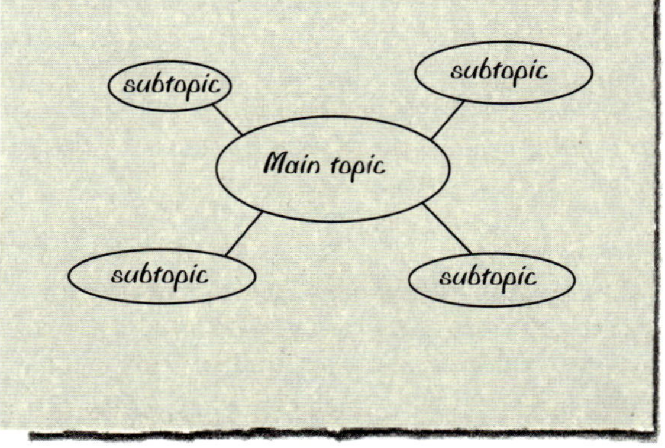

Fig. 3

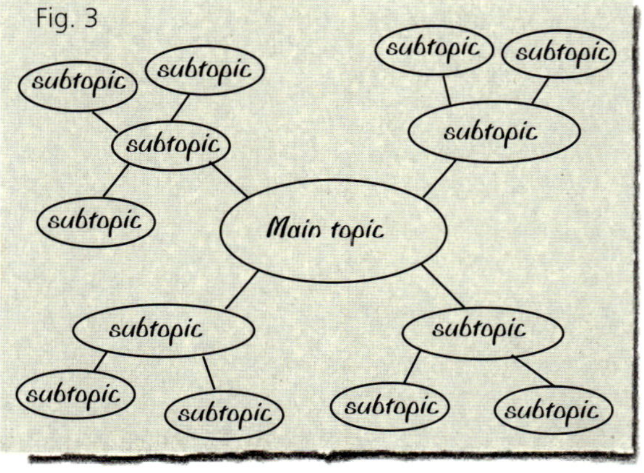

Fig. 4

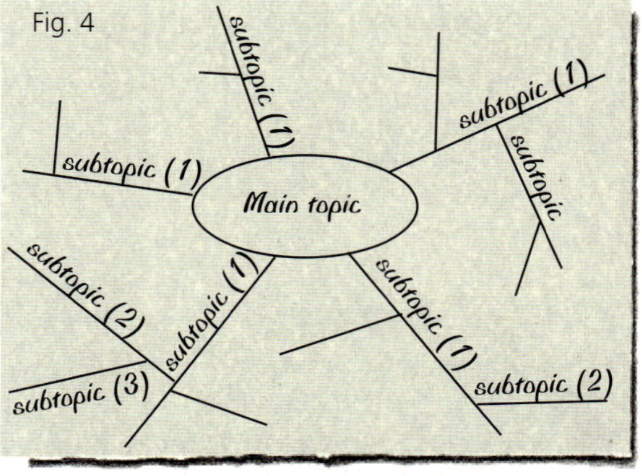

Translating

Guidelines

1. Before you start translating
- Always read the whole text before you start translating.
- Make a note of the main points in your own words in German before you start your detailed translation.

2. First version
- Write your first version in pencil so that you can change and correct things easily.
- Don't translate word for word, but do keep as close to the original as possible.
- Refer to the **Tips and tricks** and to the table of common problems on p.123.
- Don't leave any gaps! In your first version write words or phrases which you can't translate in English. Underline them so that you can find them easily.

3. Second version
- Read through your first version and try to translate any remaining English words from the context. If you can't, look them up in a dictionary.
- Check your translation word for word against the English text and make sure you haven't left anything out. Make corrections as necessary.

4. Final version
- Reread your text and decide if it sounds German. If it doesn't, you haven't translated properly. Think about what you are trying to say and decide how you would say it in German. Make corrections.
- Reread your translation and repeat these steps until you are certain your text is in good German. If you have time, leave the text for a while (e.g. overnight) before checking it for the last time.

Tips and tricks

1. Don't improve texts when you translate. For example, if one verb is used repeatedly in the text use one verb in your translation, even if you think another would sound better.

2. When translating long sentences, define the main clause and translate this first, then translate the other clauses in their order of importance.

3. Try to keep to the same number of sentences in the text and in your translation. (Don't split sentences up or join them in your translation, unless it is really necessary.)

4. Be prepared for your German text to be longer than the English original: English sentences are often shorter than German ones. One of the reasons for this is that, for example, there is often a relative clause in German where in English a participle construction (with -ing form or past participle) is used.

5. You will only be able to translate well if you read in your own language. Look for texts on similar topics to those you cover in your English lessons in German newspapers, magazines, etc. This will help you translate specific topic-related vocabulary and names of people, groups, etc.

6. Some words and phrases occur in almost all texts and are frequently difficult to translate. Collect these words and phrases in a special file. Some 'false friends' are listed below to start you off.

Common 'false friends'

actual – eigentlich (≠aktuell)
after all – doch, zum guten Schluss (≠nach allem)
brave – mutig (≠brav)
briefcase – Aktentasche (≠Brieftasche)
critic – Kritiker (≠Kritik)
gift – Geschenk (≠Gift)
gymnasium – Turnhalle (≠Gymnasium)
however – jedoch (≠wie auch immer)
to overhear – zufällig mitbekommen (≠überhören)
physician – Arzt (≠Physiker)
rent – Miete (≠Rente)
rubber hose – Gartenschlauch (≠Gummihose)
sensible – vernünftig (≠sensibel)

File continued on next page.

Translating (contd.)

Common problems

Problem / Solution	**English**	**German**
Present perfect sentences with 'since/for' are usually present tense in German.	I have had my car for 2 years now.	Ich habe mein Auto jetzt seit zwei Jahren.
Constructions using past participles and -ing forms can often be translated with a relative clause.	I thanked them for the lovely weekend spent with them. A group of American students visiting our town were at college today.	Ich dankte ihnen für das schöne Wochenende, das ich mit ihnen verbracht hatte. Eine Gruppe amerikanischer Studentinnen, die unsere Stadt besuchen, waren heute in der Schule.
The translation of 'it' is not always 'es'. It depends what 'it' refers to.	I couldn't get a seat on the train: it was totally crowded.	Ich konnte im Zug keinen Platz kriegen: er war total überfüllt.
'you' and 'they' can often be translated with the German 'man'.	In Britain you often see double decker buses.	In Großbritannien sieht man oft Doppeldeckerbusse.
'do' or 'did' in positive sentences are used to emphasize the verb. In German you usually need an adverb.	I did do my homework!	Ich habe sehr wohl meine Hausaufgaben gemacht!
'there is/are' and 'there was/were' are usually translated with 'es gibt' or 'es gab'.	There's so much to do and see in Atlanta! There was nothing to eat.	Es gibt so viel zu tun und zu sehen in Atlanta! Es gab nichts zu essen.
An adjective + noun combination in English can often be translated by one noun in German.	congressional elections (adjective + noun)	Kongresswahlen (compound noun)
'with + -ing form' is best translated with a separate clause beginning with a conjunction (weil, da, wo, wenn, wobei, etc.).	Roads are becoming busier and busier with more and more people driving cars. With winter approaching, they decided to leave.	Die Straßen werden immer voller, weil immer mehr Leute Auto fahren. Jetzt, wo der Winter sich näherte, beschlossen sie zu gehen.
Passive sentences can often be translated in the active form using 'man'.	The stolen money was found in a phone box.	Man hat das gestohlene Geld in einer Telefonzelle gefunden.
Translate proper names etc. only when there is a real German equivalent.	Henry VIII Cologne Prince Charles	Heinrich der VIII. Köln Prince Charles
Don't convert miles to kilometres, pounds to kilogrammes, etc.	She runs 5 miles every day.	Sie läuft jeden Tag 5 Meilen.

Essay writing

An essay is a clearly structured piece of writing in which important points on a topic are presented. Essays are generally written in the present tense.
In an expository essay you explain an idea or set of related facts.
In an argumentative essay you express your opinion and give arguments for and/or against a given topic.

Stage 1: Preparation

- Define the topic clearly.
- Brainstorm ideas and write down what you know about the topic in a mind map, diagram or table.
- If necessary, collect facts, arguments, statistics and other information from other sources, e.g. your library or the internet.
- Formulate your opinion on the topic.

Stage 2: Arranging your material

- Decide on the most important facts, arguments or pieces of information that you want to include in your essay (maximum 5 items).
- For each main argument try to think of two supporting arguments.
- Put your facts or arguments in a logical order.
  For example, you could:
  – start with general ideas and then go on to talk about details.
  – put things into chronological order.
  – start by giving all the arguments in favour and then give all the counter-arguments.
  – follow each argument in favour with a counter-argument.

Stage 3: Writing your essay

The introductory paragraph
- The introductory paragraph should introduce your topic and catch the reader's interest. You could:
  – give a relevant quotation.
  – make a provocative statement.
  – describe a relevant (humorous) personal experience.
- In your introductory paragraph you should also:
  – say clearly what your essay is going to be about in one or two sentences.
  – ask a question or questions which you will answer in your essay.
  – give a brief outline of the problem/topic at present and in the past.

The main paragraphs
- Start a new paragraph for each new idea.
- Begin each paragraph with a main idea or argument and then follow it up with your supporting or counter-arguments (see also Stage 2).
- Write simple sentences.
- Arrange your sentences in a logical order.
- Join your sentences using suitable connectives (see p. 125).
- Use adverbs to emphasize and tone down points.
- Use examples where possible.

The conclusion
- Do not introduce new ideas in your conclusion!
- Make a brief concluding statement summarizing what you have said in your essay.
- Include a quotation or anecdote if you can.

Stage 4: Checking your essay

- Check that all your sentences are complete and that they make sense.
- 'Proofread' your essay: check for grammar, spelling and punctuation mistakes. (Tip: Leave your essay overnight before 'proofreading' it.)
- Write or print out the final version of your essay.

Connectives

Connectives are words and phrases which you use to link sentences and paragraphs. Using connectives helps readers to follow your ideas more easily because they give your text a clear structure.
Make use of the following connectives in your texts. Keep your own list of personal favourites and add new words and phrases to it when you learn them.

To express a certain order:
to begin with • initially • first of all • first(ly)..., (second(ly)..., thirdly..., etc.) • next • then • later • finally

To add ideas:
also • as well • in addition • additionally • too • moreover • furthermore

To give examples:
for example • for instance • by way of illustration

To generalize:
as a rule • generally • in general • by and large • on the whole

to express certainty:
clearly • evidently • obviously • undoubtedly

To give a reason:
consequently • that is why • therefore • this is the reason why • as a result

To give an opinion:
in my opinion • to my mind • the way I see it • in my view

To compare or give an opposing opinion:
in the same way • similarly • likewise • equally • on the one hand ... on the other hand • in contrast • on the contrary

To conclude:
finally • in conclusion • to conclude • in summary • to sum up

Writing a summary

A summary is a short piece of writing in which you restate the main points of a text in your own words.

- A summary is almost always written in the present tense.
- Use your own words and do not copy any phrases or sentences from the text.
- Do not use statistics, numbers, figures, details or quotations from the text.
- Do not give your personal opinion.
- Your final version should be no longer than between one fifth and one third of the length of the original.

A summary of a non-fictional text
In a summary of a non-fictional text, for example, a newspaper article, a report, a factual text, etc. restate the main points or arguments presented in the text.

1. Read through the original text at least twice.
2. In your own words make a note of the main arguments or points in the text. You could:
   - Make a list of key words.
   - Write one sentence to go with each paragraph.
3. Rewrite some or all of your sentences to say what the writer's intention was. You can use the following phrases:
   The author/writer...
   – points out that ...
   – emphasizes ...
   – suggests that ...
   – describes (how) ...
   – concludes by saying that ...
4. Link your sentences with connectives (see opposite).

A summary of a fictional text
In a summary of a fictional text, for example, a short story or extract from a novel, describe briefly what happens in the story or extract and who the main characters are.

1. Briefly describe the characters and the setting.
2. Briefly describe what happens and how the events are connected. Use these phrases:
   The scene/story/extract ...
   – ... takes place in ...
   – ... is set in ...
   – ... takes place in the present/past/future.
   The main character is ...
   There are two/three/etc. main characters.
3. Link your sentences with connectives (see opposite).

Making phone calls

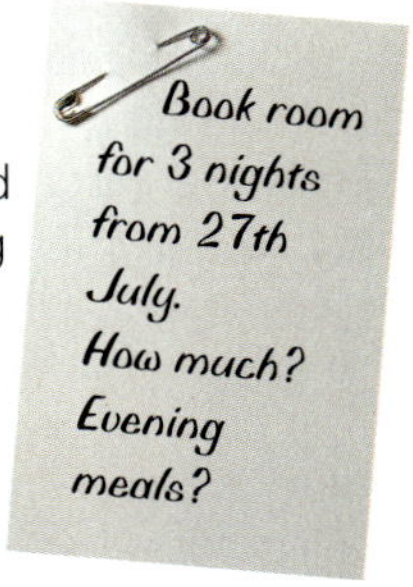

Basic guidelines

- Prepare yourself thoroughly.
  - Make notes in English or write out a rough draft of the main things you want to say or find out to give you more confidence and fluency. This is especially important when making formal or business calls.
  - If possible find out the name and number of a direct contact person in advance.
  - Think of things the contact person is likely to ask or say and work out responses.
- Speak clearly and slowly. State your requests clearly and to the point.
- Don't expect to understand every single word that is said.
- Don't worry about making mistakes.
- Be polite! Remember to say 'please' whenever you ask for information and 'thank you' whenever you have been given help. Remember:

  please = bitte
  you're welcome/not at all = bitte schön; gern geschehen
- State telephone numbers as single digits. When the same number occurs twice consecutively you can say 'double' (e.g. 33: *double 3*). 0 = *Oh* (BE & AE) or *zero* (AE)
  Example: 07145 14406: *Oh/zero – seven – one – four – five – one – double four – oh/zero – six*
- When making a social call, give your fist name only.
  When making a formal/business call give your first name and surname.
  Address people you know well (friends, people you know socially, people of your own age) by their first names.
  In a formal/business situation address people using '*Mr*', '*Mrs*' or '*Ms*' [mz] + surname.
- Be prepared to spell words, especially people's names and names of places. Useful phrases:

  Would you like me to spell …/that for you? It's spelt … • *I'll just spell that for you. It's …*
- Ask the caller to spell names, etc. for you to avoid confusion. Useful phrases:

  Could you spell …/that for me, please? • *Would you mind spelling …/that for me, please?*
- Repeat information (times, names, addresses, prices, etc.) to be sure that you have understood everything correctly. Useful phrases:

  Let me just check that I've understood all the information you've given me/asked for correctly. …
  I'll just repeat that back to you to make sure I've got everything down correctly. …
  Let me just check that I've spelt your name correctly. …
  Let me just check that I've written the dates/times/etc. down correctly. …
- If you don't understand something:
  - Ask the person to repeat what they have just said: *Could you repeat that, please?*
  - Ask the person to explain something in a different way: *I'm sorry, I'm afraid I don't understand what you mean. Could you explain that again, please?*
  - Ask the person to speak more slowly: *Could you speak a little more slowly, please?*
- If you can't hear the the caller properly, ask the caller to speak more loudly:

  I'm sorry, (it's a very bad line,) I didn't quite catch that! Could you speak up a bit, please?
- If you think you've got the wrong number, check and apologize. Don't just hang up. Useful phrases:
  Is that (+ number you want) ? • *I'm sorry, I think I've dialled the wrong number, I'm trying to call (+ number you want).* • *I'm sorry to have bothered you.*
- If the caller has got the wrong number, explain politely. Don't just hang up.
  I'm sorry, but I think you've got the wrong number. This is (+ your number/name/company name). • *I'm sorry, there's no-one here with that name. This is (+ your number/name/company name).*
- Don't interrupt! If you do interrupt, be as polite as possible. There are examples of phrases you can use to interrupt someone or deal with being interrupted in the skills file 'Useful phrases for discussions' on p. 132.

File continued on next page.

Social calls

Remember to follow the basic guidelines on p. 126. (See also ideas and useful phrases in the skills file 'Small talk' on p.128.)

Greeting

Hello! • Hello, this is…[1] .• Hello …[2].! It's me, …[1].

Starting a conversation

How are you? • How are you doing? • It's great to hear from you! • I just thought I'd call and find out how you are. • I just wanted to ring and let you know that I'll be in the States in July/etc.

Asking to speak to someone else & passing a call on

Could I speak to …[2], please? • Is …[2] in, please? • Do you know when …[2] will be back, please?

Just a second, I'll go and find him/her. • Hold on a minute, I'll see if he/she's in.

Giving and taking messages

Could you give …[2] a message, please?

I'm afraid he/she can't come to the phone right now. Can I take a message? • I'm sorry, but he/she's not in at the moment. Would you like me to take a message?

Ringing back

Would it be OK to ring back later? • What time can I ring back till? • I'll ring back in about half an hour, if that's OK. • Could you give …[2] my number, please, and ask him/her to ring me back? • Would you ask …[2] to ring me back, please?

You can try ringing again in about 20 minutes if you want to. • He/she should be back at about 10 pm. • Shall I ask him/her to call you back?

Ending a call & saying goodbye

Thanks for ringing! • It was great to talk to you/to hear from you! • Speak to you again soon, I hope. • Bye! • Take care. • All the best.

1 Your name.
2 Name of person you want to speak to.
3 State telephone number.

Formal phone calls

Remember to follow the basic guidelines on p. 126.

Greeting

*Hello/Good morning./Good afternoon. … *. (This is) ….[1] speaking. • Can I help you? • What can I do for you?*

Asking to speak to someone

Can I speak to …[2], please? • Can you put me through to …[2], please? • I'd like to speak to someone in your … department.

Holding the line & putting calls through

Please hold (the line). • One moment, please. • I'll connect you with …[2]./with the … department. • I'll put you through (to …[2]/to the … department).

When someone isn't available …

I'm sorry, …[2] isn't here/available at the moment/today/etc.

Getting the right extension, etc.

Can you give me …[2] 's extension number, please? • I'd like to receive more information about … . • I'm calling about … . • I can give you his/her extension number/voice mail number/fax number / e-mail address. It's …[3].

Giving and taking messages

Would you like to leave a message? • Can I take a message? • Would you like me to pass on a message? • Could you pass on a message, please?

Ringing back

Shall I ask him/her to call you back? • Could you call back later/in half an hour/etc., please? • Could you ask him/her to call me back, please? My number is …[3] • Can I call back later? • I'll call back later/in half an hour/etc., if that's OK. • When would be the best time to call back?

Ending a call

Thanks for your call!/Thanks for calling! • Thank you very much for your help! • Sorry I can't be of any more help. • Have a nice day! • Goodbye!

1 Your name.
2 Name of person you want to speak to.
3 State telephone/extension number.
* Name of company.

Small talk

Small talk is light (casual) conversation. It is a way of showing interest in others, communicating in a friendly way and avoiding conflict at all times! At a social event, like a party, you might spend the whole time in casual conversation. At a business meeting, on the phone, at an interview, etc. you can start (and end) with a few minutes of small talk.

Topics for small talk

- The weather (especially popular in Britain!)
- A journey (to or from the place where you are)
- Where you live./Where your conversation partner lives
- Your family and /or your conversation partner's family (if you know them)
- A recent/well-known TV programme or film
- Tips about what to see and do in a certain town or city (i.e. cultural events, attractions, restaurants, local specialities, etc.)
- Sport (e.g. a current international sports event)
- A vacation
- Where you/your conversation partner went to school or university
- What you/your conversation partner do for a living
- Hobbies and interests
- An experience/event that you and your conversation partner are both currently involved in or have been involved in
- A non-controversial item in the news

Useful phrases

Starting a conversation

Hi! / Hello!
What are you up to?
Do you mind if I join you?
Nice to see you (again)!
How are you?
How are you doing?
How are things?

Filling time

Well, …
Actually, …
Let's see, …
Let me think, …

Finding a topic

Did you see … on TV last night / at the weekend / etc.?
Have you seen the new [James Bond] film yet?
Did you read about [that terrible train crash] in the newspaper this morning?
Terrible / Beautiful weather, isn't it?
How was your journey?
How did you get here?
What made you decide to come here?
Have you ever been here before?
Who do you think is going to win [the football match] this evening?

Responding & showing surprise

Really?
I don't believe it!
That's incredible!
Well, I've never heard of anything like that before!
That's the funniest/most interesting / strangest thing I've heard in ages!
I've never thought of it like that before.
I couldn't agree more!
That's funny! Exactly the same thing happened to me the other day / two weeks ago / etc.

Using question tags

You know …, don't you?
He's … , isn't he?
It hasn't …, has it?
(See grammar file on p. 150.)

Finishing a conversation

It was nice talking to you!
Goodness / Oh no, is that the time?
Excuse me, / What a shame, I've got to go now.
Hope to see you again soon.
Hope you get home safely.
Take care.
Give my regards to … .
Don't forget to say hello to … for me!

Giving a talk or presentation

Preparation

1. Gather material on your topic.
   - Brainstorm to find ideas on the topic and make a mind map.
   - Find information from relevant sources (library, school books, the internet, newspapers, etc.)
2. Choose which main points you want to talk about.
3. Make a set of prompt cards in English, which you can look at during your talk to remind you of what you want to say. (See below.)
   - Use one card for each of your points. Give each card a suitable title.
   - Write down the key words, phrases, and vocabulary which you will need.
   - Note down any examples or quotations.
   - Note down any visual aids (OHPs, photographs, posters, flip charts, etc.) which you want to use.
   - Use colour markers to help you identify things on your cards easily when you are speaking.
4. Arrange your prompt cards in a logical order. You could present points:
   - in terms of importance, from the most to the least important (or vice versa).
   - chronologically.
   - in favour and then all those against.
   - in favour and against one after the other.
5. Make a prompt card for your introduction. To catch the listeners' attention you could start with:
   - an interesting question or fact
   - a quote or joke
   - a picture or cartoon on an OHP transparency.

   Note the key words, phrases etc. that you will need on your prompt card.
6. Make a prompt card for your conclusion.
   - Note the point(s) you want to emphasize.
   - Write down key words and phrases.
   - Make a note of a final quotation or example to use.

Giving the talk or presentation

Practise your talk or presentation out loud preferably in front of a mirror or ask a friend/relative to listen to you!

1. Speak slowly and clearly!
2. Use short, clear sentences.
3. Vary your voice so that you don't sound boring. For example, emphasize particularly important points by speaking a little more loudly.
4. Look at your audience as often as possible. Don't look at your prompt cards all the time.
5. Try not to make distracting movements such as waving your hands, etc.
6. Smile! (But don't laugh nervously!)
7. Start by introducing yourself (if necessary) and your topic. Finish by thanking your audience for listening and asking if anyone has any questions.

Useful phrases

Good morning/afternoon, my name is ...
Today I'm going to talk about ...
The subject of my talk today is ...
Can everyone hear me alright?
Can everyone see the board/screen/etc.?
Please tell me if you can't hear me properly/can't see the board/screen/etc.
I'd like to begin by (+ verb in -ing form)
Let me start by saying a few words about ...
Let me give you an example.
If you look at the chart/graph/cartoon, you'll see that ...
As you can see on the chart/graph/cartoon/etc. ...
I'd like to finish/conclude by (+ verb in -ing form)
Let me finish by (+ verb in -ing form)
Finally ...
Thank you very much for your attention.
Thank you very much for listening.
I hope you've all enjoyed my talk.
If you have any questions, please feel free to ask.
I'd be happy to answer any questions.

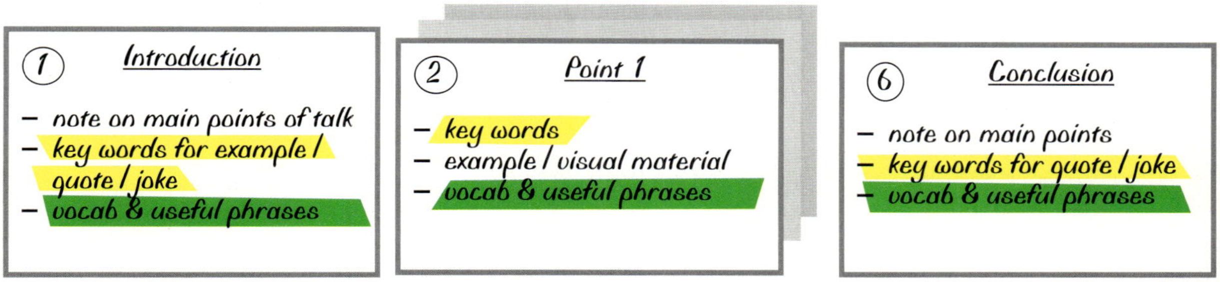

Illustrations & photographs

Types of pictures

photo(graph) • print • transparency • slide • painting • drawing • sketch • picture • illustration • image • collage • electronic image • snapshot • skyline • panorama • close-up • action photo • still (from a film)

Saying what a picture is of

This is a photo / an illustration of … .
This photo was taken in … .
The illustration shows …
In this illustration / photo you can see (that) …

Saying where things are in a picture

on the right-hand / left-hand side of the picture • in the centre • in the foreground • in the background • at the top • at the bottom • in the upper right-hand corner • in the lower left-hand corner

Adjectives of style & colour

colour • black & white • bright / dull • hand-painted / hand-drawn / drawn by hand • clear / in focus • blurred / not in focus / out of focus • lifelike • to scale / not to scale • posed / staged

Describing the impression a picture makes

- *The person in the picture looks … (+ adjective, e.g happy)*
- *The photo / illustration supports the point made in the text that …*
- *The photo / illustration gives you the impression that …*
- *The impression I get from this photo is that …*
- *The illustration makes me feel … (+ adjective: e.g. worried).*
- *The colours the artist has chosen make me feel … (+ adjective: happy / sad / worried / etc.)*
- *In my opinion the illustration would be better, if … (+ simple past: e.g. if it was more life-like)*

Cartoons

Cartoons are funny but critical. When looking at a cartoon the most important thing is to try to work out what point the cartoonist is making. Generally the point is made by a combination of the text and the illustration, so it is important to analyze and understand both.

Illustrations generally show caricatures of well-known people or particular stereotypes. To understand a cartoon, you need to recognize and define the person or group of people illustrated.

Text can be in one or all of the forms below. All text is relevant!

- A caption (a statement in quotation marks under the illustration). You need to work out who is speaking.
- A speech bubble, or speech bubbles.
- Other text, for example, on a sign or poster illustrated in the cartoon.

Phrases for talking about cartoons

Describing the cartoon

The cartoon consists of an illustration of … .
The illustration shows …
There is a caption under the cartoon, which is spoken by … .
There is a caption under the cartoon, which says "…".
In the (first) speech bubble it says "…".
The text in the speech bubble is spoken by …
The figure is a stereotype of …
The figure is a caricature of …
The drawing is detailed / clear / sketchy / abstract.

Talking about the point

The cartoonist is making fun of …
The cartoonist is satirizing …
The cartoonist is making the point that …
The cartoon is funny because of the misunderstanding between … .
The cartoon is funny because of the discrepancy between … .

Giving your opinion

I think / I don't think the cartoon is (very) funny because …
I get the joke. / I don't get the joke.
I get the point. / I don't get the point.
I think / I don't think the cartoon is easy to understand because …
I agree / I don't agree with the point the cartoonist is making because …

Talking about statistics

Useful words and phrases

To describe an increase
to rise • to increase • to have increased by • growth • an increase (in the number of …)

To describe a decrease
to decrease • to drop • to decline • a decrease • a decline • a drop (in the number of …)

Useful adjectives and adverbs
sharp(ly) • slow(ly) • steady/steadily • continuing/continual(ly) • gradual(ly) • significant(ly) • insignificant(ly) • negligible/negligibly • large • high • small

To express numbers & figures
the figures for the last year/the last month/etc. • the latest figures • the total number of … • a (significant/insignificant/etc.) number of … • a (high/etc.) percentage of … • the statistics • a majority/minority of …

Useful verbs
to show that … • to indicate that … • to suggest that … • to give information about … • to make it clear that

Types of graphs
graph • chart • pie chart • bar chart • diagram

Types of surveys
survey • opinion poll • questionnaire

Qualifiers
a total of • over • under • nearly • more/less than • between • the same number as • the same amount of • from over/under … to just over/under • half • a third • two thirds • a quarter • (25) per cent • twice as many • three times as many • on average • averagely • roughly • exactly • precisely

Having a discussion

- Use the phrases on p.132.
- Always be polite!
- Look at the people you are talking to but don't stare at them.
- Don't interrupt unless you feel it is really necessary.
- Listen carefully to what other people are saying.
- Keep to the point.
- Don't talk too much.

Leading a discussion
A discussion leader:
– introduces the discussion and the participants
- *(As you know,) our discussion today is about …*
- *On my right/left I have … (name of person or group), who is/are in favour of/against …*

– makes sure the discussion is held in an orderly way and that participants are always polite to each other.
– chooses whose turn it is to speak.
- *Who would like to open the discussion?*
- *… , would you like to open the discussion?*
- *The next person to speak is … , followed by … and then … .*

– makes sure everyone has an equal chance to speak, including people who are shy.
Is there anything you would like to say, …?
– makes sure no one person monopolizes the discussion.
- *I'm sorry to interrupt you, but I'm afraid you'll have to stop there.*
- *Sorry, but I must give the others a chance to put forward their arguments now.*

– makes sure that only one person is speaking at a time.
- *Please wait your turn, you'll have a chance to speak in a minute!*
- *If you'd just let … finish, please.*

– notes down the most important points and summarizes the discussion at the end.
- *Time is running out, so I'd like to sum up what we've been discussing.*
- *We heard from … that …*

– always remains neutral (i.e. doesn't give his/her own opinion).
– thanks everybody for taking part at the end.
- *Thank you for taking part in the discussion!*

Useful phrases for discussions

To make a suggestion:
Let's consider …
I suggest/propose that you/we …
I suggest/propose + (verb in -ing form)
What do you think about …?
If I were you, I would …

To respond to a suggestion:
That's a good idea!/Fine!
OK/Yes, why not?
OK, if you want, I don't really mind.
I think it would be a better idea to talk about/consider ….
Couldn't we look at this/do this another way? What about …?
I'm not sure (if that's such a good idea). How about …?

To ask for an opinion:
What do you think/feel about …?
What is your view/opinion on/about … ?
What would you say?

To give an opinion:
As far as I'm concerned …
I think/feel/believe/am of the opinion that …
To my mind …
In my opinion …/In my view …

To agree:
You are (quite/absolutely) right.
That's a very good point!
Absolutely!/Exactly!
I agree (with you/Susi/etc.).
You have a point.
You might/could be right.
I think you're right to a certain extent/up to a point.

To disagree:
I disagree (entirely/with some of the things you said/etc.)
I'm sorry, but I completely disagree.
Stop exaggerating!
I think you're oversimplifying things.
That's an interesting point, but …
That's not the point.
You've missed the point (entirely).

To interrupt someone:
Sorry to interrupt, but (could you please explain/repeat the point you just made).
Excuse me for interrupting, but (I don't understand what you just said).
Sorry for interrupting but (can I please say something/make a point?)

To deal with being interrupted:
Can I just finish what I was saying, please?
Just a second. I haven't quite finished.
Would you let me/allow me to make my point, please.
You could at least let me finish my sentence!

To change the subject:
There is something else that I'd like to say …
Have you ever thought of/considered …
On the other hand …
Try looking at things another way/from a different angle.
I'd like to bring up another point/point out something else.

To return to the original subject:
Lets get back to what we were saying/discussing.
Let's get back to the point.
As I was saying before, …
Getting back to what we/you/… said earlier …

To ask for further explanation:
Did I get that right?
Do you really mean that …?
Did I understand correctly that you think …?
Could you explain what you just said/the point you just made/etc. again, please?
Could you give me/us a concrete example, please?

To say that a point has been misunderstood:
I'm sorry, but …
… that's not what I meant to say (at all)!
… I think you've got the wrong end of the stick!
… you've got me (completely) wrong.
… you've (completely) misunderstood me.
… that's not what I was trying to say!
… I didn't make myself clear. I'll try and explain again.

Collecting words

Where to write new words

- On cards with the word in English on the front and the definition in English (and the German translation) on the back.
- In a vocabulary book: use a small ringbinder so that you can add pages and move pages around as necessary.
- On the computer.

Don't just write German translations to go with new English words. Always write an explanation or give a synonym or opposite in English!

Ways of collecting and organizing words

Be flexible: choose the method for collecting and organizing words which best suits your needs at a particular time!

- Alphabetically (A–Z): This is good as a reference system and you have plenty of space for definitions. You can find words easily, but you have to know what the word is in the first place. It is a good method to use in addition to the other methods listed below.
- By writing synonyms and opposites: Group together words with similar meanings, e.g. *pretty, nice, lovely,* or with their opposites, e.g. *pretty ≠ ugly*.
- In word families: When you note a new word, include the other words which can be formed from it, e.g. the verb, adjective, adverb, etc. Also make a note of the word with its prefix or suffix (see opposite). This is a good way of quickly increasing your word power!
- In collocations: Make a note of words which are often written together (verb + preposition, verb + noun, etc.) Always try to learn words with their collocations, e.g. *to make allowances, to break the news.*
- In semantic fields: Group words according to topics. Include nouns, adjectives, verbs, idioms, phrases, etc., e.g. *School: to attend, to be absent from, to play hockey; classroom, hall, staff room, gymnasium; etc.*
- In mind maps by topic (see p.121): Start with the topic heading and add all the words which come to mind in a logical way. This is a good way of collecting words on a particular theme, however you generally don't have much space in a mind map for definitions.

Prefixes

A prefix is added to the beginning of a word to change its meaning.

To give a word a **negative** or **opposite** (≠) meaning add:

Prefix	Example
in-	active ≠ ***in***active
im-	possible ≠ ***im***possible
il-	literate ≠ ***il***literate
ir-	relevant ≠ ***ir***elevant
un-	happy ≠ ***un***happy
dis-	to like ≠ to ***dis***like
de-	to stabilise ≠ to ***de***stabilise

To show an **increase** (+) or **decrease** (-):

Prefix	Example
over- (+)	to heat – ***over***heat
out- (+)	to grow – *to* ***out***grow
super- (++)	natural – ***super***natural
under- (–)	to pay – *to* ***under***pay
sub- (–)	standard – ***sub***standard

Others:

Prefix	Meaning	Example
inter-	between/among	***inter***national
pre-	before	***pre-***school
post-	after	***post-***war
trans-	across	***trans***atlantic
counter-	against	***counter***revolution
pro-	for	***pro-***abortion
anti-	against	***anti-***smoking
re-	again/back	***re***read
mis-	wrong/bad	*to* ***mis***understand

Suffixes

A suffix is added to the end of a word to give it a different meaning, usually to make a verb or adjective into a noun:

Suffix	Example
-ence	to differ – differ***ence***
-ment	to improve – improve***ment***
-ion/-ation/-ision	to nationalize – national***ization***
-er/-or	to teach – teach***er*** / to act – act***or***
-ing	to begin – beginn***ing***
-ness-	happy – happ***iness***
-(i)ty	difficult – difficul***ty***
-th	true – tru***th***

Surviving without a dictionary

The following techniques will help you to 'survive' without a dictionary, when you come across words you don't know:

- Always read a text once through without looking up any words. Try to understand the gist, i.e. the basic meaning of a text. You don't need to understand all the details at first and sometimes the gist alone is enough.
- See whether the words and sentences before and after the word (the context) can help you to understand it! Can you guess the meaning by the context? Or can you understand the sentence without needing to understand that particular word?
- Try to identify the word family. Part of the word may well be related to another English word which you already know. Look out for prefixes, suffixes and compounds, e.g. *disapproval* = *approve* + prefix & suffix.
- Many English words are of French or German origin, so think about whether there is a similar word in your own language or other foreign languages you know, e.g. discipline – *Disziplin*.
- Does the sound of the word help? Say the word out loud, e.g. "Ping!".

Using an English-English dictionary

A good English-English (monolingual) dictionary gives you much more information than just the meaning of a word. It will provide you with:

- the different forms of a word.
- the class of the word (noun, verb, adverb, etc.).
- the pronunciation (phonetics).
- the different meanings.
- grammatical information, e.g. if the word takes an object; whether a noun is countable; etc.
- examples showing how the word is used in context.
- the prepositions, etc. commonly used with the word.
- idioms, etc. in which the word is commonly used.

Tips for using an English-English dictionary

- Before looking up a word identify whether it is a verb, noun, adjective, adverb, etc.
- When you have found the entry for the word make sure you look at the meaning for the correct class of word.
- Read any examples and/or additional information which the dictionary gives you about the word.
- Take your time to read the entry carefully. Don't just look at the first entry or entries. Make sure you find the entry which matches the use of the word in the given context.

In the dictionary entry on p. 135 the following additional information is given in the extra column.

◆◆◆◇◇ = importance of a word. The more black squares, the more important the word is.
ADV = adverb
PHRASE = common phrase using the word
PRAGMATICS = a word is used in a particular way to show more than meaning There is a definition of when and how to use the word or phrase, the feeling created and an example.
ADV after v = the word is an adverb used with a particular verb. The adverb always comes after the verb in the sentence.
N-COUNT= word is a countable noun and must be used in the singular with a determiner (the/a/my/etc.).
INFORMAL = word or phrase is usually used in informal conversations, personal letters, etc.
ADJ: ADJ n = word is an adjective and must be used in front of the noun or noun phrase.
N-SING: prep *the* N = a singular noun which always has 'the' in front of it and has a preposition before it.
SPOKEN, BRITISH = used mainly in speech and mainly in Britain (not in America)
N-UNCOUNT = uncountable noun. Uncountable nouns do not have a plural form and always take verbs in the singular.
AMERICAN = used mainly in America (not in Britain)
VERB = word is a verb.
V *onto* n = word is a verb which takes the preposition *onto* followed by a noun.
V-ERG = verb which can be used with or without an object.
V n = verb followed by a noun.
COMB = combining form. Word is joined to another usually with a hyphen (-).
be V-ed = word is used in the passive.

Dictionary page

This dictionary entry was taken from *PONS Cobuild English Learner's Dictionary*, Klett number: 517922

back 1 adverb uses

back /bæk/. In addition to the uses shown below, **back** is also used in phrasal verbs such as 'date back' and 'fall back on'. ◆◆◆◆◆

1 If you move **back**, you move in the opposite direction to the one in which you are facing. *The photographers drew back... She stepped back from the door... She pushes back her chair and stands.* [ADV] **2** If someone moves **back and forth**, they repeatedly move in one direction and then in the opposite direction. *He paced back and forth. ...tossing a baseball back and forth.* [PHRASE]

3 If someone or something goes **back** somewhere, they return to the place where they were before. *I went back to bed... Smith changed his mind and moved back home... I'll be back as soon as I can.* [ADV] **4** If someone or something is **back** in a particular state, they were in that state before and are now in it again. *Denise hopes to be back at work by the time her daughter is one.* [ADV] **5** If you give or put something **back**, you return it to the person who had it or to the place where it was before you took it. If you get or take something **back**, you then have it again after not having it for a while. *She handed the knife back... Put it back in the freezer... You'll get your money back.* [ADV] **6** You can say that you go or come **back** to a particular point in a conversation to show that you are mentioning it again. *Going back to the school, how many staff are there?* [ADV, PRAGMATICS] **7** You use **back** in expressions like **back in London** or **back at the house** when you are giving an account, to show that you are going to start talking about what happened or was happening in the place you mention. *Meanwhile, back in New York, Sid was back to his old tricks.* [ADV, PRAGMATICS] **8** If something is or comes **back**, it is fashionable again after it has been unfashionable for some time. *Consensus politics could easily come back.* [ADV]

9 If you put a clock or watch **back**, you change the time shown on it so that it shows an earlier time. [ADV: ADV after v]

10 If you talk about something that happened **back** in the past or several years **back**, you are emphasizing that it happened quite a long time ago. *The story starts back in 1950, when I was five. ...that terrorist attack a few years back.* [ADV, PRAGMATICS] **11** If you think **back** to something that happened in the past, you remember it or try to remember it. *I thought back to the time in 1975 when my son was desperately ill.* • to **cast your mind back**: see **mind**. [ADV]

12 If you write or call **back**, you write to or telephone someone after they have written to or telephoned you. If you look **back** at someone, you look at them after they have started looking at you. *If the phone rings say you'll call back... Lee looked at Theodora. She stared back.* [ADV]

13 If someone or something is kept or situated **back** from a place, they are at a distance away from it. *Keep back from the edge of the platform.* [ADV] **14** If something is held or tied **back**, it is held or tied so that it does not hang loosely over something. *Her hair was tied back.* [ADV: ADV after v]

15 If you lie or sit **back**, you move your body backwards into a relaxed sloping or flat position. *She leaned back in her chair and smiled.* [ADV: ADV after v] **16** If you look or shout **back** at someone or something, you turn to look or shout at them when they are behind you. *Nick looked back over his shoulder... He called back to her.* [ADV]

back 2 opposite of front; noun and adjective uses

back /bæk/ **backs. 1** A person's or animal's **back** is the part of their body between their head and their legs that is on the opposite side to their chest. See picture headed **human body**. *She turned her back to the audience. ...the victims were shot in the back.* ◆◆◆◆◆ [N-COUNT]

2 If you say that something was done **behind** someone**'s back**, you disapprove of it because it was done without them knowing about it, in an unfair or dishonest way. *You eat her food, enjoy her hospitality and then criticize her behind her back.* [PHRASE, PRAGMATICS] **3** If you tell someone to **get off** your **back**, you are telling them angrily to stop criticizing you or putting pressure on you. [PHRASE, INFORMAL]

4 If you say that you will be glad **to see the back of** someone, you mean that you want them to leave. [PHRASE, INFORMAL] **5** If you **turn** your **back on** someone or something, you ignore them, leave them, or reject them. *Stacey Lattisaw has turned her back on her singing career.* [PHRASE] **6** If someone or something **puts** your **back up** or **gets** your **back up**, they annoy you. [PHRASE, INFORMAL]

7 If you **break the back of** a task or problem, you do the most difficult part of what is necessary to complete the task or solve the problem. *We've broken the back of inflation in this country.* [PHRASE]

8 The **back** of something is the side or part of it that is towards the rear or farthest from the front. *...a room at the back of the shop. ...the back of her neck... Her room was on the third floor, at the back.* [N-COUNT] **9 Back** is used to refer to the side or part of something that is towards the rear or farthest from the front. *...the back door. ...the back seat of their car. ...the back garden.* [ADJ: ADJ n] **10** You can use **back** in expressions such as **round the back** and **out the back** to refer generally to the area behind a house or other building. *He had chickens and things round the back.* [N-SING: prep the N, SPOKEN, BRITISH] **11** You use **back** in expressions such as **in the back** and **out back** to refer to the area behind a house or other building. You also use **in back** to refer to the rear part of something, especially a car or building. *He would be out back on the patio cleaning his shoes... I sat in back.* [N-UNCOUNT: prep N, AMERICAN] **12** If you are wearing something **back to front**, you are wearing it incorrectly, with the back of it at the front of your body. If you do or write something **back to front**, you do or write it the wrong way around. *He wears his baseball cap back to front... The picture was printed back to front.* [PHRASE]

13 The **back** of a chair or settee is the part that you lean against when you sit on it. [N-COUNT]

14 The **back** of a piece of paper or an envelope is the side which is less important. *...the back of a postcard.* [N-COUNT: the N]

15 The **back** of a book is the part nearest the end. *...the index at the back of the book.* [N-COUNT: the N]

16 In team games such as football and hockey, a **back** is a player who is concerned mainly with preventing the other team from scoring goals. [N-COUNT]

17 • **off the back of a lorry**: see **lorry**. • **to have your back to the wall**: see **wall**.

back 3 verb uses

back /bæk/ **backs, backing, backed. 1** If a building **backs** onto something, the back of it faces in the direction of that thing or touches the edge of that thing. *...a ground floor flat which backs on to a busy street.* ◆◆◆◆◆ [VERB: V onto n] **2** When you **back** a car or other vehicle somewhere or when it **backs** somewhere, it moves backwards. *He backed his car out of the drive... The train backed out of Adelaide Yard.* [V-ERG: V n, V] **3** If you **back** a person or a course of action, you support them, for example by voting for them. *...a new witness to back his claim that he is a victim of mistaken identity.* [VERB: V n] ♦ **-backed** *...government-backed loans to Egypt.* [COMB]

4 If you **back** someone in a competition, you predict that they will win, and usually you bet money that they will win. *It is upsetting to discover that you have backed a loser.* [VERB: V n] **5** If a singer **is backed** by a band or by other singers, they provide the musical accompaniment for the singer. [VERB: be V-ed] **6** See also **backing**.

Letter writing: Personal letters

A personal letter is a letter you write to someone you know well on a personal basis, e.g. a friend or relative. There are no special rules which you have to follow when you write to people you know well. The model letter below shows you what an informal letter generally looks like in English. You can use informal language in a personal letter, as if you were speaking to the person.

> *Oinkelstr. 1*
> *70183 Stuttgart*
> *Germany*
>
> *May 3, 200…*
>
> *Dear Frank,*
>
> *Just a few lines to let you know I'm still alive! Sorry for not having written for so long, but I've been very busy at college with exams.*
>
> *How are things with you? What are you doing for the summer? Unfortunately my applications for jobs in the States have all been turned down so far. Oh well, I'll keep trying…*
>
> *Please drop me a line when you have a minute. We really must keep in touch. Give my regards to your family.*
>
> *All the best,*
>
> *Thomas*
>
> *P.S. If I do get to the States, I'll let you know my address. Maybe we'll be able to meet up!*

Your address goes in the top right hand corner.

Write the date under the address.

Start the letter: *Dear + name,*

Use a capital letter for the first word.

Group your news, etc. in paragraphs.

Finish the letter with one of these phrases:
All the best,
Best wishes,
Bye for now,
Love,
Lots of love,

Salutations & complimentary closes

The salutation you choose in a formal letter (see p. 137) depends on whether you know a person's name, sex, etc. The complimentary close depends on the salutation you have used. Follow the guidelines below.

! Americans usually close formal letters with: *Sincerely yours* or *Yours truly*

Salutation	When used	Complimentary close
Dear Sir or Madam	to a company and when you don't know person's name or sex	*Yours faithfully*
Dear Madam	to a woman, when you don't know her name	*Yours faithfully*
Dear Sir	to a man, when you don't know his name	*Yours faithfully*
Dear Mr Brown	to a man, whose name you know	*Yours sincerely*
Dear Ms Brown	to a woman, whose name you know	*Yours sincerely*
Dear Jenny	to a person you know well	*Best wishes / Yours*

Salutation the way a person is addressed at the beginning of a letter

Complimentary close the phrase used before signing off

Letter writing: Formal letters & commercial correspondence

A **formal letter** can be a letter of application, a reservation, a request for information, etc.
Commercial correspondence refers to formal letters written in a business context, i.e. from one company to another.
There are different ways of layouting these types of letters. The model letter below is in 'block form', which is probably the best to use because it is accepted everywhere.
The parts in blue are only necessary in commercial correspondence.

! Punctuation: In 'block style' you don't use commas in the address, salutation or complimentary close.

Weltweit Services
Vinckestr. 1
70183 Stuttgart
Germany

Tel: 0711 768232
Fax: 0711 768233

→ Writer's address. In commercial correspondence you should include the company name, telephone and fax number.

Personnel Manager
Import Export
11270 White Blvd.
Los Angeles CA 91430
USA

→ Addressee, including name and position, if known.

Your ref:
Our ref: TW

→ In commercial correspondence include references. 'Our ref:' is usually the initials of the person who wrote the letter. (TW = Thomas Wagner)

11 January 2000

→ Date: The British write day, month, year (11.1.00). Americans write month, day, year (1.11.00). So it is best to write the date in full to avoid confusion.

Dear Sir or Madam

→ Salutation: See box on p. 136 for further details.

Re: Your advertisement in the Sun Times of April 28

→ In commercial correspondence include a subject line beginning 'Re:'

With reference to your advertisement in the Sun Times of April 28, I would like to apply for the position of bilingual buying assistant.

I am particularly interested in this job as I would very much like to gain work experience abroad. As well as speaking fluent English and Spanish, I have a working knowledge of French. My mother tongue is of course German.

I can supply references from former employers if you wish.

I enclose my curriculum vitae. Please do not hesitate to contact me if you should require further information.

→ Main part of letter, in which you state your reason for writing in formal, polite language. Group your points in paragraphs.

Yours faithfully

→ Complimentary close: See box on p. 136 for further details.

TWagner

→ Signature

Thomas Wagner

→ Name in full

Trainee buyer

→ In commercial correspondence: Writer's position in company.

Enc.

→ Enc. = Enclosures: indicates that additional material is being sent with the letter.

Writing a CV

CV is short for 'Curriculum Vitae'. There are no rules about how to write a CV in English. Use the following 'Dos and Don'ts' and the model CV below as a guide.

Dos and Don'ts

Do include skills and interests which are relevant to the job, if possible.
Do give the English equivalents of German terms, where possible.
Don't write more than one page.
Don't necessarily include a photo, unless asked to.
Don't use handwriting for your CV.
Don't sign your name at the end.

Curriculum Vitae

Name:	Thomas Wagner
Address:	Dinkelstr. 1, 70183 Stuttgart, Germany
Telephone:	++ 49 / 711/234567
E-mail:	t.wagner@e-mail.de
Date of birth:	6.5.1982
Nationality:	German
Schools:	1992–1998: Pfeiffer Comprehensive School *(Realschule)* 1998–2000: College of Languages, Stuttgart
Qualifications:	School leaving certificate *(Realschule) (1998)* Diploma in English & Spanish for bilingual secretaries (2000)
Work experience:	July 1999– September 1999: cashier at McDougall's, Stuttgart July 2000– September 2000: office assistant in the export department of Busch, Stuttgart
Further skills:	Fluent in English and Spanish, working knowledge of French Good computer skills (Word, Excel) Driving licence
Hobbies:	Tennis, member of local theatre group responsible for posters and advertising

References:

Mr Peter Meier, Export manager Busch, Jahnstraße 11 70023 Stuttgart	Ms Hannelore Schwarz, Personnel Manager McDougall's, Königstraße 128 70031 Stuttgart

Projects & group work

Finding information

Set up an 'information centre' in your classroom (or of your own) in which you keep a record of where to find information.

Find and keep a record of:

- the name, address, e-mail address, telephone and fax number of:
  - your local library.
  - the nearest university or college library.
  - your twin-town association (if your area has one).
  - the nearest newsagent or bookshop which stocks English newspapers and magazines. (Tip: Try your nearest main station.)
- the website addresses of:
  - search engines in America and the UK.
  - schools and colleges in America and the UK.
  - youth organizations in America and the UK.
  - political parties in America and the UK.
  - newspapers, magazines in America and the UK.
  - government agencies in America and the UK.
- the names of any members of your class who have contacts (penfriends, relatives, friends, etc.) in the English speaking world, and who might be willing to help you.
- the names of any members of your class or in your neighbourhood who have an English-speaking parent/parents and who might be willing to help you.

Collect brochures from travel agencies and tourist information bureaus.

Collect material while you are on holiday (leaflets, magazines, postcards, advertisements, menus, timetables, etc.).

Add information and addresses to your files whenever you find new material.

Projects in *Challenge 21*

1. Creating a poster (p. 19)
2. Producing a brochure (p. 35)
3. Making a promotional leaflet (p. 55)
4. Making a dossier (p. 68)
5. Making an information folder (p. 85)
6. Giving a talk (p. 105)
7. Having a panel discussion (p. 119)

Doing a project

How you go about doing a project will depend on the assignment. These tips are very general.

1. Read the information you are given about the assignment carefully.
2. In your groups, brainstorm to find ideas about:
   - what you all already know about the topic.
   - which aspects you want to concentrate on.
   - where you can find information.

   (See *skills file* on p. 121.)
3. If necessary, decide which points are more important (concentrate on these) and which are less important (and can possibly be left out).
4. Decide which tasks each member of the group are going to do. Make sure the workload is divided equally amongst you.
5. If not specified in the assignment, decide how you want to present your material. You can produce:
   - a talk using visual aids. (See *skills file* on p. 129.)
   - a video.
   - a cassette or CD.
   - a leaflet.
   - a brochure.
   - a file of written information.
   - a poster or wall chart.
   - a written report. (See *skills file* on p. 124.)
6. Remember to keep a record of your sources, i.e. where you found material, where quotes or extracts from original material are taken from, etc.

Useful websites (general information)

Search engines

www.altavista.digital.com
www.excite.com
www.lycos.com
www.yahoo.com
www.google.com

GB

www.searchuk.com (*Search engine for GB only*)
www.bta.org.uk (*British Tourist Association*)
www.britcoun.org (*British Council*)

USA

www.usia.gov (*US Information Agency*)
www.whitehouse.gov (*US Government*)
www.nytimes.com (*New York Times*)

Find more websites in the '*Check the web*' boxes in each chapter.

Questionnaires & surveys

Before doing a survey

It is important to have a clear idea of what kind of information you hope to get from your survey.

1. Write one or two sentences describing your topic and explaining why you are doing the survey. (Later you can include these sentences at the start of your questionnaire so that the people you ask (interviewees/participants) have a clear idea of what the survey is about.)
2. Briefly state what you expect the results of your survey to be – or give alternatives.
   I think the survey will show / prove that …
   The survey might prove that … . On the other hand, it might show that …
3. Decide how many people you want to interview and which social groups they should belong to. For example, is the age of participants important? Should they be male or female? Should they have a certain job or hobby?

The questionnaire

The success of a survey depends largely on how good your questions are. If possible, ask an independent person to answer your questions before you carry out the survey to make sure your questions are clear.

1. Decide what type of questions you want to ask.
   - Your choice of question type will depend on the type of information that you hope to get and on the amount of time that you want to spend on the survey.
   - The most common types of questions are described in the box opposite.
   - Your questions need not all be of the same type, but it is best not to include too many different types.
2. Always keep the aim of your survey in mind when you are formulating questions.
3. Word your questions clearly and concisely. Use formal language.
4. Don't ask too many questions (between 10 and 15 is usually enough).
5. Put your questions in a logical order.
   - Group questions relating to particular aspects together.
   - Start off with simpler, more general questions and then go on to more detailed questions.
   - Your last question can be an open-ended question giving interviewees the opportunity to give further information on the topic.

Types of questions

- **Multiple choice questions**

The interviewee chooses from one (or more) of a given set of answers.

Which of the following is not a US state?
a) Hawaii ❑
b) Texas ❑
c) Bangladesh ❑
d) North Dakota ❑

- **Yes/No questions**

Questions that can be answered 'Yes' or 'No'.

Do you exercise more than three times a week?
❑ *YES*
❑ *NO*

- **Graded questions**

The interviewee has to choose to what extent they agree/disagree with, do/don't do, like don't like, etc. the thing in question.

How often do you eat fruit and vegetables on average per day?
❑ *never*
❑ *less than three times*
❑ *more than three times*

- **Open-ended questions**

Questions to which the interviewees must give their own answer. These questions usually beginning with a question word: who, what, when, where, why or how.

How, in your opinion, could the recycling system in your area be improved?

____

____

- **Advantages (+) & disadvantages (–)**

  Multiple choice, yes/no and graded questions:
  + Can be answered quickly and easily. Are easy to evaluate.
  – Answers are not detailed or personal.

  Open-ended questions:
  + Answers are detailed, personal and individual.
  – Questions take much longer to answer. Answers are more difficult to evaluate.

File continued on next page.

Questionnaires & surveys (contd.)

Carrying out the survey

1. Don't try to make people take part in the survey or to answer particular questions if they don't want to. Participation should always be voluntary.

2. Explain to interviewees why you are doing the survey, who you will be presenting the results to and in what form you will be presenting them.

3. It is usually best to conduct anonymous surveys: that is, without keeping a record of the names of the people you interview. However, in order to evaluate the results it can be important to make a note of certain personal details, for example, age and sex. If you do need this information, explain why to the interviewee.

4. Explain exactly what interviewees are expected to do.
   - Be prepared to give more details if necessary.
   - Be prepared to explain what certain questions mean as the interviewee is doing the survey.

5. If you want to make an audio or visual recording of the interview (and especially if you want to use the recording in your presentation), ask participants for their permission.

6. Smile and always be polite!

Useful phrase for talking to interviewees:
- *Excuse me, I'm carrying out a survey on … for a school project. Would you be prepared to answer a few questions?*
- *It shouldn't take long.*
- *It should only take a few minutes.*
- *Don't hesitate to ask me if any of the questions are unclear.*
- *Ask if you're not sure what any of the questions mean, won't you?*
- *Thank you very much for your participation.*
- *Thank you very much for taking part in the survey.*

Analyzing and presenting results

1. Combine all your results on one sheet of paper.

2. Where possible, present your findings in graphic form using graphs, diagrams, pie charts, bar charts, etc. (See *skills files* on p. 131.)

3. Look for similarities and differences in the responses. Try to come to basic conclusions and explain why you think particular results were found.

4. Compare the results with the results that you predicted. If there are differences, think of reason(s) why you think this might have occurred.

Useful phrases for talking about the results of a survey:
- *The objective/aim/goal of our survey was to …*
- *In this survey we wanted to find out …*
- *(Approximately) one-fourth/one-third/20%/only two of the participants said …*
- *Our findings indicate that …*
- *A(n) (overwhelming/slight) majority/minority of the participants indicated that …*
- *The survey results prove/show/suggest that …*
- *As we expected, the survey showed …*
- *Surprisingly, …*
- *The results of the survey were completely different to the results we had expected.*
- *On the basis of these results, we have come to the conclusion that …*
- *As a result, …*
- *We are of the opinion that …*

Grammar files: *Table of tenses*

PAST ← NOW → FUTURE

FUTURE PERFECT	For future activities that are finished [1] before other future activities take place [2]. *The train will have gone [1] before you even get to the station [2].*	
FUTURE PERFECT PROGRESSIVE	To describe an action that has begun [1] or will begin [2] and that wil continue up to or beyond a future event [3]. *They will have been studying English for eight years [1/2] before they take the exam [3].*	
SIMPLE 'WILL' OR 'GOING TO' FUTURE	The 'will' future is used most often to predict events that will happen at a certain time in the future. *Tomorrow the weather will be fine.*	The 'going to' future is used most often for planned future events: *Tomorrow I'm going to go to the cinema.*
FUTURE PROGRESSIVE	To talk about future events that will be in progress [1] when another future event occurs [2]. *You will be sleeping [1] by the time I get home [2].*	
SIMPLE PRESENT	Used for sequences of present time events [1], general statements, habitual & everyday activities [2] and firmly scheduled future events [3].	[1] *When the bus stops, people get off first, then others get on.* [3] *The play opens in a month.* [2] *Hilary gets up at 7.30 every day.*
PRESENT PROGRESSIVE	Used for activities that start in the recent past, are still going on and will continue for a certain time [1]; and for scheduled future events instead of the 'going to' future [2].	[1] *James is cooking dinner.* [2] *They are coming here next Friday.*
SIMPLE PRESENT PERFECT	[1] *I've seen that film three times and I never want to see it again.* [2] *We've known them since 1998.*	Used for events that happened in the past but whose effects are relevant in the present [1]; and for events that began in the past and continue up to the present (and sometimes into the future) [2] especially with 'since' and 'for'.
PRESENT PERFECT PROGRESSIVE		For activities that began in the past and have been going on continuously since then and are still going on. *We've been looking for a camping site all day.*
SIMPLE PAST		For activities that took place at a certain time in the past [1] and/or that began and ended in the past [2]; often used to tell stories ("narrative past"). [1] *Columbus discovered America in 1492* [2] *Anne lived in America from 1997 to 1999.*
PAST PROGRESSIVE		For past activities which were going on [1a] when another past activity occurred [1b] or when several activities were in progress at the same time [2]. *They were watching TV [1a] when the phone rang [1b].* [2] *Anne was watching TV and Peter was reading the paper.*
PAST PERFECT		For a past activity [1] that occurred before another one in the past [2]. *The film had already started [1] when I arrived at the cinema [2].*
PAST PERFECT PROGRESSIVE		For activities in the more distant past that were in progress [1a] when another past activity occurred [1b] (see also past progressive). *Jill had been waiting for Nigel for an hour [1a] before he finally arrived [1b].*

single activity or event — activity which begins and ends at a particular time — activities that occur one after the other — activity which continues over a period of time — activity that has ended but has an effect on the present

How to form & how to use tenses

How to form	Examples of typical use
Simple present	
• he/she/it + s Add 's' to the infinitive in the third person singular (he/she/it): *he/she/it looks*. But *I/you/we/they look*. • Irregular verbs have to be learnt! • Form questions and negative sentences with do/does + infinitive: *How much do you spend on clothes?* *The government doesn't spend enough money on education.*	• *Humans need approximately eight hours of sleep a night.* (For facts and general statements) • *Does Jill always read in the evening?/Jack leaves the house at 7 am* (For everyday activities or habits.) • *The two knights fight, the Queen screams, and then the King saves her.* (For a set sequence of events or actions.) • *The play opens at the Monty Theatre in a month.* (For scheduled future events with an adverbial phrase of time.)
Present progressive	
• am/are/is + -ing (present participle) *I'm learning/you're reading/she's watching* • Form questions by inversion: *What are you doing?* • Form negatives by adding 'not': *They aren't coming.* • Some verbs are never used in the progressive form, especially many that express feelings or belief, e.g. *believe, love, hate, seem, have* (in the sense of own), *feel, notice, realize*.	• *Greg is cooking dinner (now)./We are building a house.* (For an activity that is going on right now and will continue for a certain limited or temporary period of time.) • *They are visiting us in three weeks.* (For planned future events with an adverbial phrase of time.)
Simple past	
• verb + -ed: Regular verbs add 'ed' to the infinitive: *look – looked.* • Irregular past forms have to be learnt! *go – went* • Form negatives and questions with did/didn't + infinitive: *Did you watch Big Brother on TV last night?* *We didn't go to the cinema on Saturday.* • With was/were: Form negative sentences by adding 'not' and form questions by inversion: *Karen wasn't very happy about her grades.* *Where were you last night?*	• *Columbus discovered America in 1492./They returned from the Canary Islands a week ago.* (For activities that began and ended at a specific time in the past.) • *As the train left the station, Helen looked around the compartment. There was no-one else in sight. She took out the letter and started to read.* (For a series of events in the past as in a story, often called the "narrative past".)
Past progressive	
• was/were + -ing (present participle) *They were playing football.* • Form negative sentences by adding 'not': *They weren't playing football.* • Form questions by inversion: *Were they playing football?*	• *They were cleaning the house when the guests arrived.* (For an activity in the past that was already in progress when something else happened.) • *While Patty was mowing the lawn, Sid was cleaning the windows.* (For several activities or events that were happening at the same time in the past.)

File continued on next page.

<table>
<tr><th>How to form</th><th>Examples of typical use</th></tr>
<tr><td colspan="2">Present perfect simple</td></tr>
<tr><td>

• has/have + past participle:
Monica has found her English book.
• Form the past participle of regular verbs by adding '-ed' to the infinitive:
play – played.
• Learn the past participles of irregular verbs!
• Form negative sentences by using 'hasn't/haven't':
Monica hasn't found her English book.
• Form questions by inversion:
What has Monica lost?

</td><td>

! With the present perfect simple the result of the action is usually more important than the action itself.
! Never use the present perfect with adverbs of past time, e.g. yesterday, <u>last</u> week, three years <u>ago</u>, in 1999.
• *They have moved to Stratford.*
(For activities that happened recently, and whose effects are still felt in the present.)
• *The test results have just arrived. / I have had good marks so far this year. / Have you ever been to Atlanta?*
(With certain adverbs: *just, so far, ever, never, recently.*)
• *I haven't eaten chocolate for three weeks! / I haven't seen Melanie since 1998.* (With 'for' and 'since', for activities that started in the past and are continuing.)

</td></tr>
<tr><td colspan="2">Present perfect progressive</td></tr>
<tr><td>

• have/has + been + -ing (present participle):
He has been looking for a job for three years now.
• Form negative statements by using 'hasn't/haven't':
You haven't been looking properly.
• Form questions by inversion:
Have you been looking properly?

</td><td>

! The present perfect progressive is used in much the same way as the present perfect simple, but the activity is more important than the result.
• *We have been looking for a camping site all day.*
(For activities that have been going on either continuously or at intervals up to the present, often with adverbials of time such as 'all day', 'for a week', etc.)
• *It's been raining.*
(With no mention of time, the activity has taken place very recently and the result is clearly visible.)

</td></tr>
<tr><td colspan="2">Past perfect simple</td></tr>
<tr><td>

• had + past participle:
He had found ...
• Form negative sentences with 'hadn't':
He hadn't found ...
• Form questions by inversion:
What had he found?

</td><td>

• *When we arrived at the station the train had already left.* (For an activity that happened before another activity in the past, showing the connection between the two activities.)
• *Jane admitted that she had forgotten to do her homework.* (In indirect speech, when the original statement is in the past or present perfect.)

</td></tr>
<tr><td colspan="2">Past perfect progressive</td></tr>
<tr><td>

• had been + -ing (present participle):
They had been working.
• Form negative sentences with 'hadn't':
They hadn't been working.
• Form questions by inversion:
What had they been doing?

</td><td>

! The past perfect progressive is used in much the same way as the past perfect simple, but the activity is more important than the result.
• *He was tired because he had been working so hard. / I saw her red eyes and knew immediately that she had been crying.*
(For a past activity that occurred before another and there is a direct relation to the activity that followed.)
• *He said that he had been working hard.*
(For indirect speech, when the original statement is in the present perfect progressive.)

</td></tr>
</table>

File continued on next page.

How to form	Examples of typical use
'Going to' future	
• am/are/is + going to + infinitive: *I'm going to buy the new Mad Dogs CD at the weekend.* • Form negative sentences with 'not': *Mark isn't going to buy the new Mad Dogs CD at the weekend.* • Form questions by inversion: *Are you going to buy the new Mad Dogs CD at the weekend?*	• *She is going to phone her friend this afternoon. / Bill says he's going to lose 2 kilos before summer.* (For planned events or intentions.)
Future simple ('will' future)	
• will/shall + infinitive: *It will rain tomorrow.* • Form negative sentences with 'won't': *It won't rain tomorrow.* • Form questions by inversion: *Will it rain tomorrow?*	! English 'will' = German 'werden/wird' German 'will' = English 'want/wants' • *You'll be a great movie star some day.* (For things that are likely to happen at a defined or undefined time in the future.} • *On Saturday there will be rain and snow for most of the day.* (For forecasts, such as the weather forecast.)
Future progressive	
• will + be + -ing (present participle): *They will be doing …* • Form negative sentences with 'won't': *They won't be doing …* • Form questions by inversion: *What will they be doing?*	• *You will be sleeping by the time I get home.* (For events – often planned – that will be going on at a certain time in the future when another event occurs.)
Future perfect simple	
• will + have + past participle: *Joanna will have finished.* • Form negative sentences with 'won't': *Joanna won't have finished.* • Form questions by inversion: *Will Joanna have finished?*	• *Joanna will have finished the college course by the time she is 18.* (For future activities that take place before other future activities to show a relation between the activities. The simple present is used for the other activities.)
Future perfect progressive	
• will + have been + -ing (present participle): *They will have been studying.* • Form negative sentences with 'won't': *They won't have been studying.* • Form questions by inversion: *Will they have been studying?*	• *They will have been studying English for eight years before they take the exam.* (Used in the same way as the future perfect simple but placing more emphasis on the activity.)

If-clauses

There are three main types of 'if-clauses' (or conditional sentences) in English. They are used in basically the same way as conditional sentences in German.

Type 1 – future situations (probable/possible)
- *If you study hard, you will pass the exam.*
  – If-clause: simple present
  – Main clause: will future
  German equivalent: *Wenn du fleißig lernst, wirst du die Prüfung bestehen.*
- *If you have studied hard, you will pass the exam.*
  – If-clause: present perfect
  – Main clause: will future
  German equivalent: *Wenn du fleißig gelernt hast, wirst du die Prüfung bestehen.*
- *If you study hard, you can pass the exam.*
  German equivalent: *Wenn du fleißig lernst, kannst du die Prüfung bestehen.*
- *If you study hard, you might pass the exam.*
  German equivalent: *Wenn du fleißig lernst, wirst du eventuell die Prüfung bestehen.*

Frequently made mistakes

! Don't use 'will' in the 'if-clause', except to express willingness, e.g.:
They can come to Britain if they'll work.
! Don't use 'would' in the 'if-clause' except when you are making a polite request, e.g.:
I would be grateful if you would do your homework in future.
! Be careful with commas:
If you start with the 'if-clause', use a comma.
Don't use a comma if you don't start with the 'if-clause'.

Type 2 – future situations (improbable / unlikely)
- *If you studied hard, you would pass the exam.*
  – If-clause: simple past
  – Main clause: conditional I (would + infinitive)
  German equivalent: *Wenn du fleißig lernen würdest, würdest du die Prüfung bestehen.*
- *If you studied hard, you could pass the exam.*
  German equivalent: *Wenn du fleißig lernen würdest, könntest du die Prüfung bestehen.*

Type 3 – past situations (unreal / impossible / hypothetical)
- *If you had studied hard, you would have passed the exam.*
  – If-clause: past perfect
  – Main clause: conditional II (would + have + past partiple)
  German equivalent: *Wenn du fleißig gelernt hättest, hättest du die Prüfung bestanden.*
- *If you had studied hard, you could have passed the exam.*
  German equivalent: *Wenn du fleißig gelernt hättest, hättest du die Prüfung bestehen können.*
- *If you had studied hard, you might have passed the exam.*
  German equivalent: *Wenn du fleißig gelernt hättest, hättest du eventuell die Prüfung bestehen können.*

Exceptions to the rules & further examples
- In general statements and for repeated activities or habits use the present tense in both clauses, e.g.:
  If plants don't get enough water, they die.
  If she has time, she goes running.
- For recommendations and advice use 'were' in the 'if-clause' and conditional I (would + infinitive) in the main clause, e.g.:
  If I were you, I would study a bit harder.
- 'If' can be left out when the order of the verb and subject are reversed, e.g.:
  Had I studied harder, I would have passed the exam.

The passive

The passive is often used when the action is more important that who or what performed it. The passive is frequently used in scientific and technical writing.

Forming the passive

The passive is formed using a form of 'to be' + past participle.

- **Simple present**
  am/is/are + past participle:
  The workers are always paid on the first of the month.
- **Present progressive**
  am/are/is + being + past participle:
  The offices are being decorated at the moment.
- **Present perfect**
  have/has been + past participle:
  The car hasn't been repaired since we bought it.
- **Past tense**
  was/were + past participle:
  The book was written by Thomas Wagner.
- **Past progressive**
  was/were + being + past participle:
  My computer was being repaired so I couldn't send an E-mail.
- **Future**
  will + be + past participle:
  Do you think he will be awarded the first prize?
- **Future perfect**
  will + have + been + past participle:
  Next time you come the number will have been changed.
- **Modal verbs in the passive**
  modal + be + past participle (for the present);
  He can be found at Millie's Restaurant every Friday.
  modal + have been + past participle (for the past):
  The essay should have been handed in on time!
- **The passive after verbs of saying, thinking, etc.**
  After passive forms of verbs of saying and thinking (*to say, to think, to report*, etc.) an infinitive construction is used:
  He is said to be lazy.
  (These kind of sentences are best translated using '*sollen*', an adverb like '*angeblich/vermutlich*' or '*man sagt, dass*'. E.g. *Er soll faul sein./Angeblich ist er faul./Man sagt, dass er faul sei.*

The agent

The 'agent' is the person who does an action or the thing that causes it. Passive sentences can be formed with or without an agent. The agent usually takes 'by', e.g.:

This book was published in 2000. (no agent)
This book was published by Ernst Klett Verlag in 2000.
(by + agent 'Ernst Klett Verlag')

Making passive sentences active

Examples

- Passive with agent
  The bill should have been paid by my wife yesterday.
- Active
  My wife should have paid the bill yesterday.
- Passive, no agent
- If no agent is mentioned, a suitable one must be found. You can often use '*someone*'.
  The bill should have been paid yesterday.
- Active
  Someone/my wife/you/etc. should have paid the bill yesterday.

Making active sentences passive

Examples

- Active
  My grandparents built this house in 1955.
- Passive with agent
  This house was built by my grandparents in 1955.
- Passive, no agent
  This house was built in 1955.

Summary of changes

Passive	⟷	**Active**
tense of 'to be'/modal	⟷	tense of main verb
by + agent	⟷	subject
no agent	⟷	s.o., s.th., etc.
subject	⟷	object

Relative Clauses

- A relative clause usually begins with a relative pronoun:
  who or whom, which, that, whose.
- Relative clauses are used to describe people or things.
- There are two kinds of relative clauses:
  defining relative clauses and non-defining relative clauses.

Defining relative clauses

- A defining relative clause is important for the meaning of the sentence. Without the relative clause the sentence would not make sense.
- Defining relative clauses are not set off from the rest of the sentence by commas.
- The pronoun 'that, which, who(m)' can be left out if the pronoun is the object of the relative clause. This type of relative clause is known as a 'contact clause'.
  - *The house that/which we live in is very old.*
    or
    The house we live in is very old.
  - *I am giving the job to the woman who I interviewed yesterday.*
    or
    I am giving the job to the woman I interviewed yesterday.
  - *This is the boy whose bike was stolen.*
- Prepositions usually come at the end of a defining relative clause in everyday English.
  - *This is the book (that) I have heard so much about.*
- In formal English, the preposition can be placed directly before the relative pronoun:
  - *This is the book about which I have heard so much.*

Non-defining relative clauses

- In non-defining relative clauses the information is additional descriptive information. The sentence is clear even without the relative clause.
- Non-defining relative clauses are set off from the rest of the sentence by commas.
  - *My grandmother, who will be 85 in December, has asked me to take over the family farm.*
- In everyday English, a preposition is placed within or at the end of the relative clause:
  - *My friend Janet , who I stayed with last summer, has just moved to Australia.*
- In formal English the preposition comes directly before the relative pronoun:
  - *My friend Janet, with whom I stayed last summer, has just moved to Australia.*

Adjectives

Using adjectives

Adjectives describe people and things (nouns):
the tall man – bright lights

Comparative and superlative forms

- Regular comparative and superlative forms are formed as follows:

cold	*colder*	*the coldest*
hot	*hotter*	*the hottest*
funny	*funnier*	*the funniest*
modern	*more modern*	*the most modern*
expensive	*more expensive*	*the most expensive*

- Remember the following irregular forms:

good	*better*	*the best*
much	*more*	*the most*
bad	*worse*	*the worst*
far	*further*	*the furthest*

Making comparisons

- Use 'more/-er than', 'not as … as' and 'as … as' to make comparisons:
  The blue car is newer than the red one.
  The red car is not as new as the blue one.
  The white car is as new as the blue one.
- Always use 'the' before a superlative:
  This is the hottest summer we've had in years.

Adjectives used as collective nouns

- 'the + adjective' can be used to refer to a particular group of people as a whole:
  We raised money for the blind.
  The very young and the very old are particularly at risk.

Participles as adjectives

- The present participle (-ing form) and past participle of verbs can often be used as adjectives:
  an interesting book • the finished product

Verbs followed by adjectives

- Verbs are usually followed by adverbs, however some verbs are followed by adjectives. The most common verbs which are followed by adjectives are:
  to be: Sally was tired. • to become: Anne became ill. • to feel: Thomas felt happy. • to get: The child got dirty. • to look: Mary looks sad. • to seem: Her new boyfriend seems very nice. • to smell: That smells good. • to sound: The new CD sounds good. • to taste: This cake tastes delicious.

Adverbs

Using adverbs

Adverbs describe actions (verbs):
He walked quickly.
She spoke slowly.
Adverbs are also used:
- before other adjectives.
  This is an extremely good essay.
- before other adverbs.
  The traffic was moving unbelievably slowly.
- before past participles.
  My name is wrongly spelt.

Forming adverbs

- Many adverbs are formed by adding '-ly/-ily' to an adjective:
  safe – safely • quick – quickly • real – really • happy – happily • reasonable – reasonably
- Remember the following irregular adverb forms:
  good – well
  fast – fast
  hard – hard

Some useful adverbs

- *always • usually • often • frequently • sometimes • seldom • rarely • never*
- *recently • soon • lately • in the past • in the future*
- *largely • for the most part • partly • probably • possibly • hardly*
- *definitely • obviously • clearly*
- *basically • consequently • as a result*
- *fairly + adjective • really + adjective • totally + adjective • quite + adjective*

Comparison of adverbs

- In most cases 'more' + adverb (+ than) is used for comparisons and 'the most' + adverb is used for superlatives.
  Anne speaks French more fluently than her brother.
  Alison speaks it the most fluently.
- Note these irregular comparative and superlative forms:
  well – better – the best
  badly – worse – the worst
  fast – faster – the fastest

Question tags

A question tag is added to the end of a sentence turning it into a question. In German you use expressions like "…, *nicht wahr?*" "…, *oder?*" in a similar way.

Statement (+)	**Tag (-)**
Dave knows Paul,	*doesn't he?*
It rained hard,	*didn't it?*
Jill will be at the party,	*won't she?*
Sheila has bought a new car,	*hasn't she?*
You can speak English,	*can't you?*

Statement (-)	**Tag (+)**
You don't know Stephanie,	*do you?*
Andrew didn't ring,	*did he?*
The students weren't listening,	*were they?*
You haven't got a coin,	*have you?*
We can't stop here,	*can we?*

- If the statement is positive, the question tag is negative.
- If the statement is negative, the question tag is positive.
- The subject of the verb is the same in the statement and the question tag. Proper names (e.g. Dave) become pronouns (e.g. he).
- If the statement is in the simple present or simple past tense, the question tag uses 'do/don't' or did/didn't'.
- If the statement uses an auxiliary verb (e.g. to be, to have, will, etc.) or a modal (e.g. can, must, etc.) use the modal or auxiliary in the same tense in the tag.

-ing forms

- The -ing form is used in the progressive tenses (present progressive, past progressive, etc. See pp. 142–145):
  Mary is playing the guitar. • The plane was flying at a height of 10,000 metres.
- The -ing form can be used as an adjective:
  the winning party • a growing child
- The -ing form is used after prepositions (in, about, at, etc.):
  You're very good at speaking English. • I'm very excited about going to America
- The -ing form is often used after these verbs: *like, hate, enjoy, love, mind, prefer.*
  I don't mind watching TV but I prefer reading and I also enjoy playing computer games.
- The -ing form can be used as a noun:
  Laughing is good for you. • Studying is very important.
- Some verbs have the construction 'verb + preposition + -ing form'. The most common are:
  to be afraid of • to look forward to • to feel like • to talk about • to insist on • to decide against • to think about/of • to succeed in • to apologize for. *I'm afraid of flying. / We are looking forward to meeting you.*
- The -ing form can be used to shorten clauses, often after a preposition, e.g. after, while, before, when, by.
  I was riding my bike to work when… → *While riding my bike to work…*
  … I saw a woman who was wearing a silly hat. → *… I saw a woman wearing a silly hat.*
  After we had been to the cinema we went home. → *After going to the cinema we went home.*
  Before you answer the questions reread the text. → *Before answering the questions reread the text.*
  Although I felt tired I couldn't sleep. → *Although feeling tired I couldn't sleep.*
- When the following expressions (underlined) are followed by a verb use the -ing form.
  There's no point in waiting any longer.
  It's not worth going to see the new James Bond film.
  A waste of money/time: It's a waste of time talking to you.
  to spend/waste time/money: He spent all his money playing fruit machines.

Reported Speech

- Reported speech (or indirect speech) is used to report what someone has said without quoting them.

Direct Speech	**Reported Speech**
Sally said: "I want to go home."	*Sally said that she wanted to go home.*

Changing direct speech to reported speech

- If the reporting verb is in the past tense (which it most commonly is) the tense of the reported speech changes:

simple present	simple past
"I walk the dog every day."	*Sally said (that) she walked the dog every day.*
present progressive	past progressive
"I am walking the dog."	*Sally told me that she was walking the dog.*
future	conditional
"I will walk the dog every day."	*Sally mentioned that she would walk the dog every day.*
simple past	past perfect
"I walked the dog last night."	*Sally answered that she had walked the dog the night before.*
past progressive	past perfect progressive or past progressive
"I was walking the dog."	*Sally said she had been walking / was walking the dog.*
simple present perfect	simple past perfect
"I have walked the dog today."	*Sally said that she had walked the dog that day.*
present perfect progressive	past perfect progressive
"I have been walking the dog."	*Sally replied that she had been walking the dog.*
past perfect	past perfect
"I had walked the dog."	*Sally said that she had walked the dog.*

- Questions follow the same tense changes as statements. Note the word order in reported speech:

"Where did you park the car?"	*The policeman asked the man where he had parked the car.*
"Is this your car?"	*The policeman asked the man whether it was his car.*

- For requests use ask + object + infinitive

"Could you take me to the movies?"	*Billy asked his brother to take him to the movies.*

- Imperatives become infinitives (with 'to') in reported speech:

"Hurry up!"	*Jenny told Michael to hurry up.*
"Don't shout like that!"	*Jenny told Michael not to shout that way.*

- For proposals use 'suggest + verb + -ing' or ' suggest that + pronoun + infinitive'.

"Let's go to the cinema."	*Alex suggested going to the cinema.*
	Alex suggested that we go to the cinema.

- Some adverbs of time and place also change in reported speech, for example:

now	*then*
here	*there*
today	*that day*
yesterday	*the day before / the previous day*
last year	*the year before / the previous year*
tomorrow	*the next day*

- If the reporting verb is in the present, present perfect or future tense, the tense stays the same

"Watching TV is bad for your eyes!"	*Mr Jones says that watching TV is bad for our eyes.*

- Statements involving truths and facts do not have to change:
  My teacher said: "Isaac Newton discovered the principles of gravity."
  My teacher said that Isaac Newton discovered the principles of gravity.

Reporting verbs

Use these verbs as reporting verbs. Add to the list as you come across new examples:

say • tell • know • think • learn • mention • claim • answer • reply • state (for written statements) • ask • want to know • wonder

Glossary: *abbreviation – non-fictional*

This glossary explains literary terms and terms which you need to understand when working with texts and completing tasks in English.

abbreviation short form of a word or phrase made by leaving out some of the letters or only using the first few letters of a word, e.g. 'Rd' is the abbreviation for 'Road'.

acronym short form of a phrase in which a new 'word' is made by using the first letters of the words in the phrase. For example, AIDS is an acronym for Acquired Immune Defiency Syndrome.

alliteration repetition of sounds, especially consonants, either at the beginning of each word in a group or on certain syllables within each of the words, e.g. 'seven singing sisters'.

antagonist the character who is opposed to or in conflict with the main character in a novel, play or story (protagonist).

antonym see glossary entry for 'opposite'.

assignment piece of work that you are given to do as part of your work or studies.

assonance repetition of the same or similar vowel sounds within stressed syllables of neighbouring words, e.g. 'on the dole with nowhere to go'.

atmosphere feeling or mood created by a writer. It may be gloomy or pleasant, peaceful or violent.

character person in a piece of fiction whose personality develops through action, description, language and way of speaking.

cliché description of a group of things or people in a way that has been done so often before that it is no longer interesting. See also glossary entry for 'stereotype'.

climax the moment in a text when the conflict is most intense.

comment short essay giving your opinion on a topic (usually about 200 words).

connotation additional meaning of a word beyond its dictionary definition(s).

curriculum vitae (CV) short formal written account of personal details, education, work experience, etc. usually sent with a letter when applying for a job. (See *Skills file* on p. 138.)

denotation actual meaning of a word as defined in a dictionary.

drama piece of fiction, also known as a play, usually written for performance on stage, in films or on TV. It is characterized by dialogue and stage directions. It may be written as poetry or prose.

essay piece of writing usually between 300–600 words.

euphemism stylistic device used to make something unpleasant sound nicer by expressing it in a more pleasant, less direct way, e.g. 'to pass away' is a euphemism of 'to die'.

exposition structural element at the beginning of a longer text, in which the main characters are introduced, the setting is described, and first indications of the atmosphere and tone are made.

falling action structural element of a fictional text. In this part of a text there is a clear reduction of suspense.

fictional not real, invented by an author.

figurative language words used in an abstract context rather than in their usual definition(s); used in metaphors, similes and symbols, e.g. 'girls are like cats'.

flashback interruption of the chronological order of a text in order to go back in time and show what happened earlier.

foreshadowing anticipating events that will occur later in the story.

formal language used to address people you don't know very closely. Formal style shows detachment and respect. Typical of it are the use of precise and often difficult vocabulary, full forms and frequently long, complex sentences.

genre type of text, e.g. poetry, drama and fiction, non-fiction.

hyperbole statement which is exaggerated for effect, e.g. 'The way he put his car keys on the desk indicated that he had a fleet of Cadillacs parked outside'.

informal language relaxed, personal and subjective communication. Typical of it are the use of fairly simple language, short forms, uncomplicated sentence patterns and fillers.

irony in its strictest sense, a statement expressing the opposite of what is really meant, whereby the reader is expected to realize the true meaning, e.g. saying: "What a lovely day!", when the weather is terrible.

literal meaning meaning of a word as defined in a dictionary.

literary devices see glossary entry for 'rhetorical devices'.

metaphor way of describing something by saying it is something else, e.g. journalists are vultures.

narrator the narrator is the person who tells a story in a novel or short story. The narrator is not identical with the author. If the story is written as if someone was telling it themselves, using the 'I' form, the narrator is a first-person narrator. The first-person narrator can only tell you what he/she does, thinks, and feels, so he/she always has a limited point of view. A third-person narrator is not a character in the story, but stands outside it. The story is told in the third person (he/she/they). The point of view of a third-person narrator can be limited or omniscient (unlimited).

non-fictional true to life; the writer refers only to real people and places and to events that do or did take place.

 enumeration – Aufzählung

note making writing down in short form information you are given from a written source.

note taking writing down in short form information you are given from a spoken source.

novel long and complex fictional story, written in prose.

opposite (also known as **antonym**) word or term which has roughly the opposite meaning of another word, e.g. soft ≠ hard.

parody fictional text which imitates the form or language of a well-known piece of writing.

personification technique of presenting animals, plants, objects, the forces of nature or abstract ideas as if they were human beings and possessed human qualities, e.g. "Atlanta was young for her years."

plot the arrangement of the events in a story as decided by the author.

point of view perspective or position from which the narrator presents the story to the reader. (See also glossary entry for 'narrator'.)

project a major assignment which usually involves some kind of research.

protagonist the main character in a novel, play or story.

quotation a quotation is a sentence or phrase taken word for word from another source. If you **quote** someone or quote from a text you use the exact words spoken or written, usually to support an argument.

pun play on words, e.g. 'The sole has no feet and therefore no soul, poor soul.'

report factual text written objectively describing a particular event or point.

rhetorical devices (also referred to as 'literary devices') use of language in a non-literal sense or in an unusual way. The following are all literary devices: alliteration, assonance, contrast, hyperbole, irony, metaphor, personification, rhetorical questions (questions to which an answer is not expected), simile, understatement (see glossary entries).
Rhetorical devices used in talks: key words can be repeated to stress/emphasize an idea; quotations and proverbs can be used to support a statement; rhetorical questions can be asked to keep the listeners' attention and get them thinking; personal pronouns (we/our/you) can be used to make the audience feel personally involved.

rising action structural element of a fictional text, marked by an increase in suspense and an intensifying of the conflict.

sarcasm bitter or aggressive remark used to express disapproval or mockery.

satire fictional text intended to criticize certain conditions, events or people by making them appear ridiculous.

science fiction literary genre in which fantastic adventures take place on Earth and on other planets, mostly in the future.

setting the place and time in which the action in a piece of writing occurs.

short story short fictional narrative which has a tight plot, and is limited in theme, setting, number of events and characters.

simile a simile describes someone or something as being like something else, e.g. she runs like a hare.

stage direction author's notes in a drama on how it is to be performed.

stanza group of lines in a poem. (Also known as a verse.)

stereotype a fixed set of general characteristics that people believe are typical of a particular group of people or things. (See also glossary entry for 'cliché'.)

style refers to the kind of language the writer employs.

suspense feeling of tension and expectation about what is about to happen in a book, play or film, etc.

symbol an object which stands not only for itself but for some abstract idea as well, e.g. the dove is often used as a symbol of peace.

synonym a word or term that means the same or nearly the same as another, e.g. clever/intelligent.

technical term word or phrase used in a special field of knowledge, e.g. word processor.

text form kind of text, e.g. comment, novel, report, manual.

text type classification of texts based on the writer's intentions, i.e. argumentation, description, exposition, instruction, narration.

tone writer's attitude towards his theme, character(s) and especially towards the reader, as reflected in the text. The tone can be serious or playful, humorous or solemn, arrogant or modest.

turning point structural element of a fictional text, marking a change in the conflict or suspense.

understatement statement that is deliberately weak, putting less emphasis or importance on s.th. than it deserves, often used in the form of irony.

utopia fictional text dealing with an ideal society, place or world.

A–Z : A – C (consistently)

The words explained in the annotations in this book are listed here in alphabetical order with their German meanings. The German meaning is given for the use of the English word in the given context. Some words appear in the book more than once. The page numbers refer to the first occurrence of the word.

A

abandoned (p. 102) verlassen
about to (p. 86) im Begriff
accountable to (p. 39) jdm gegenüber verantwortlich sein
accounting (p. 52) Buchführung, -haltung
Act (p. 36) Gesetz
to address a problem (p. 96) Problem angehen
adhesive (p. 8) Klebstoff
adverse (p. 102) ungünstig
affiliated [ə'fılıeıtıd] (p. 114) *hier:* angeschlossen – **affiliated to** (p. 89) nahe stehen
to afflict (p. 82) betrüben
agony ['ægənı] (p. 117) Qual
aid Hilfe
ain't *(slang: isn't)* (p. 120) ist nicht
aisle [aıl] (p. 101) Gang
alert (p. 61) Notalarm
all-embracing (p. 82) vereinnehmend
allotted (p. 67) *hier:* zugeteilt, zugewiesen
to make allowances (p. 49) berücksichtigen
alluring (p. 92) verführerisch
to amble (p. 50) schlendern
to amend (p. 87) ändern
angled (p. 28) schräg
appeal (p. 8) Berufung, Revision
application (p. 41) Bewerbung
appropriate (p. 51) passend, geeignet
to approve (p. 87) billigen, genehmigen
archery (p. 52) Bogenschießen
architecturally (p. 92) architektonisch
archive ['ɑ:kaıv] (p. 55) Archiv
armadillo (p. 81) Gürteltier
armed forces (p. 36) Streitkräfte
aside (p. 79) außer
to assume (p. 81) annehmen
astounded (p. 27) höchst erstaunt
at the top of their lungs (p. 110) so laut wie möglich
attachment (p. 81) *hier:* emotionale Bindung
to attribute [ə'trıbju:t] **to** (p. 13) zurückführen auf
auction ['ɔ:kʃn] Versteigerung
authority (p. 13) Behörde
to no avail (p. 60) vergebens, vergeblich
on average (p. 12) im Durchschnitt
avid (p. 45) begeistert
to raise awareness (p. 12) das Bewusstsein wecken
azalea [ə'zeılıə] (p. 92) Azalee

B

to turn one's back on (p. 12) ignorieren
to bag (p. 101) in Tüten verpacken
bald [bɒ:ld] (p. 73) kahl
bar chart Balkendiagramm
bass [beıs] (p. 44) Bass
to batter (p. 77) *hier:* schlagen
to beat s.o. to a pulp (p. 107) jdn brutal zusammenschlagen
beehive (p. 94) Bienenstock
benign [bı'naın] (p. 26) gütig, freundlich
to bet (p. 86) wetten
bewilderingly (p. 73) verwirrend
to bicker (p. 111) sich zanken
Bill (p. 36) Gesetzentwurf
Bill of Rights (p. 86) US Grundgesetz
biscuit (p. 26) Keks
Go to blazes! (p. 50) Scher' dich zum Teufel!
blow (p. 50) Schlag
to feel blue *(informal)* (p. 84) traurig sein
boarding school (p. 43) Internat – **full boarding** (p. 52) Internat, in dem Schüler auch an Wochenenden bleiben – **weekly boarding** (p. 52) Internat, in dem Schüler an Wochenenden nach Hause gehen
to boast [əʊ] (p. 94) prahlen, angeben
bok choy (p. 101) asiatisches Gemüse
boom (p. 61) *hier:* Donner, Knall
to be given the boot *(informal)* (p. 72) rausgeschmissen werden
botanical (p. 93) botanisch
to bother (p. 13) *hier:* sich Sorgen machen
to be bound up with (p. 81) verbunden/verknüpft sein mit
to brag *(negative)* (p. 94) prahlen, angeben
branch (p. 86) Teil
brand new (p. 120) nagelneu
to breach (p. 118) durchbrechen
to break the news (p. 31) jdm etwas sagen
bridal shop (p. 102) Brautmodegeschäft
to bring up (p. 17) *hier:* großziehen
brochure Broschüre, Prospekt
BSc/BA Degree (Bachelor of Science /Arts) (p. 41) akademischer Grad, Diplom
BTEC (p. 41) Diplom in Betriebswirtschaft, Naturwissenschaft und Technologie
bud (p. 92) Knospe
bunch (p. 96) Menge, Gruppe
burst (of applause) (p. 50) *hier:* Beifallsturm
bustling ['bʌslıŋ] (p. 92) belebt, voller Leben

C

cabbage (p. 101) Kohl
capable ['keıpəbl] (p. 46) fähig, kompetent
carcass (p. 64) Kadaver
on the cards (p. 58) zu erwarten
to caress [kə'res] (p. 110) streicheln, liebkosen
carrier (p. 94) *hier:* Flugzeug
to carry out research (p. 44) Forschung anstellen
case study (p. 41) Fallstudie
to cast (p. 89) (ab)geben
casual (p. 13) *hier:* zwanglos, flüchtig
caution ['kɔ:ʃn] (p. 11) Verwarnung – **cautious** ['kɔ:ʃəs] (p. 24) vorsichtig
cavalier (p. 96) unbekümmert
to cede s.th. *(formal)* (p. 104) etw. abtreten
glass ceiling *(fig.)* (p. 24) unsichtbares Hindernis gegen das berufliche Weiterkommen
census (p. 102) Volkszählung
centipede (p. 81) Tausendfüßler
cereal ['sıərıəl] (p. 101) Frühstücksflocken
ceremonial (p. 36) zeremoniell
chairman (p. 98) Vorsitzende(r)
chandelier [ˌʃændə'lıə] (p. 110) Kronleuchter
to change tack (p. 30) die Methode ändern
to charge (p. 30) berechnen
charity (p. 44) Wohltätigkeitsverein
charlady (= charwoman) (p. 66) Reinmachefrau, Zugehfrau
cheeky (p. 16) frech, dreist
Cherokees (p. 104) nordamerikanischer Indianerstamm
chestnut ['tʃesnʌt] (p. 92) Kastanie
chores [tʃɒ:z] (p. 67) (tägliche) Pflichten/Arbeiten
chronic ['krɒnık] (p. 26) scheußlich, schlecht
chunk (p. 96) Batzen, Brocken
citadel *(here: fig.)* (p. 48) Hochburg, Bastion
claw (p. 64) Klaue
to clear the way (p. 77) *hier:* etwas möglich machen
clustered (p. 81) gedrängt
to coast (p. 72) *hier:* hinunterfahren
coffee shop (p. 111) Café
collar (p. 8) Halsband
colonnaded (p. 92) von Säulen getragen
to combat (p. 48) kämpfen
comedic [kə'mi:dık] (p. 112) komisch
when it comes to *(informal)* (p. 11) bezüglich
to commandeer [ˌkɒmən'dıə] (p. 72) beschlagnahmen
commerical station (p. 114) kommerzieller Sender
to commission (p. 13) beauftragen
commitment (p. 36) Versprechen, Verpflichtung
to compel s.o. (p. 26) jdn zwingen
competing (p. 114) konkurrierend
compulsory (p. 38) Pflicht-
to conceive (p. 72) sich denken, sich vorstellen – (p. 93) *hier:* planen
to condemn [kən'dem] (p. 104) verurteilen, verdammen
conditioning (p. 48) Konditionierung
condo *(AE)* (p. 73) Eigentumswohnung
to conduct [kən'dʌkt] (p. 13) durchführen
to confer *(formal)* (p. 94) verleihen
confidence (p. 48) Vertrauen
to confirm (p. 92) *hier:* übereinstimmen
congested (p. 79) überbevölkert
Congress (US) (p. 112) *s. S. 88* – **congressional** (US) (p. 79) Kongress- *(s. S. 88)*
to conk *(informal)* (p. 26) hauen
conservatory (p. 93) Wintergarten
to conserve (p. 97) erhalten
consistently (p. 92) durchweg

constituency (p. 36) Wahlkreis
constitution (p. 36) Verfassung
consumer (p. 110) Verbraucher
continuity [ˌkɒntɪˈnjʊɪtɪ] (p. 87) Kontinuität
to contract [ˈkɒntrækt] (p. 13) sich eine Krankheit zuziehen
control (truck) (p. 117) Sendewagen
convention (p. 36) Abkommen – (p. 86) Versammlung, Konferenz, Tagung
to converge (p. 82) sich einander annähren, zusammenlaufen
to cook tea *(BE)* (p. 15) Abendessen machen
cookoff *(AE)* (p. 92) Kochwettbewerb
coronation (p. 94) Krönung
couch potato *(slang)* (p. 117) jmd, der viel fernsieht
coup [ku:] (p. 94) Coup
to crackle (p. 60) knacken, knistern
to cram (p. 66) hineinstopfen
crew-cut (p. 81) Bürstenschnitt
crucial [ˈkru:ʃl] (p. 79) äußerst wichtig
crude (p. 104) roh, rau
to crumble (p. 82) zerfallen
crumpet (p. 26) süßes, pfannkuchenartiges Gebäck
to crumple (p. 72) zusammendrücken
cul-de-sac [ˈkʌldɪˌsæk] (p. 98) Sackgasse
culinary [ʌ] (p. 92) kulinarisch
cure (p. 120) Heilmittel
curfew (p. 77) Ausgangssperre
curiosity [ˌkjʊərɪˈɒsətɪ] (p. 103) Neugier
curriculum Lehrplan – **national curriculum** (p. 48) zentraler Lehrplan

D

dash (p. 92) Schwung, Elan
dead (p. 19) *hier:* ernsthaft
(to meet a) deadline (p. 44) Termin/Frist (einhalten)
to decline (p. 13) sich weigern
defiantly [dɪˈfaɪəntlɪ] (p. 28) starrköpfig
degree (p. 41) akademischer Grad – **to the tiniest degree** (p. 26) bis ins Kleinste
to delay (p. 36) aufschieben
demanding (p. 24) anspruchsvoll
demise [dɪˈmaɪz] *(formal)* (p. 79) Ende
to deny (p. 8) abstreiten
to deplore (p. 82) missbilligen
depot [ˈdepəʊ] (p. 104) Lager(haus), Depot
designation (p. 94) Bezeichnung
desperate [ˈdesprət] (p. 50) hoffnungslos
destiny (p. 93) Schicksal, Vorsehung
to deteriorate (p. 60) sich verschlechtern – **deterioration** (p. 73) Veschlechterung
devastated (p. 77) zerstört
devolution (p. 37) Dezentralisierung; Übertragung politischer Macht von einer Zentralregierung auf die Regionen
devoted (p. 28) *hier:* gewidmet
diary [ˈdaɪrɪ] Tagebuch; (Termin-)Kalender
to differentiate (p. 28) unterscheiden
dignitary *(formal)* (p. 94) Würdenträger
dignity (p. 103) Würde
directory Verzeichnis
dire [ˈdaɪə] (p. 28) schlimm
discursive (p. 44) *hier:* (logisch) folgernd (*sonst:* weitschweifig)
to dismantle (p. 26) auseinander nehmen
to dismiss (p. 8) entlassen
to dispense with (p. 92) *hier:* verzichten auf
disproportionate (p. 38) in keinem Verhältnis (zu etw.) stehen
disreputable (p. 73) in Verruf gekommen
distaste (p. 103) Abneigung
distinctiveness (p. 82) Verschiedenheit
distraught [dɪsˈtrɔ:t] (p. 61) außer sich
distress alert (p. 61) Notalarm
disturbance [dɪˈstɜ:bns] (p. 7) Störung,
to ditch *(coll.)* (p. 61) notlanden
to be diverted (p. 61) umgeleitet werden
dogwood (p. 92) Hornstrauch
dominant (p. 94) beherrschend
donation (p. 114) Spende
to let s.o. down (p. 16) jdn enttäuschen
downpour [ˈ--] (p. 77) Platzregen, Wolkenbruch
to drawl (p. 82) mit langgezogenen Vokalen sprechen
dreaded (p. 86) gefürchtet
to dress down (p. 12) zwanglose Kleidung tragen – **to dress up** (p. 12) *hier:* offizielle Kleidung tragen (*sonst:* sich verkleiden)
to drive (p. 104) *hier:* hineintreiben
drizzly [ˈdrɪzlɪ] (p. 26) nieselregnerisch
to drone (p. 60) brummen
due (p. 72) *hier:* direkt – **to pay one's dues** (p. 64) seinen Verpflichtungen nachkommen
Duke of Edinburgh's Award *(GB)* (p. 52) Freizeitprogramm für junge Leute zwischen 14 und 25
dumb [dʌm] (p. 50) sprachlos, stumm
to dump (p. 60) abladen, ablassen
dynamism [ˈdaɪ] (p. 92) Dynamik

E

eagerly [ˈi:gəlɪ] (p. 94) gespannt
earshot (p. 73) Hörweite
at ease (p. 13) locker, gelassen
eaves (p. 73) *hier:* Ecken
edgy *(informal)* (p. 82) unsicher
to edit s.th. (p. 117) bearbeiten
editor Herausgeber(-in) – **letter to the editor** Leserbrief – **editorial** redaktionell
eel (p. 101) Aal
in effect (p. 77) in Kraft sein
egret (p. 81) Wasservogel der Reiherfamilie
to embrace (p. 93) *hier:* willkommen heißen
emergence (p. 82) *hier:* Entwicklung
to encourage s.o. to do s.th. (p. 49) jdn ermuntern, etwas zu tun
to endorse (p. 11) bestätigen, bekräftigen
engaged (p. 82) angestellt
enigma [ɪˈnɪgmə] (p. 26) Rätsel
enlightened (p. 26) aufgeklärt, fortschrittlich
entire [ɪnˈtaɪə] (p. 110) ganz, vollständig
entrepreneur (p. 102) Unternehmer
epic (p. 72) gewaltig, riesig
to erode (p. 13) (langsam) untergraben, *hier:* verändern
erroneous(ly) [ɪˈrəʊnɪəslɪ] (p. 13) irrtümlicherweise
to eschew [ɪsˈtʃu:] *(formal)* (p. 24) vermeiden
estate agent (p. 13) Immobilienmakler
estimate (p. 79) Schätzung
evidence (p. 44) Beweis
evocative (p. 92) sinnträchtig, beziehungsreich
to evoke (p. 92) heraufbeschwören; wachrufen
executive search firm (p. 96) Headhunterfirma
extent (p. 48) Ausmaß
exuberance [ɪgˈzju:bərəns] (p. 92) Überschwänglichkeit
EZ-OFF EZ-ON [i:z] (p. 73) (EZ = easy) verkehrsgünstig

F

facility (p. 41) Einrichtung
to fade [feɪd] (p. 12) nachlassen, schwinden
familiar (p. 48) bekannt
to fan (p. 103) fächern
fancy dress (p. 12) (Masken-) Kostüm
to fare (p. 103) ergehen
fate [feɪt] (p. 118) Schicksal
featured (p. 81) auftauchen
federal (p. 86) Bundes- – **federal aid** (p. 77) staatliche Hilfe
fee-charging (p. 43) gebührenpflichtig
to feed off *(informal)* (p. 24) essen
feeder road (p. 72) Zubringerstraße
to feel blue *(informal)* (p. 84) traurig sein
to fell (p. 96) fällen, schlagen
fence Zaun – **picket fence** (p. 73) Bretterzaun, Lattenzaun
fencing (p. 52) Fechten
fête [feɪt] (p. 26) (Wohltätigkeits-) Fest
to figure largely (p. 93) ein wichtiger Aspekt sein
file Aktenordner – **to file** (p. 44) Akten ablegen
firmly (p. 51) fest, bestimmt
First Amendment (p. 112) Teil der US Verfassung: Recht auf Redefreiheit
first and foremost (p. 94) vor allem
fives *(GB)* (p. 52) Ballspiel
fixture (p. 110) zum Inventar gehörend
flexitime Gleitzeit
to flock (p. 79) in Scharen gehen
to focus on (p. 49) sich auf etw. konzentrieren
fondness (p. 81) Vorliebe
forecaster (p. 24) jmd, der (wissenschaftlich) Entwicklungen untersucht und voraussagt
to foreclose (p. 73) (an-)kündigen
form *(BE)* (p. 51) Klasse
foundation [faʊnˈdeɪʃn] (p. 114) Stiftung
fragrant [ˈfreɪgrənt] (p. 92) duftend
frankness (p. 28) Ehrlichkeit
frantic (p. 110) wild, mitreißend
freakish (p. 58) verrückt
to frown (p. 27) die Stirne runzeln
to fuel (p. 94) *hier:* steigern, größer werden
funding (p. 43) finanzielle Förderung
fundraising (p. 12) Geldbeschaffung (für einen guten Zweck)

G

Ga. 400 (p. 102) Autobahn in Georgia
to run the gamut (p. 93) die ganze Palette anbieten
gateway (p. 93) Eingang, Tor

GCSE (General Certificate of Secondary Education) (p. 44) Schulabschluss ähnlich der Mittleren Reife
gem [dʒem] (p. 94) Juwel; *hier:* Prachtexemplar
gender (p. 24) Geschlecht
General Elections (p. 36) Parlamentswahlen
Generation X (p. 96) Ausdruck für zynische und selbstsüchtige junge Leute zwischen 15 und 35, die Autoritäten in Frage stellen
gentility (p. 92) Höflichkeit
to get on with (p. 44) sich gut verstehen
gig (p. 44) *hier:* Konzert
ginger ['dʒɪndʒə] (p. 101) Ingwer
to give s.o. a drubbing *(informal)* (p. 27) jdm eine Tracht Prügel verpassen
to give s.th. a thumbs up/down *(informal)* (p. 87) etwas genehmigen/etwas ablehnen
given the boot *(informal)* (p. 72) rausgeschmissen
glance (p. 101) Blick
glimpse (p. 79) *hier:* Eindruck
glittering (p. 92) glitzernd
glue (p. 8) Klebstoff
GNVQ (General National Vocational Qualification) (p. 41) Berufsschulabschluss
gonorrhoea [ˌgɒnə'ri:ə] (p. 12) Gonorrhöe, Tripper
Good Friday (p. 39) Karfreitag
good ol' boys *(AE; informal)* (p. 81) junge männliche Einwohner; Kumpel
gore [gɔ:] (p. 64) (geronnenes) Blut
gorgeous ['gɔ:dʒəs] (p. 93) herrlich
to grace (p. 94) ehren
graciousness ['greɪʃəsnəs] *(formal)* (p. 92) Höflichkeit
to graduate (p. 86) Abschlussprüfung bestehen
grass roots (p. 89) (Partei-)Basis
grave [greɪv] (p. 50) ernst
grimy ['graɪmɪ] (p. 28) schmutzig
groan (p. 60) Ächzen, Stöhnen
grocery store (p. 101) Lebensmittelgeschäft
on grounds that (p. 8) wegen
to guess (p. 87) annehmen, schätzen
guidance (p. 41) Anleitung
gunrack (p. 81) Gewehrhalterung
gust (p. 77) (Wind-)Böe

H

hack *(coll.)* (p. 64) Schreiberling
hairdo ['hɛəˌdu:] (p. 8) Frisur
to split hairs (p. 27) Haarspalterei betreiben
half a crown *(GB, old)* (p. 51) alte britische Münze, im Wert von zwölfeinhalb Pence
to hammer (p. 13) *hier:* einhämmern, einbleuen
handcuffed (p. 118) mit Handschellen an gefesselt
to handle (p. 94) *hier:* abfertigen
hap *(old)* (p. 72) Glück
hard and fast (p. 13) bindend, verbindlich
to hatch (p. 104) ausbrüten
haunt [hɔ:nt] (p. 120) dauernd verfolgen
hazard Gefahr – **safety hazard** (p. 8) Gefahr für die eigene Sicherheit
headstrong (p. 104) eigensinnig, dickköpfig
heart's-ease *(AE)* (p. 73) Sorgenfreiheit
hereditary (p. 36) erblich, Erb-
hero (p. 26) Held
to hiss (p. 16) zischen
to hitch (p. 72) *hier:* befestigen
honeysuckle (p. 92) Geißblatt
to hoover *(BE)* (p. 15) staubsaugen
hospitality (p. 82) Gastfreundschaft/Gastfreundlichkeit
to hold an event (p. 91) Ereignis/Veranstaltung ausrichten
to host (p. 91) Gastgeber sein, Ereignis ausrichten
hostility (p. 81) Widerstand
hub (p. 92) Zentrum, Mittelpunkt
hush (p. 50) (plötzliche) Stille
to hustle *(informal)* (p. 94) sich ins Zeug legen
hype [haɪp] (p. 13) Hysterie

I

idiosyncratic [ˌɪdɪəʊsɪŋ'krætɪk] (p. 27) eigentümlich
to idle (p. 72) langsam fahren, bummeln
IHOP (p. 102) Pfannkuchenrestaurant
impetuous (p. 104) ungestürm, stürmisch
implication (p. 13) Bedeutung – **to imply** (p. 110) andeuten
inauguration (p. 89) Amtseinführung
incentive (p. 96) Anreiz
in-depth (p. 44) eingehend, gründlich
industrial tribunal (p. 8) Arbeitsgericht
inexorable (p. 82) unerbittlich
to infuriate (p. 67) zur Raserei bringen
innovation [ɪnə'veɪʃn] (p. 91) Neuerung
innovative ['ɪnəvəˌtɪv] (p. 92) originell, neu
insight (p. 44) Einblick
to insist on (p. 13) bestehen auf
instantly (p. 50) sofort
to institute *(formal)* (p. 94) einrichten
interaction (p. 98) Zusammenarbeit
intermediate (p. 94) Zwischen-, Mittel-
interstate (p. 72) US Autobahn
to intervene (p. 117) einschreiten
intractable (p. 27) hartnäckig
to involve (p. 44) *hier:* einschließen
irrespective (p. 49) unabhängig von, ungeachtet
Isle of Dogs (p. 66) Insel in der Themse; neue Adresse vieler führender Zeitungen

J

to jam (p. 11) blockieren
jeopardy ['dʒepədɪ] (p. 60) (Lebens-) Gefahr
Jerry *(BE)* (p. 27) britischer Spitzname für die Deutschen im 2. Weltkrieg
jigsaw (p. 48) Puzzle
joint *(AE, informal)* (p. 81) Restaurant
jolly well *(BE, old)* (p. 50) einfach, ebenso
to jostle (p. 72) *hier:* konkurrieren
judicial [dʒu:'dɪʃl] (p. 86) rechtssprechend
judiciary [dʒu:'dɪʃərɪ] (p. 36) Rechtswesen
to juggle (p. 24) jonglieren
junction (p. 93) Kreuzung

K

KFC (Kentucky Fried Chicken) (p. 102) Fast-Food-Kette
kin (p. 84) Familie; Verwandte(r)
to knock out (p. 77) *hier:* lahmlegen

L

to lack sophistication (p. 81) niveaulos/einfach sein
lacrosse [lə'krɒs] (p. 52) ein Feldspiel
lame [eɪ] (p. 96) *hier:* schwach
to lament *(formal)* (p. 111) beklagen
to lash (p. 77) *hier:* peitschen (gegen)
league [li:g] (p. 92) Liga
to leap (leaped/leapt) to life (p. 104) ins Leben springen
leech (p. 64) Blutegel, Blutsauger *(fig.)*
legacy (p. 93) Erbe
to go legal (p. 73) *hier:* sich an die Geschwindigkeitsbegrenzung halten
legislation (p. 39) Gesetzgebung
to lend (p. 81) *hier:* geben (*sonst:* ausleihen)
to let s.o. down (p. 16) jdn enttäuschen
levee (p. 77) Damm
to license (*BE* **to licence**) (p. 112) eine Lizenz/Konzession vergeben an
lid (p. 16) Deckel
loads of *(informal)* (p. 16) massenhaft
to log (p. 49) Buch führen, eintragen
to loom (p. 61) bedrohlich näherrücken
loop (p. 72) Schlaufe
low-density (p. 98) geringe Dichte
to lumber (p. 73) trampeln; stolpern

M

to make it up (p. 18) wieder gutmachen (nach einer Auseinandersetzung)
manacled ['mænəkld] (p. 117) gefesselt
to manage (p. 97) verwalten, organisieren
marital (p. 24) ehelich
Marmite *(Markenname)* (p. 26) salziger Brotaufstrich (Hefeextrakt)
to match (p. 48) *hier:* sich messen können; (p. 111) ähnlich sein, entsprechen
mature [mə'tjʊə] (p. 41) erwachsen, reif
median strip *(AE)* (p. 72) Mittelstreifen
medical geographer ['medɪkl dʒɪ'ɒgrəfə] (p. 12) Epidemiologe
merchant (p. 102) Kaufmann
merit (p. 51) *hier:* Leistung
metropolitan (p. 92) hauptstädtisch, weltstädtisch
mighty *(informal)* (p. 104) extrem
mob (p. 50) Mob
moccasined (p. 104) Mokassins tragend
mock exam (p. 15) Probearbeit, Probeexamen
to monitor (p. 49) überwachen
moor (p. 28) (Hoch-) Moor
moth [mɒθ] Motte – **moth-eaten** (p. 72) *hier:* schäbige Kleidung tragend
motorcade ['--ˌkeɪd] (p. 94) Fahrzeug-, Wagenkolonne
to mould (p. 8) formen

mown [məʊn] (p. 73) gemäht
mutha *(vulgar, negative)* (p. 118) (mother) Dummkopf
mutual (p. 39) gegenseitig

N

native (p. 81) gebürtig
naval Marin- – **naval hero** (p. 26) Anspielung auf Horatio Nelson, der in der Seeschlacht bei Trafalgar starb (1805)
New Deal (p. 81) wirtschaftliches und soziales Reformprogramm von F. D. Roosevelt (1933–1941)
nitrogen dioxide ['naɪtrədʒən daɪ'ɒksaɪd] (p. 30) Stickstoffdioxyd
not on the end of a barge pole *(informal)* (p. 50) Ohne Frage!/Niemals!
n'oubliez jamais *(Französisch)* (p. 120) Vergiss nie

O

obsolete ['ɒbsli:t] (p. 55) veraltet
to occupy (p. 82) *hier:* innehaben
onrushing (p. 82) anstürmend
oppressed (p. 82) unterdrückt
order Bestellung – **a tall order** *(informal)* (p. 27) schwer zu machen
Ordnance Survey *(GB)* (p. 26) Landesvermessungsamt
to oscillate (p. 73) schwanken
to oust [aʊst] (p. 55) etwas verdrängen
out of date (p. 31) unzeitgemäß
(retail) outlets (p. 81) Einzelhandelsgeschäft
overdue (p. 49) überfällig
overextended (p. 72) *hier:* länger als gewöhnlich
overwhelmingly (p. 39) *hier:* mit überwältigender Mehrheit

P

pace (p. 55) Tempo
pager (p. 66) Piepser
palmtop (p. 54) handgroßer Computer
panhandle Stiel einer Pfanne – **Florida Panhandle** (p. 77) Bezeichnung für Florida, weil Florida die Form eines Pfannenstiels hat
parchment (p. 73) Pergament
parental [pə'rentl] (p. 112) elterlich
particle (p. 30) Staubteilchen in der Luft
party (p. 81) Gruppe
to pass (a law) (p. 112) (ein Gesetz) verabschieden
passion (p. 120) Leidenschaft
pattern (p. 81) *hier:* Trend
peculiar (p. 81) ungewöhnlich
peeled (p. 101) geschält
peer (p. 36) Person mit einem Titel; *hier:* Mitglied des Oberhauses im englischen Parlament – (p. 106) Gleichaltrige(r) – **to peer** (p. 73) starren
perpetually (p. 82) ständig
perspective (p. 98) Blickwinkel
to pick up (p. 79) *hier:* dazugewinnen – **to pick s.o. up** (p. 84) *hier:* aufheitern – **pick-up** (p. 81) Kleintransporter
picket fence (p. 73) Bretterzaun, Lattenzaun
pie [paɪ] (p. 26) Pastete, spezielles Backwerk – **pie chart** Kreisdiagramm
pier [pɪə] (p. 26) Pier
pile (p. 73) *hier:* Flor
pitch (p. 52) Sportfeld
to place a bid (p. 110) einen Preis vorschlagen
placement (p. 43) Praktikum
placidly (p. 103) ruhig, gelassen
playwright (p. 31) (Theater-)Schriftsteller(in)
plinth (p. 73) Sockel
plot (p. 73) kleines Stück Land, Parzelle
to plunge (p. 60) stürzen
poised (p. 82) bereit
population Bevölkerung – **population drain** (p. 79) Abwanderung
port (p. 8) Hafenstadt
to pose (p. 77) *hier:* sein, darstellen
potted *(informal)* (p. 72) kleiner/verkürzt
pottery (p. 52) Töpfern
to pour [pɔ:] (p. 72) *hier:* fahren (*sonst:* einschenken)
to praise (p. 7) loben
precarious (p. 61) gefährlich
predominantly (p. 37) überwiegend
preference ['prefrns] (p. 7) Vorliebe
pressure cooker (p. 15) Schnellkochtopf
prestigious (p. 92) Prestige-
pretence (p. 27) Täuschung; Anschein
primary source (p. 44) (aus) erste(r) Quelle
produce ['--] (p. 101) (Farm-)Erzeugnisse
productivity (p. 98) Produktivität
to prohibit (p. 112) verbieten, untersagen
to project [prəd'ʒekt] (p. 8) hervorstehen
to promote (p. 96) *hier:* (Gebrauch) anregen, fördern
proportional representation (p. 38) Verhältniswahl(recht)
proposal (p. 38) Vorschlag
protracted (p. 27) sich hinziehend
pursuit [pə'sju:t] (p. 24) Beschäftigung
pushy *(informal)* (p. 104) penetrant
to put s.th. on (p. 73) *hier:* (einen Akzent) annehmen

Q

to queue (p. 11) Schlange stehen

R

racket (p. 18) Krach, Lärm
to raise (awareness) (p. 12) das Bewusstsein wecken
to rant (p. 64) wettern, zetern
rattletrap *(informal)* (p. 72) alt und klapprig
outer reaches (p. 98) Randgebiete
to reckon (p. 13) glauben, annehmen
to recommend (p. 104) empfehlen
reconstruction (p. 91) Wiederaufbau
to recruit [rɪ'kru:t] (p. 96) einstellen, anstellen
Rednecks (p. 81) ungebildete weiße Arbeiter und Bauern der Südstaaten der USA
reference point (p. 111) Anlaufstelle
reflection (p. 79) Widerspiegelung
refugee [refʊ'dʒi:] (p. 102) Flüchtling
refurbished (p. 93) renoviert
regardless (p. 48) ohne Rücksicht auf
to regret bedauern – **to have no regrets** (p. 120) nichts bereuen
relaunch (p. 58) Neuanfang
release (p. 12) *hier:* (Ballons) fliegen lassen
relentless (p. 77) *hier:* nicht nachlassend
reluctance (p. 81) Widerwillen, Abneigung
to remark on (p. 7) eine Bemerkung machen über
reminder (p. 49) Mahnung
replica ['replɪkə] (p. 93) Nachbildung
reproach (p. 50) Vorwurf
to require *(formal)* (p. 107) verlangen
research (p. 48) Forschung – **to carry out research** (p. 44) Forschung anstellen
to reshape (p. 79) verändern
respectively (p. 37) beziehungsweise
respiratory ['respərɪtrɪ] (p. 30) Atmungs-
restrained (p. 13) beherrscht, vernünftig
resurgens *(AE)* (p. 93) wieder auflebend
retail Einzelhandel- **retail outlet** (p. 81) Einzelhandelsgeschäft – **retail price** (p. 110) Einzelhandelspreis
to retain (p. 36) (bei-)behalten
retake ['--] (p. 16) Wiederholung (eines Examens)
revision (p. 16) Lernstoffwiederholung
to rewrite (p. 49) neu schreiben
ribbon (p. 12) Schleife
rig (p. 73) Ölbohrinsel
(economic) roll (p. 82) wirtschaftlicher Aufschwung
rollered ['rəʊləd] (p. 73) gewalzt (Rasen)
root Wurzel – **grass roots** (p. 89) (Partei-) Basis
roughly (p. 98) *hier:* ungefähr
row [raʊ] (p. 18) Streit
in a rush (p. 16) in Eile

S

sacred (p. 117) heilig
safeguard (p. 13) Schutz
safety hazard (p. 8) Gefahr – **safety valve** (p. 18) Sicherheitsventil
scabby (p. 73) schäbig; *hier:* zerfetzt
scale (p. 11) Ausmaß, Umfang
scrutiny (p. 50) musternder oder prüfender Blick; (p. 67) Untersuchung
sea change (p. 13) totale Veränderung
seasoned (p. 101) gewürzt
sedate (p. 72) gemächlich
to see s.o. (p. 16) *hier:* jdn treffen
to seek (sought, sought) (p. 98) *hier:* bekommen wollen
self-indulgence (p. 51) Maßlosigkeit
selfish (p. 24) egoistisch
self promoter (p. 94) jmd, der geschäftig in eigener Sache wirbt; tüchtiger Eigenwerber
semblance (p. 104) Anflug; Anschein
semi-literate (p. 96) jmd, der kaum lesen und schreiben kann
to sense (p. 81) *hier:* fühlen

sensitive (p. 50) sensibel
to serve (p. 73) *hier:* überreichen
to set to *(informal)* (p. 73) beginnen
to settle down (p. 12) häuslich werden
(shotgun) shack *(AE)* (p. 81) kleines Holzhaus
to shake up (p. 72) *hier:* umorganisieren
sheer (p. 82) rein, völlig
shelter (p. 77) Schutz, Unterstand
to shudder (p. 102) schaudern
siege [siːdʒ] (p. 118) Belagerung
to sigh (p. 50) seufzen
significant (p. 24) bedeutend
to slam (p. 17) zuschlagen; (p. 61) aufschlagen
slant (p. 43) *hier:* Schwerpunkt, Richtung
to slap (p. 17) einen Klaps geben, eine Ohrfeige geben
slave (p. 12) Sklave
sleek (p. 92) elegant
slick (p. 63) gewieft, clever
slovenly (p. 73) verwahrlost
to sneer at *(negative)* (p. 82) spötteln
snug [snʌg] (p. 28) geschützt
to sob (p. 117) schluchzen
sober(ly) (p. 7) *hier:* einfach, schlicht
soggy (p. 15) matschig
solitude (p. 73) Einsamkeit
sophistication (p. 92) Kultiviertheit – **to lack sophistication** (p. 81) niveaulos/ einfach sein
source Quelle – **primary source** (p. 44) aus erster Quelle
sovereign ['sɒvrɪn] (p. 27) hoheitlich regiert
spectrum (p. 92) Palette, Skala
spike (p. 8) Spitze, Stachel
to split hairs (p. 27) Haarspalterei betreiben
sponsored run/walk (p. 12) gesponserte Aktivität, bei der die Teilnehmer gehen/ laufen und dafür Spenden für wohltätige Zwecke bekommen
to spool *(informal)* (p. 73) vorbeiziehen, wie ein Film ablaufen
to sport (p. 8) *hier:* anhaben, herumlaufen mit
to sprawl (p. 94) sich (planlos) ausdehnen
spud *(informal)* (p. 15) Kartoffel
to squabble (p. 96) zanken, streiten
squid (p. 101) Tintenfisch
stake (p. 104) Pfahl, Pfosten
to stand for (p. 11) stehen für, bedeuten
(up to) standards (p. 8) den Anforderungen entsprechend
stark (p. 48) offensichtlich
startling (p. 28) überraschend
statelet *(informal)* (p. 73) kleiner Staat
state-of-the-art (p. 93) modern
station (p. 114) Sender
stationary ['steɪʃnrɪ] (p. 77) unbeweglich,
to steepen (p. 73) steiler werden
to stem from s.th. (p. 48) von etwas herrühren, von etwas kommen
stinging nettle (p. 26) Brennessel
to stow [əʊ] (p. 72) *hier:* verstauen
to stretch the truth (p. 103) absichtlich übertreiben, schwindeln
strip Streifen – **median strip** *(AE)* (p. 72) Mittelstreifen
stronghold (p. 48) *hier:* Domäne
studded (p. 8) mit Ziernägeln besetzt
to submerge (p. 77) unter Wasser setzen
to subscribe to s.th. (p. 24) etwas abonnieren
substantial (p. 98) beträchtlich
successively (p. 104) nacheinander
SUPERCOMM (p. 91) jährliche Konferenz und Ausstellung
superficial (p. 46) oberflächlich
supervisor (p. 8) Leiter; Kontrolleur
to supplant (p. 94) ersetzen
supportive (p. 41) unterstützend
surf (p. 73) *hier fig.:* regelmäßiges Geräusch (vorbeifahrender Autos)
surge (p. 77) Anschwellen – **to surge** (p. 72) *hier fig.:* vorbeieilen, vorbeirasen
to swallow (p. 18) einnehmen, schlucken
to swirl (p. 61) wirbeln
to be sworn in (p. 89) vereidigt werden

T

to tackle (a problem) (p. 49) (ein Problem) angehen
to take wing (p. 93) fliegen
a tall order *(informal)* (p. 27) schwer zu machen
tan (p. 72) hellbraun
target (p. 48) Ziel, Norm, Maßstab
tarmac (p. 60) Asphalt
techno-mecca (p. 96) Hochburg für Technologie
to teem with (p. 92) strotzen vor
temperate (p. 92) gemäßigt
tenant (p. 94) Mieter, Pächter
thick *(informal)* (p. 17) dumm, doof
thoroughly (p. 41) gründlich
to thrive (p. 104) (wirtschaftlich) blühen
to throng (p. 61) sich drängen
thus *(formal)* (p. 106) so, auf diese Art
tide (p. 82) *hier:* Ansturm
tiniest degree (p. 26) bis ins Kleinste
tinted (p. 72) getönt
tiny (p. 101) winzig
toddler (p. 48) Kleinkind
torrential (p. 77) sinnflutartig
in totemic fragments (p. 73) in charakteristischen Bildfragmenten
to tow [əʊ] (p. 72) ziehen
trade union (p. 24) Gewerkschaft
tribunal [traɪ'bjuːnl] Gericht – **industrial tribunal** (p. 8) Arbeitsgericht
triumphantly [traɪ'ʌmfəntlɪ] (p. 48) triumphierend
tube [tjuːb] (p. 18) Schlauch
tug [tʌg] (p. 81) Ziehen, Zerren
tune [tjuːn] (p. 11) Melodie – **to tune** (p. 73) einstellen
turf [tɜːf] (p. 73) Boden
to turn one's back on (p. 12) ignorieren
turnout ['--] (p. 11) Besucher, Zuschauer
tutor ['tjuːtə] (p. 46) Tutor, Mentor

U

under-achievement (p. 48) schwache Leistung
understanding (p. 110) Abmachung, Vereinbarung
to undertake (p. 44) etwas durchführen
unique [juː'niːk] (p. 101) einzigartig
universal suffrage (p. 36) das allgemeine Wahlrecht
unkempt (p. 73) ungepflegt
to unleash (p. 77) freisetzen
unplace *(informal)* (p. 72) irgendwo, irgendein Ort
unproductive (p. 98) unergiebig
upbeat (p. 82) optimistisch
uproar (p. 50) *hier:* Stimmengewirr; Geschrei
upset [-'-] (p. 18) ärgerlich; betrübt
to usurp [juː'zɜːp] *(formal)* (p. 106) *hier:* mehr Zeit als nötig beanspruchen

V

valve Ventil – **safety valve** (p. 18) Sicherheitsventil
to veer (p. 77) (sich) drehen
vendor (p. 101) Verkäufer
to venerate s.th. *(formal)* (p. 92) verehren, hoch achten
venue ['venjuː] (p. 11) Veranstaltungsort
verdant (p. 92) grün
vibrant [aɪ] (p. 92) lebendig, voller Leben
vigorous (p. 104) kräftig, kraftvoll
vinyl ['vaɪnl] (p. 45) *hier:* Schallplatte
virginity (p. 13) Jungfräulichkeit
virtually (p. 37) praktisch
viz. (p. 27) nämlich
vocational (p. 43) beruflich
vulture (p. 64) Geier

W

to wade (p. 77) waten
to weigh (p. 94) *hier:* nachdenken über
to be well along in years (p. 103) relativ alt sein
whatsit *(informal)* (p. 87) Dingsbums, Dingsda
when it comes to *(informal)* (p. 11) bezüglich
whereas (p. 86) wohingegen
whey-faced (p. 72) blass
Winnebago *(AE)* (p. 72) Handelsname eines Wohnmobils
to withdraw (p. 42) *hier:* abmelden, freistellen
to be wont to do *(old)* (p. 104) gewöhnt sein zu tun
worship (p. 42) Andacht, Gottesdienst
worthy (p. 92) würdig
to wreak *(formal)* (p. 77) (Zerstörung) anrichten

Y

Yep *(informal)* (p. 87) ja

Index

Skills files

Grammar files

List of abbreviations

adj.	adjective
AE	American English
BE	British English
b.	born
cf.	compare, see
e.g.	for example
esp.	especially
etc.	et cetera, and so on
fig.	figuratively
i.e.	that is
l./ll.	line/lines
lit.	literary
o.s.	oneself
p./pp.	page/pages
s.o.	someone
s.th.	something
usu.	usually

Acknowledgements

The editors wish to thank all authors, publishers and literary agencies who have given permission to use copyright material. Sources are given next to the texts. The following list acknowledges copyright holders who are not identical with the publishers quoted and also gives specifications requested by copyright holders.
Every effort has been made to locate owners of copyright material, but in a few cases this has not proved possible and repeated inquiries have remained unanswered. The publishers would be glad to hear from any further copyright owners of material reproduced in this book.

p. 7: Copyright © D.J. Enright, Chatto & Windus, original publishers, Watson, Little Ltd, licensing agents; p. 8: Copyright © 1990 by Monica Hoose and Carolyn Naifeh. Reprinted by permission of William Morris Agency, Inc. on behalf of the Author; p. 11: Copyright © 1997, *The Guardian*; pp. 12–13: © *Times Newspapers Limited,* 1999; pp. 15–19: Reproduced by permission of The Agency (London) Ltd, Copyright © Steve Barlow and Steve Skidmore, 1989. First published in *New Plays 1: Contemporary One-Act Plays* edited by Peter Terson, Oxford University Press, 1989. All rights reserved and enquiries to The Agency (London) Ltd, 24 Pottery Lane, London W11 4LZ, fax: 0171 727 9037; p. 24: Copyright © 1999, *The Observer*; pp. 26–28: © Bill Bryson 1995. Extracted from *Notes from a Small Island* published by Black Swan, a division of Transworld Publishers Ltd. All rights reserved; pp. 30–31: Copyright © 1999 *The Observer*; p. 50–51: Included by permission of The Peters Fraser and Dunlop Group Limited on behalf of The Estate of Evelyn Waugh; p. 52–53: Fettes College, Edinburgh; p. 55: Copyright © 1997 *The Guardian*; pp. 58–59: Copyright © 1998 *Press Gazette,* research in part by Shaw PR; p. 60: Copyright © 1998 *The Guardian*; p. 61: © 2000 MSI/Distr. Bulls; p. 63: Copyright © 1998 *The Guardian;* pp. 66–67: © Telegraph Group Limited, London; p. 69: © Telegraph Group Limited, London; p. 77: Copyright © 1998 Mark Tran, first published in *The Observer*; p. 78: Population Estimates Program, Population Division, U.S. Bureau of the Census; pp. 81–82: © *The Economist,* London, December 10, 1994; pp. 92–93: Reprinted with the permission of Macmillan General Reference, a division of IDGBooks Worldwide, Inc. from *Frommer's Atlanta*, by Rena Bulkin. Copyright © 1993 by Simon & Schuster/Macmillan; pp. 96–98: Reprinted with permission from *Atlanta Business Chronicle*; pp. 101–102: Reprinted with permission from *The Atlanta Journal* and *The Atlanta Constitution*; pp. 103–104: Copyright © 1936 by Macmillan Publishing Company, a division of Macmillan, Inc. Copyright renewed © 1964 by Stephens Mitchell and Trust Company of Georgia as Executors of Margaret Mitchell Marsh. Reprinted by permission of William Morris Agency, Inc. on behalf of the Author; pp. 117–118: Copyright © 1996 by Stand Up Limited, From *Popcorn* by Ben Elton, Reprinted by permission of St. Martin's Press, LLC

Picture Credits

Every effort has been made to locate owners of copyright material, but in a few cases this has not proved possible and repeated inquiries have remained unanswered. The publishers would be glad to hear from any further copyright owners of material reproduced in this book.

Cover photos: 1 Klett-Archiv; 2 Corbis/Picture Press; 3,4 Hanjo Schmidt; 5 www.klett-verlag.de; p. 6: 1,2,4 und 6: Cash, London; 3 und 5: Greenhill, London; p. 7: Greenhill, London; p. 8: Greenhill, London; p. 10 Copyright 1997 *The Guardian;* p. 11: Cash, London; p. 12: © AVERT 1999. AVERT, 4 Brighton Road, Horsham, West Sussex RH13 58A ENGLAND Tel: 01403 210202, e-mail: avert@dial.pipex.com, internet site: http://www.avert.org/; p. 15: Mauritius, Stuttgart; p. 20: Bryn Colton/ Corbis/Picture Press (Welsh flag); Cash, London (breakfast, cottage, back-to-back houses, cricket, Birmingham lane, beach); PhotoDisc (House of Parliament); Imagine (rainy day); Harding, London (red busses, avenue); Rupert Horrox/Corbis/Picture Press (policeman); Dave Bartruff/Corbis/Picture Press (hikers, telephone); Nathan Benn/Corbis/Picture Press (soccer fans); Annie Griffith Belt/Corbis/Picture Press (milk); AA Publishing 1998 (map); p. 22: Cash, London; p. 23: Martin Jones/Corbis/ Picture Press; Cash, London; Colin Gerratti/Corbis/Picture Press; p. 25: Pilbrow. *The Spectator Cartoon Book*; p. 27: AA Publishing 1998; p. 28: Cash, London; p. 31: Antonio Olmos, London; p. 34: Cash, London; p. 34: Annie Griffith Belt/Corbis/ Picture Press; p. 36: Reproduced from *The Spectator*; p. 40: Central College of Commerce, Glasgow; p. 41: Eastbourne College of Arts and Technology, Eastbourne; p. 47 Greenhill, London; p. 48: Copyright 1998 *The Observer*; p. 50: Dpa, Stuttgart; p. 52-53: Fettes College, Edinburgh; p. 56: Rüdiger Knieknecht, Unterriexingen; p. 59: Rüdiger Knieknecht, Unterriexingen; p. 62: Rüdiger Knieknecht, Unterriexingen; p. 63: Dpa, Stuttgart; p. 64: Bryn Colton/Corbis/Picture Press, p. 66: Greenhill, London, p. 67: Rüdiger Knieknecht, Unterriexingen; p. 69: Robert Thomson. Reproduced from *The Spectator*; p. 70: 1 Virginia Maier, Stuttgart; 2 Klett-Archiv/Schwenk; 3-5 Steenmans, Mönchengladbach; 6 Bavaria, Gauting; 7 Shostal; 8 USTS; 9-12 Shostal; p. 72/73: Bavaria, Gauting; p. 74: Steenmans, Mönchengladbach; p. 75: Steenmans, Mönchengladbach; p. 76: Dpa, Stuttgart; p. 80: 1-2 Steenmans, Mönchengladbach; 3 USTS; p. 82: Foto-presse Timmermann, Möhrendorf; p. 84: Roger Ressmeyer/ Corbis/Picture Press; p. 90: 1 Kevin Fleming/Corbis/Picture Press; 2 Joseph Sohm/Corbis/Picture Press; 3 Flip Schulke/Corbis/ Picture Press; 4 Corbis/Bettmann/Picture Press; 5 Marta/Rapid Rail Systems, Atlanta; p. 91: 1 Franz Marc Frei/Corbis/Picture Press; 2 National Archives; p. 92: *Atlanta Now*/Atlanta Convention and Visitors Bureau, July/August 1998; p. 98: James L. Amos/Corbis/Picture Press; p. 100: Kevin Fleming/Corbis/Picture Press; p. 104: Noreen O'Donovan Hage, Pforzheim; p. 107: *Punch*; p. 108: Yobs. Reproduced from *Private Eye*; p. 113: Nick Downes. Reproduced from *The Spectator*; p. 116: Hislop and Newman. Reproduced from *Private Eye*; p. 117: Pocket Books, London; p. 118: Kevin Woodcock. Reproduced from *Private Eye*.